246

wasn't much of a market for [...] frocks and the lazy [...] dreams of past-time whores. But he gathered what he could and he sold what he could and he waited for the moment when the [...] would begin to stir.

In the meantime, he marvelled at what he overheard and at what he found on the walls. Round and round the rumours went and the hands that wrote them were never seen. Who were these phantoms, whose sources you could never check, who could only be identified by what they wrote, but who always wrote it in the dark, like God. The only trouble is, he thought, recalling the eternal twilight of the world's lavatories and the rows of feet beneath the cubicle doors — the only way I'd know it's God is if I recognized His shoes.

To the west of the town of [...] lies the island of Andros — far enough away to lie below the horizon. Not that any [...] person in [...] could [...] of anything due west no matter how close it might be, since the

INSIDE
MEMORY

Pages from a writer's Workbook

Also by Timothy Findley:

Novels
The Last of the Crazy People
The Butterfly Plague
The Wars
Famous Last Words
Not Wanted on the Voyage
The Telling of Lies

Short Fiction
Dinner Along the Amazon
Stones

Plays
Can You See Me Yet?
John A. — Himself

INSIDE
MEMORY

Pages from a writer's Workbook

TIMOTHY FINDLEY

HarperCollins*Publishers*Ltd

Toronto

First published 1990
by HarperCollins Publishers Ltd.
Suite 2900, Hazelton Lanes
55 Avenue Road
Toronto, Ontario M5R 3L2

designed by Styles Design Inc., Toronto

The quotations from "I Daniel" by Phyllis Webb have been used by permission of the author. "I Daniel" appears in The Vision Tree: Selected Poems by Phyllis Webb, published by Talonbooks, 1982. Quotations from Margaret Laurence used by permission of the Estate of Margaret Laurence. Quotations from Marian Engel used by permission of Charlotte Engel. "I Get a Kick Out of You" (Cole Porter) © 1934 Warner Bros. Inc. (Renewed) All Rights Reserved. Used by permission.

Canadian Cataloguing in Publication Data

Findley, Timothy, 1930-
    Inside memory

ISBN 0-00-215697-0

1. Findley, Timothy, 1930- — Biography.
2. Canadian literature (English) — 20th century —
History and criticism.* 3. Novelists, Canadian
(English) — 20th century — Biography.* I. Title.

PS8511.I573Z53 1990   C813'.54   C90-094829-9
PR9199.3.F548Z47 1990

90 91 92 93 94 95 RRD 5 4 3 2 1

Acknowledgements

My thanks to William Whitehead, whose help in selecting and collating this material was incalculable. Also, thanks to Anne Goddard at the National Archives in Ottawa, who retained her sanity and monitored ours throughout the process. Finally, my thanks to Stanley and Nancy Colbert, whose faith in this book preceded and encouraged my own.

Timothy Findley
Stone Orchard,
April 1990.

For Mary Adachi
and
in memory of Ken Adachi

And so we will remember him all our lives. And even if we are occupied with most important things — if we attain to honour or fall into great misfortune — still let us remember how good it was here, when we were all united by these loving feelings which made us, for the time we stood together, better perhaps than we are.

Alyosha, *The Brothers Karamazov*

·CONTENTS·

· I ·

REMEMBRANCE

Stone Orchard
November 11, 1970
Radio
In the plays of Anton Chekhov, there is always a moment of profound silence, broken by the words: "I remember. . . ." What follows inevitably breaks your heart. A woman will stand there and others will sit and listen and she will say: "I remember the band playing and the firing at the cemetery as they carried the coffin. Though he was a general, in command of a brigade, yet, there weren't many people there. It was raining. Heavy rain and snow."

Or some such thing. And she is transformed, this woman, by her memories — absolutely transformed. And as you watch her and listen to her, you are transformed, too — or something inside you is. You change. Your attitude changes. In a way — if it has been well done — your life changes. Why should this be?

I think one reason must be that Chekhov discovered the dramatic value of memory — that a woman in tears remembers happiness; that a smiling, laughing man re-

3

members pain. This gives you two views in one: depth and contrast. But, there's more to it than that. Memory, Chekhov also discovered, is the means by which most of us retain our sanity. The act of remembrance is good for people. Cathartic. Memory is the purgative by which we rid ourselves of the present.

Because memory is what it is, the first thing we tend to "remember" is that time passes. In going back, we recognize that we've survived the passage of time — and if we've survived what we remember, then it's likely we'll survive the present. Memory is a form of hope.

If the memory is a bad one, say of pain or of a death — then it's clouded. The sharpness is blunted. We remember that we were in pain. But the pain itself cannot be recalled exactly. Not as it was. Because, if we could recall it, then we'd have to be in pain again — and that, except where there's psychological disorder, is a physical and mental impossibility. If you've ever had a bad accident, then you'll remember that you can't remember what happened. But you can recall joy. You can make yourself laugh again and feel again something joyous that happened before.

Of course, you can make yourself cry again, too. But the tears aren't as valid as the laughter, because the tears you conjure have as much to do with the passage of time as with the sadness you remember. Still, a sad memory is better than none. It reminds you of survival.

Most of the activity in your brain relies on memory. That takes energy. Have you ever noticed that when you're tired and there's silence in your brain, you begin to sing? That's good health taking over. The tensions of serious thought are being released through play.

Today is Remembrance Day, and it's a strange thing to me that we confine ourselves to remembering only the dead — and only the war dead, at that. If they were able, what would *they* be remembering? Us. And we're alive. Here we are. Maybe it's sad — I suppose it is — that the dead should be remembering the living and the living remembering the dead. But the main thing is, we all remember when we were together. We remember what we were in another time. Not now, but *then*. Memory is making peace with time.

They say that loss of memory is not to know who you are. Then, I suppose, it has to follow that we *are* what we remember. I can believe that. I mean, it's very easy for me to imagine forgetting my name. That wouldn't worry me. And it wouldn't worry me to forget how old I am (I wish I could!) or to forget the colour of my eyes and have to go look in a mirror to remind myself. None of that would worry me. Because I can skip all of that. None of those things are who I am.

But it would worry the hell out of me if I couldn't remember the smell of the house where I grew up, or the sound of my father playing the piano, or the tune of his favourite song. I remember my brother, Michael, as a child. And the child I remember being myself is as much a remembrance of him as it is of me. More, in fact — because I saw him every day and did not see myself. I heard him every day — and did not hear myself (except singing). So, to be a child in memory means that I conjure Michael, not the child in photographs who bears my name.

I am my Aunt Marg, for instance, telling me not to lean into the cemetery over the fence at Foxbar Road. I am not me leaning over the fence, I am her voice — because that is what I remember. And I am all the gravestones I was looking at when she called me. And the fence boards that supported me. And the sun on my back. But I am not that little boy. I don't remember him at all. I remember

5

him falling and being picked up — but I am the distance he fell and the hands that lifted him, not the bump in between. I remember the sound of my own voice crying — but not the feel of it. That voice is gone. And I am the gloves my mother wore when she held my hand and the tones of her laughter. And I remember and will move forever, as all children do, to the heartbeats of my mother. That remembrance is the rhythm of my life. So memory is other people — it is little of ourselves.

I like Remembrance Day. I'm fond of memory. I wish it was a day of happiness. I have many dead in my past, but only one of them died from the wars. And I think very fondly of him. He was my uncle. He didn't die in the War, but because of it. This was the First World War and so I don't remember the event itself. I just remember him. But what I remember of my uncle is not the least bit sad.

I was just a child — in the classic sense — a burbling, few-worded, looking-up-at-everything child. Uncle Tif — who died at home — was always in a great tall bed — high up — and the bed was white. I would go into his room, supported by my father's hands, and lean against the lower edge of the mattress. There was a white sheet over everything, and I can smell that sheet to this day. It smelled of soap and talcum powder. To me, Uncle Tif was a hand that came down from a great way off and tapped me on the head. He smoked a pipe. And there was something blue in the room — I don't know whether it was a chair or a table or my father's pant legs — but there was something blue and that has always been one of my favourite colours.

And high above my head, there was a tall glass jar on a table and the jar was full of hard French candies. They had shiny jackets and were many colours. And Uncle Tif's hand would go out, waving in the air above my gaze and

lift up the lid of the jar and take out a candy and slowly —
it was always slowly — he would pass the candy down
into my open mouth. Then I would lean against the bed,
or fall on the floor, and taste the candy for about two
hours — or what, to a kid, just seemed two hours —
while the adult voices buzzed above my head.

I know he sacrificed his youth, his health, his leg and
finally his life for his country. But I'd be a fool if I just
said *thanks* —*I'm grateful*. I might as well hit him in the
mouth as say that. Because my being grateful has nothing
to do with what he died for or why he died. That was part
of his own life and what I am grateful for is that he had
his own life. I am grateful he was there in that little bit of
my life. And I am grateful, above all, that he is in my
memory. I am his namesake. He is mine.

Remembrance is more than honouring the dead. Remembrance is joining them — being one with them in
memory. Memory is survival.

· 2 ·

FROM
STAGE TO PAGE

Stone Orchard
March 1990
He is smiling. She is laughing. They are standing somewhere in limbo. People are the landscape of memory. Without the benefit of time and place, they are forced to play the scenery themselves. All the information they can give you is there in their faces and in their names.

Thornton Niven Wilder. Ruth Gordon Jones. I cannot think of one without the other. I met them both in the summer of 1954 and ever since, I have always imagined them standing side by side.

Ruth is small. She ticks like a clock — or, rather, like a watch. A ticking watch is less sedate and has more verve than a ticking clock. If a clock stops ticking, everyone rushes to wind it up. If a watch stops ticking, everyone runs for cover. You wait for the explosion. That was Ruth Gordon at her best — the pause between the ticking and the bang.

Thornton is big, until you measure him. He seems

11

immensely tall and infinitely round — yet, alive, he was neither. Even his tailors could not define his shape. His suits were always cut as if Orson Welles had ordered them. The collars rose with a life of their own whenever Thornton sat down. He was forever leaning forward in his chair. His clothes were forever pulling him back. He favoured single-breasted jackets, vests and suspenders. All his clothes were grey or blue or white.

He had impeccable taste, but he made no show of having it. He knew exactly how to present himself for every occasion; knew it, but would forget. He came down, once, to the lobby of his hotel in evening dress. Our meeting was pre-arranged and I was embarrassed when I saw him. I had arrived in slacks and sports jacket — quite inelegant.

"Aren't we going to the Savoy?" he said when he saw me.

"No," I reminded him. "We're going on a pub crawl."

"Oh," said Thornton. "Yes. I remember, now."

As he turned to go back to his room in order to change, he suddenly took in his surroundings.

"Good God!" he said. "I'm *at* the Savoy!"

After Thornton died, Ruth told how, once, he had asked her to marry him. This was early in the 1930s. Ruth and Thornton were relatively young. The proposal came at a time when her fortunes were low. She couldn't get a job — she couldn't pay her bills — and the man she had wanted to marry was not forthcoming. I suspect this man was Jed Harris, the father of Ruth's son, Jones.

Whenever Ruth Gordon told a story, she liked to drop a lot of names into it — *sort of like spicing up the sauce!* she said. But the only name she ever put in this story was Thornton Wilder's. The other players remained anonymous. Anyway, the long and short of it is — she turned him down. Not because she didn't cherish him. It was because she knew that Thornton's proposal had more to do with friendship than with love. He was offering a friend's way out of her predicament.

Ruth had a lot of practical courage. She took a look around her and decided that with friends like Thornton Wilder, she would survive the present crisis. Yes — she had begun to panic. But Thornton's proposal had calmed her. She had never been one to win her wars by doing what was expected of her. She did what she expected of herself — which was to be herself at any cost.

The subject of marriage between them did not come up again. Ruth went on to ever-brighter stardom and Thornton went on to take the theatre by storm. Jed Harris, incidentally, went on to direct Wilder's masterpiece *Our Town*.

I take great comfort from this story. When I heard it first, it told me something about independence I hadn't recognized before, which was: being cared for by someone doesn't mean you lose your independence. Under the best of circumstances, you gain it.

Ruth said: *be yourself — but know who you are. Being yourself is not a licence. It's a responsibility.*

Not all that easy, when you begin as Ruth Gordon Jones or Thornton Niven Wilder. Not all that easy for anyone born with talent, once you have seen what must be done with who you are.

Ruth also said: *lots of people have talent, darlin'. But look how many people throw it away. It boils down to this: having talent is not enough. You also have to have a talent for having talent.*

Ruth dropped the *Jones* from her name when she went into the theatre. But she kept it in her heart. It was the name she chose for her son. *But* — she said — *the name*

13

of Jones was not going to conquer the world when I came down out of Wollaston, Massachusetts in 1916!

Thornton dropped the *Niven* from his name — but not the initial. When you got to know him — after a while, he would ask you to call him *T.N.* That was how he signed his letters: *cordial regards, T.N.*

I don't know why, but I never cottoned to this form of address and always — except in occasional letters, called him Thornton. He always called me *Timothy* — or *Findley*. He never cottoned, either, to my being called *Tiff*.

"It's my initials," I told him.

"Yes. But that doesn't make it your *name*."

He was adamant concerning names. "You can't call someone *Tiff*," he said. "It's a verb!"

"What would you call me if my name was Tiffany?" I asked.

"*Tiffany*," he said.

And that was that.

Most, but not all, of their major achievements were behind them when I met them first in 1954. Thornton had long since written *The Bridge of San Luis Rey, The Ides of March, Our Town* and *The Skin of Our Teeth*. Ruth had already given what everyone agreed was the definitive performance of Nora in *A Doll's House*, adapted by Thornton from Ibsen's play in 1937. There had also been *Abe Lincoln in Illinois*, in which Ruth played Mary Todd, the president's unhappy and unstable wife. And Natasha in the all-star production of Chekhov's *Three Sisters* in 1942. And there was more, of course — all the way back to Nibs in *Peter Pan. Seventeen* and *Clarence. Ethan Frome, The Country Wife* and *Over Twenty-one*.

These were the legendary achievements that appealed to me, the young actor, who met Ruth Gordon and

Thornton Wilder that warm July morning on the mezzanine of a West End theatre. I think it was the Globe, on Shaftesbury Avenue.

I was one of sixteen who had been gathered there to commence rehearsals of Wilder's play *The Matchmaker*. I remember now that, when I got the call to come and read for the producers, I had thought it was going to be a play about someone who manufactured wooden matchsticks. Turn-of-the-century tragedy stuff . . . everyone freezing to death in the snow . . . and then some character invents the safety match. Fires would be lighted — the human race would survive — and! . . .

Mister Wilder had already written that one. He'd called it *The Skin of Our Teeth*.

In *The Matchmaker*, Miss Gordon played Dolly Levi. She played her in seventeen layers of pink organdy and seven shades of red hair. Her mouth was painted a mile wide and it didn't shut from the moment she came onstage until the final curtain. Her performance was a masterpiece of over-statement and vulgarity. Without any doubt, it was one of the century's greatest comic creations. Anyone who saw it will tell you so. Of course, when they made the movie, they gave the role to someone else. The real Dolly Levi went to the grave with Ruth, who probably had to drag her down and lie on top of her to make her quit.

The director of the play was Tyrone Guthrie. I had worked for him in Canada. That had been the previous summer, in the inaugural season of the Stratford Shakespearean Festival in Ontario. Wilder, who was a pal of Guthrie's, had come up to Stratford from Connecticut to see those first productions — *Richard III* and *All's Well That Ends Well* — but I had not been aware of his presence. On that morning, however, in July of 1954, his presence could not be denied. Though he tried his damnedest to play it in a minor key, he did not succeed.

He sat in a corner, more in shadow than not. The light spilled through the dusty windows and landed on his feet. He wore black shoes, I remember, but he wore them carelessly. One of his laces was undone. Balanced on his knees, his hands seemed disembodied. He constantly passed his cigarette back and forth between one set of fingers and another. Instantly, you recognized — not nerves — but energy. He always seemed to be at war with stillness.

The smoke from his cigarette curled up and obscured his face and all I could really see was the flare from his glasses and the pale grey tufts of hair that framed his head. I'm afraid I must have smiled at him from my place in the semi-circle of actors' chairs. This was intolerable. He turned away and made a show of looking for an ashtray.

It was much too soon to say hello.

I nearly got fired that afternoon — the first of a half-dozen episodes in which I nearly got fired while playing in *The Matchmaker*. Life with Ruth Gordon was like that. Volatile.

That afternoon, I was reading the role I'd been hired to understudy. The part I was playing was Rudolph, the flamboyant waiter. The understudy role was Ambrose Kemper, a boy who was courting Mister Vandergelder's niece, Ermengarde. Mister Vandergelder was the misanthropic miser who had hired Dolly Levi to find him a wife. Ambrose was the character with whom Dolly Levi played her first expository scene.

Playing straight man in an expository scene is never much fun. I'd had my share of such roles over time and thought I had learned how to survive with my dignity intact. Every actor has to play the straight man at some point in his career, and the way to do it is to resolutely face out front and direct all your questions at the audience.

What is the point, Mrs Levi? (Staring at the balcony.) *Married to you, Mrs Levi?* (Staring at the mezzanine.) *What are you suggesting, Mrs Levi?* (Staring at the box, stage left.) Et cetera.

In the meantime, upstage, Mrs Levi is telling you her life story.

Books in hand, we set out to block the scene. (I was standing in because the actor hired to play Ambrose was unavailable that day.)

Tony Guthrie said: "all right, Findley — you're over there for this."

I stood *over there*.

Ruth at once said: "no, Tony. No."

"No to what, Ruth?" Guthrie asked.

"Mister Findley cannot stand over there, " said Ruth. "He's much too far upstage."

Too far upstage? I was practically standing in the footlights. "Mister Findley," said Ruth Gordon — turning to me — "please stand further down."

I looked behind me and laughed. "You mean in the orchestra pit, Miss Gordon?" I said.

This was my big mistake. Ruth was not amused.

"You should be grateful, Mister Findley, that I didn't mean *the street*," she said.

Lesson number one: never play for laughs when the star is staking out her territory.

We took a break and when we returned to the scene, I assumed the prescribed position — with my back to the house. I played the whole scene that way.

Miss Gordon was finally satisfied. Guthrie, however, was not. But he was crafty. . . .

17

He clapped his hands when the scene was over and snapped his fingers.

"Very nice," he said. "Very nice." Then he looked at Ruth and added — deadpan — "Mister Findley has lovely wide shoulders, Ruth. *Very, very* wide shoulders. The audience will love them!"

Ruth bit her lip. "I see," she said. "Yes."

When the scene was finally blocked, Ambrose Kemper stood facing stage right — effectively turning him sideways to the house. I got to play this role quite often during the run. I was slimmer then, and I always wondered if I could be seen at all. Ruth, on the other hand, had no such worry. Playing to my paper-thin shadow, she was, to all appearances, the only person on stage.

"What is the matter with all you people?" said Ruth, one day.

We were on the road and playing in Manchester. This was prior to our opening in London and we had already played in Newcastle, Edinburgh, Glasgow and Liverpool.

All you people meant people under thirty years of age and I was one of them. Twenty-three and loving it. I had never felt more alive.

We had been to see an exhibition of paintings, all of which had been created by artists in their twenties. It was called *The New Generation Shows Its Colours!* or some such thing. The colours were fairly uniform. Black, brown and deep shades of blue. Many storms and a lot of *drang*. It was wonderfully depressing and, if you were twenty-three, profound as hell itself.

"Can't any of you people say *yes* to anything?" Ruth asked. "Say *yes* to one another? Say *yes* to life?"

"Well, yes," I said.

Ruth laughed. "I'll *bet!*" she said. "Your face is a sight, right now. You *loved* it in there, didn't you. Loved it and

18

revelled in it! I was watching you. Oh — *you people!*"

We were walking in the street.

"I wish you'd stop saying *you people* like that," I said. "It isn't fair to lump us all together."

"*Lump* is a very good word, my darlin'," she said. "And *you* said it."

I was hurt by this. She obviously thought that mine was a generation of depressed defeatists. The exhibit of paintings had truly upset her. She did not believe in defeat. She did not believe in darkness. She knew, of course, that defeat and darkness existed — but she refused their blandishments. "Too easy, too easy," she said. "It's just too easy to accept defeat. You know what, darlin'? Laughter is the hardest thing in all the world to bring to your troubles. But it will save you. Get up! Stand up! And laugh!"

Get up. Stand up. And laugh.

"That should be your generation's motto," she said. This was the mid-1950s. Mine was the generation whose childhood had been interrupted by the war. We grew up through that time, deprived, one way and another, of normal life. Our fathers went to war. Our cities were bombed. And some of us went to Auschwitz. Our childhood ended with the dropping of the Hiroshima bomb. What darkened our moods — above all, I guess — was the vision we had been forced to endure of what people really do to one another — and, as children, we had been powerless to stop it.

I went home to my digs and thought about it. I thought about it for days — the juxtaposition of all those dark paintings and the darkness from which they had emerged.

It didn't come to me at once — but, finally, I caught a glimmer of what Ruth had meant by *get up, stand up and laugh*. She had meant that after darkness, something must be done about the need for light.

19

If the future was just another dark place — then how could you ever hope to survive it?

Something like that.

I began to work it out — and to write it down.

I wrote Ruth a story. Fiction. I wrote about a woman who was afraid of storms and of darkness and whose way of "getting up and laughing" was to think of the storms and the darkness as salvation. It was loosely based on the story of a woman I had known when I was a child. She believed that Jesus would arrive to save the world from its wars and its other torments in a great, green storm — preceded by thunder and lightning. I called this woman Effie and I gave the story to Ruth.

"What's this," she said.

"I wanted to prove," I said — with an overdose of pomposity, "that some of us in my generation can still say *yes*."

This, of course, is not what I had written at all. It was what I had wanted to write. The story — called *About Effie* — was just as dark and just as depressing as any of the paintings in that infamous exhibition. Coupled with this was the fact that I had copied it out on plain white paper and the lines all fell away sideways towards the lower right-hand corner. My writing, at the best of times, is illegible — but I had no typewriter and had done the best I could. Every third word — on an average — could be read.

Ruth Gordon's dresser in England was a woman called Dodie. Dodie was blonde and wise and funny. And she was small. She was smaller, if that was possible, than Ruth herself. Everyone in the company was in love with her and we called her "The Bird." She had, however, one devastating mark against her.

The Bird was Ruth Gordon's messenger from hell.

The times to be wary of Dodie's arrival at your dressing-room door were during the half-hour call before the play and after the final curtain. Her fingernail knock and her whispering voice announcing that *Miss Gordon would like to speak with you* were downright chilling. If you asked The Bird why Miss Gordon was calling, her small round face would remain expressionless. *All I know is*, Dodie would say, *she wants to see you.*

We had already lost one actor this way.

The knock came for me with the half-hour call, the evening after I had handed Ruth my pages.

"Yes?"

"Miss Gordon would like to speak with you after the performance."

And me without unemployment insurance.

Had Ruth misinterpreted what I had written? *HOW DARE YOU SUGGEST THAT EFFIE IS LUSTING AFTER THE BODY OF JESUS CHRIST!* Had she been able to read my handwriting? *WHAT IS THIS INDECI-PHERABLE GARBAGE?* (Throwing the pages in the air.)

What if she thought it was pornographic? *THAT WOMAN EXPOSES HERSELF TO JESUS CHRIST IN HER NIGHTIE!*

. . . *Miss Gordon would like to speak with you.*

All through the performance, Ruth betrayed nothing of what her verdict might be. A person dared not approach her once she had stepped inside Dolly Levi — and, once she had stepped inside Dolly Levi, she stayed there until her dressing-room had been gained. Garson Kanin, Ruth's husband, told someone in an interview that life with Ruth had been relative hell while Dolly Levi trod the boards.

"She started being Dolly two hours before the curtain went up," he said, "and, most nights, we took Dolly home with us. I even had to sleep with her!"

Doubtless, this must have been exhausting. Eight

hours of minor explosions — waiting for the big one.

The moment came.

Still wearing my costume, I approached Ruth's dressing-room. My costume (this was Rudolph — the waiter) consisted of black trousers, white shirt and a long, white apron. I wondered what to do about blood stains. . . .

Dodie sat on her little chair outside Ruth's door.

"Can I go in?"

"Yes."

"*Should* I?"

"I don't know," said The Bird.

She stood up and went into the *sanctum*. I heard my name being spoken. There was a pause and The Bird returned.

She nodded at the open door.

As I went inside, I glanced at Dodie and said: "good-bye."

The door closed behind me.

Ruth, still in costume but minus her wig, was seated at her dressing-table. The back of her chair was tied with several little velvet bows. The smell of make-up and the warm, rich scent of Ruth's perfume eddied round me. Ruth was watching me in the mirror. Her eyes reflected light — a cat's eyes, brightly focused.

When she spoke, she had all her usual bluntness about her. "Oh, *darlin'!*" she said — and she got up out of her chair and threw her arms around me. "You must give up acting just as fast as you can!"

I stood there alarmed and paralysed.

Ruth was weeping and smiling and she held on tight to the back of my neck — locking me in place as she looked up into my face. "Your story is wonderful!" she said. (There were many exclamation points that night.) "*Wonderful!*" She let go and went to her dressing table, where she picked up my pages and flourished them. "*This*

22

is what you are! *This* is what you are! A writer — not an actor!"

I blinked — and I heard myself say: "thank you."

But my heart was sinking. What had I done to myself?

There I was, twenty-four years old by now, and heading straight for stardom. Or so I had thought. But now this other thing — this writing — was standing in my way. *You must give up acting just as fast as you can.*

My talent for having talent was nowhere in sight.

"It was just an exercise," I said. "I didn't mean it to do any more than make a point. . . ."

But Ruth wasn't listening. She was dragging out an old, boxed portable typewriter and putting it at my feet.

"The first thing you have to learn," she was saying, "is how to use one of these. I nearly killed myself trying to make out what you had written on those pages. So Garson and I — we just bought a new one — we're giving our old one to you."

Smith-Corona.

Tap-tap-tap.

My acting career — to all intents and purposes — was over.

Or so I thought that night.

I had this image of Ruth sending messages to all the West End producers: DO NOT HIRE THIS MAN. HE IS NOT AN ACTOR.

But it was not to them that she sent this message. It was to me — and she didn't stop sending it for the next two years.

If writing *About Effie* was the beginning of the end of my acting career, Ruth's giving it to Thornton Wilder was almost the beginning of the end of my writing career.

He said: "have you tried a play, Findley?"

I said: "no."

"Then let me urge you to try one."
He should not have said that.

If the play you are in achieves a long run, there are consequences — good and bad. On the positive side — *the money*. You can pay your debts. You can celebrate.

The first few weeks of this are heaven on earth. You begin to eat oranges again and you take home Twinings Earl Grey tea instead of flavourless tea bags. You eat in restaurants. You buy new records and books and presents for your friends. You get new trousers and a sweater. You have that extra piece of cake. . . . But, in time, this binge of spending ends and your comforts become more compatible with reality.

The Matchmaker ran forever. Or so it began to seem — and this is where the consequences took on a negative edge. I was not being stretched. The role I was playing was fun but it didn't offer much scope. Rudolph, the waiter, is an arrogant, angry piece of work — and while these qualities afford the actor playing him lots of opportunities for comedy, they do not afford him many opportunities for variation. To be more or less arrogant, more or less angry according to each night's audience was pretty well the end of it. That, and the necessary hold on technique to achieve the intricate moves required without screwing up the intricate moves of your fellow actors. The play is a farce — and Guthrie had asked us all to maintain a breakneck pace from start to finish. This required everyone to move like Olympic athletes. In essence, we went to the theatre every night and performed the decathlon. A person had to be in very good shape.

I kept getting calls to read for other plays — and, finally I wanted very much to be doing something else. My greatest heartbreaks were missing out on *Bell, Book and Candle* with Lilli Palmer and Rex Harrison (in which

I would have played Palmer's brother) and a European tour and West End engagement with Gielgud and Ashcroft in *Much Ado* and *Lear* — in which I had been asked to play one of the Watch (superb comedy) and Oswald (the perfect villain). But Ruth would not let me go. She wanted her company kept intact and the producers bowed to her will. No one was released.

The weeks and the months stretched on. We played at one of London's oldest and most charming theatres, the Haymarket, and it was always a pleasure to go there to work. There was a ghost who appeared from time to time in one of the upper galleries. Not a rampaging ghost — but benign and rather sad. It was said he had been an actor and had died of a foiled ambition. There was also a book which everyone who had ever played the Haymarket had signed. *Everyone* — and in the long run, everyone included me. I wrote my name where Kean had written his and Barrymore, Gielgud, Ellen Terry and Mrs Pat. . . .

Autumn came and went. And winter. Christmas. New Year's. . . .

Now it was 1955.

Ever since Ruth had said *you must give up acting* and *this is what you are — a writer*, I had been trying to write more stories. Two of them, called "War" and "The Name's the Same," have subsequently been published. Nothing else I wrote then was worthy of publication — but it was all worth doing as an exercise. I began a novella which I then called *Harper's Bazaar*, and dedicated it to Ruth. This, in time, became *Lemonade* — but that was later.

I also wrote a play.

Perhaps there is such a piece in every writer's background — overwritten — over-serious — overbearing and over-everything! I called it, with what I thought was stunning understatement, *A Play.*

A group of actors are locked in a theatre with God. . . .

That's right. A group of actors are locked in a theatre with God. They have been playing "God's play." It was their last chance to *get it right* — and they have failed. God has enemies everywhere. The actors try to encourage him — but God is very old and has lost the will to try again. Besides which, the enemies are coming to do God in. They surround the theatre — break down the doors and arrest not only God but all his actors, too — and everyone in the audience.

See what I mean?

Well. This was the play I offered to Thornton Wilder.

"Try one," he had said.

So, I tried one.

The poor man was honour-bound to read the thing. I got a card from Switzerland: *am reading play. We will talk when I return. . . .*

Another card from Aix-en-Provence: *am reading play. Don't know what to make of it yet. . . .*

And from Berlin: *have finished play. Hope the acting goes well. . . .*

Then he was back in London: *greetings. Now prepared to discuss your play. Gird your loins. I talk tough. Dinner. Savoy. Sunday. T.N.*

I had, as every actor had, an audition suit. Blue. Somewhat baggy — but presentable. Late Sunday afternoon, I dressed for my "audition" for the Master. I polished my shoes and borrowed a better tie than the one I owned and I looked many hours at myself in the mirror. Would he approve of what he saw? Why should it matter? He'd seen me dozens of times already at rehearsal and in performance. Yes, I told myself — *but that was the actor he was looking at. This is the writer. . . .*

Did I look like a writer?

Well?

What does a writer look like?

Thornton Wilder. Hemingway. Shakespeare. Emily Brontë. . . .

No luck there. All I got back from the mirror was me — and somehow, that wasn't good enough.

Gird your loins. I talk tough.

What should I gird my loins with?

Three pairs of jockey shorts.

And Fowler's Extract. It keeps your bowels in place.

I was living then in Tedworth Square with Alec Mc-Cowen — an actor who played a leading role in *The Matchmaker*. Alec's friendship endures and we correspond and talk on the phone to this day. Whenever I go to London, it is Alec with whom I spend the longest time. He is one of the centrepieces of my life. *But this is not about that* — as Ruth would have said — *this is about the other. The other* being my meeting with Thornton Wilder.

Up from Tedworth Square, along Royal Hospital Road and then up to Sloane Square Station. I am going to Charing Cross on the Circle Line. None of my precautions are working. My stomach churns with apprehension — my blue suit shines with a dreadful gloss beneath the lights — my hair, which is cut in the Junker's style for my role in the play, is standing on end and crackling with electricity. My palms are sweating and my feet are cold. I have all the sophistication of a spotted disease.

I get off and allow the escalator to carry me further towards my fate. Here, in this place — or roughly, so I have been told — there was once a teeming mass of activity known as Hungerford Market. Now, there are all the gleaming tiles and the hollow silence of a tube station.

It was to Hungerford Market that Dickens, as a little boy, was sent to work in a blacking factory. The blacking factory had been right there — bleak in the shadow of the Hungerford Stairs, which climbed up out of the mud flats by the river to the Strand. The Strand was then much closer to the Thames than it is now, with all its hotels and shops.

Today and yesterday. Me and Charles Dickens. What was the point of thinking any other way? If you were going to be a writer, the only kind of writer to be — or try to be — was the best. That thought made me feel better. That and the thought that Dickens, on his way up out of the rat-infested blacking factory, had started further down at the bottom than I had ever been forced to go. My only connection to the blacking factory had been the polish on my shoes.

To achieve the foyer of the Savoy Hotel, you walk in off the Strand through a courtyard. By the time I got to the doors of Thornton's rooms, I had passed a lot of glass in which I could watch my ghost in the process of materializing. Everything was going to be all right. Thornton Wilder was just another human being. He wasn't going to bite my head off.

I stood up taller and squared my "wonderful" shoulders. (These were my only visible asset.) The whole of me prepared to knock. But the door flew back, like a comedy door, before my knuckles had touched the wood. I was impelled into the light — fist raised and lurching. Somewhat blinded, I collided with my host and inadvertently forced him back against a table. All he said was:

"Timothy Findley, I presume."

He was laughing.

So was I. This was proof that, whatever he had to say about my work, I would survive it. With his laughter, I sensed I might already have been forgiven for its excesses.

Filet mignon. Roast potatoes and broccoli under silver

covers. Shrimps on ice. Melba toast and a bottle of wine.

"*Eat!*" said Thornton. "You treat your body as if it was your servant, Findley. *You* are your *body's* servant. Feed it. *Eat!*"

The food had arrived on a cart about ten minutes after I had fallen through the door. Thornton had ordered it long before my arrival. If I had failed to materialize, he doubtless would have offered it to the waiter.

"You eat, I'll talk," he said. He never sat down once the whole first hour I was there. He didn't eat, himself. Perhaps he already had. At any rate — I sat there and ate alone while Thornton walked up and down the room and drank his Scotch and water from a stubby tumbler.

Beyond the windows, the sun was setting beyond the city, way beyond the visible skyline. London was still a mass of chimney pots then, and every chimney gave off smoke. The sunset colours infused this smoke with reds and yellows smudged with grey, and all you could see was colour and light and the gradual coming on of lamps as the darkness increased.

This fading light and growing darkness have remained for me an integral part of Thornton's presence and his words that night. But the darkness was neither threatening nor depressing.

"Be confident," he said, "that whatever I say is said as one writer to another. I do not mince words — but neither do I mince writers. You are a writer, Findley. That's a certainty. What you have written, on the other hand. . . ."

What I had written, on the other hand, was everything I had feared it was and hoped it was not:

an intellectual forum in which your
characters talk their problems to death —
not an active exploration of their lives —
— an arrogant tirade, written from a

position of ignorance, not — as it should
be — an impassioned questioning written
from a position of bafflement —
The characters in a play must never know
what is going to happen next. In a play,
the moment is always now. Do you know what
is going to happen in the next five
minutes, Findley?
No, sir —
Well, then —

On the other hand, he conceded that I could handle dialogue.

— and some of your images are
good. Good enough to suggest that more good
images will be forthcoming —

All the while he spoke, he paced and smoked and drank. His cigarette ashes fell helter-skelter. Drops from his glass were spewed out over the carpet every time he turned his pacing in a new direction. But the words he spoke were spare and well considered.

He was always out of breath. His voice had edge — but the edge kept cracking.

He pulled at his tie. His collar wilted. He forgot — or seemed to have forgotten — where he was. He might have been on a hill in Athens five hundred years before the birth of Christ — he might have been blind, dictating to his daughters — he might have been sitting in an eighteenthth century drawing-room, wrapped in flesh and warts — he might have been musing out loud on the fate of roses in a Paris garden, circa 1910. He was all great teachers in one. The only assumptions he made were that knowledge was important and that I cared.

"Pay attention, Findley. Pay attention. That is all you have to do. Never, for an instant, leave off paying attention."

So it was. That evening, my attentions garnered the following:

I could write — but had written a travesty.
Talk is cheap — but you pay a hefty price
for the written word.
Come down from all high-minded places — no
one down here can hear you.
A writer — however good he may be
intrinsically — cannot communicate without
a sense of craft. In writing — the craft is
all.

After he had spoken and I had eaten, he gave me back my pages and urged me to put them away in a drawer.

"When you write again, write something new," he said. "Ordinarily, I say the wastepaper basket is a writer's best friend — but keep these pages as a reminder of how intentions go awry. Otherwise, forget it. Don't even mourn it, Findley. You've more important things to do than that."

He walked me to the elevator.

After I had thanked him, he wanted to know if I was going to go home on the bus or on the tube.

"I'm going to walk," I said.

Which I did.

It took me about two hours. But every step was worth it. All the way home, I smiled.

You only have such an evening once in your life. There isn't room for two.

The relationship begun with Ruth and Thornton in

London lasted through the years in places such as Berlin and Boston, Edinburgh and New York, San Francisco and Chicago, Washington, D.C. and Los Angeles. There was never a moment, for me, that wasn't rewarding — even when arguments, misunderstandings and temperament stood in the way.

Thornton remained my mentor until he died in 1975. We wrote long letters often and saw each other on occasion. I never failed to pay attention.

The last time I saw Ruth, in person, was at the memorial service given for Thornton. This was in January 1976 at Yale's Battell Chapel. We all stood then, together, having come inside from the wind and snow of a New Haven winter and we sang the hymn from *Our Town* — "Blessed Be the Ties That Bind." What I remember most from that service is the enduring smell of melting ice and the sound of radiators cracking with heat as we sang. We stood in our boots and galoshes — overcoats over our shoulders against the draft and scarves draped round our necks. Ruth's opening words, when she got up to speak to all of us, were *have you got a minute?*

There it was — the essence of Thornton Wilder.

Have you got a minute? Have you got a lifetime?

Let's talk.

Late in the summer of 1955, Thornton and I went on one of our pub crawls. These could take place anywhere. You named a street — a district — a town — and you tried to drink in all its pubs and bars. Highfalutin hotel bars were out. You drank in them when you were on the road. A pub crawl was where you drank for pleasure — not for business reasons.

The pub crawl this time took us to Fleet Street.

"If you start at Temple Bar — which is where Fleet Street begins," said Thornton, "and end at St Paul's churchyard, you can practically touch the whole of English literature. . . ."

Daniel Defoe was pilloried there at Temple Bar — and across the road at Child's Bank, Samuel Pepys and John Dryden kept their money — Henry Fielding, William Congreve, Oliver Goldsmith and William Makepeace Thackeray all were feted there in the Temple Hall — and this is where Charlotte Brontë was introduced to the London literary scene, riding in Thackeray's carriage along this street. Conrad wrote here. There — in the courtyard up that alley, is Doctor Johnson's house, where he created his dictionary. . . .

On and on they went — the names.

"Know where you enter," Thornton said. "Know where you enter into the literature of your language. . . ."

We stood, at the far end, having drunk many glasses of wine and many tumblers of Scotch — and, looking up at the massive doors of St Paul's Cathedral, we devised a staging of the *Agamemnon* of Aeschylus. "The great doors open and Clytemnestra appears with her husband's body. . . ."

We were like two excited children, suddenly falling on a world of life-sized toys.

This was a part of Thornton never to be forgotten. The joy he took in recognizing other people's joy.

"Shakespeare's publisher set up his stall in the church-yard, there," he said — pointing through the fence at the gardens. "How Shakespeare loved to come into this city! All this was food and drink to him, Findley. The great trees that would have been here then — the sellers' stalls — the people buying books — the colour of it all — the dawning of universal knowledge — and he was at the centre of it. God — he *was* the centre!"

Thornton tooted every horn but his own.

One last image of Ruth.

This is in New York.

I have rejoined the cast of *The Matchmaker*, having stayed behind in England when the production was moved to America. This would be sometime in 1956. Perhaps October or November.

The mails have brought me a copy of *The Tamarack Review*, from Canada, in which "About Effie" has been published. This is my first publication, anywhere, ever, of anything.

I am sick with excitement.

I tear the envelope open and look inside. There it is. There is even an illustration.

Ruth must see this. Ruth made it happen. This is how it all began.

I clattered down the stairs — tying the strings of my apron — holding the magazine in my mouth.

I race along the hall and around the corner. There is The Bird.

She rises from her little chair.

"No," she says. "Don't!"

Heedless — I rap just once on Ruth's door — and fling it open.

Goodness. . . .

Ruth is standing there, wearing her slip and pulling on her stockings. She has — at sixty — the most beautiful legs I have ever seen.

She looks at me and yells with a terrible loudness: "GET THE HELL OUT OF HERE!"

I fling the magazine onto her dressing-table and lunge for the doorway.

I go somewhere and hide.

Now — for certain — I will be fired.

Nothing happens. Dreadful silence ensues. The first act plays and I am not in it. I lock my dressing-room door.

At last, the call comes: *Act Two beginners, please.*

I go down onto the stage.

Since everyone is in this scene, the whole company is now assembled. Ruth will come — and fire me in front of all my friends.

She sweeps out onto the stage. The curtain is down. We can hear the audience.

"Listen, everybody!" Ruth says. "I have something to tell you all about Mister Findley. . . ."

Oh, God.

She turns towards me and smiles. The whole shebang. She has the kind of smile that kills.

"Darlin'," she says. "I want them all to know."

Then she turns and says to the others: "Tiffy has been published! And here it is, in my hand!"

She shows the magazine and turns back to me and pulls me down and kisses me on the top of my head.

"Next time you're published, darlin' — I only hope I'm stark naked!"

Gone, now. Both of them.

Whirlwind and teacher.

Stone Orchard
March 1990

Another memory from London in the mid-1950s: I had just been up on the top floor of Harrod's — I can't remember why. What I do remember is coming down in the elevator. Reaching the third floor, the elevator stopped and the doors opened.

There stood — unmistakably — Beatrice Lillie: Lady Peel.

She was wearing her famous toque hat, her leopard skin coat and a pair of dark glasses.

I was the only passenger in the lift.

Miss Lillie paused. I can still see her eyes behind those tinted lenses. She was looking at me sharply.

I was thinking: *how wonderful! I adore this woman: she's probably the funniest human being alive. I come from Toronto. She comes from Toronto. I am an actor. She is an actress. What a delightful conversation we will have!*

I smiled.

Miss Lillie raised her glasses for a better look. She swept the length of my body with her eyes — and then:

"No thank you," she said.

She lowered her glasses and folded her hands.

The elevator doors closed.

For weeks after that, I studied myself in the mirror — but I couldn't work it out. In fact, to this very day, I'm stymied. Perhaps — somehow — she guessed I was from Toronto.

Stone Orchard
March 1989

I was twenty-four years old — an actor still, before my writing days — and working London's West End. The play I was in was called *The Prisoner*, written by Bridget Boland and starring Alec Guinness and Wilfred Lawson. I had earlier worked with Guinness at Stratford's first summer, in 1953. After an evening performance in March of 1954, Guinness called me to his dressing room and asked if I would be willing to play the role of Charles Surface in a rehearsal of the famous screen scene from Sheridan's *School for Scandal*. The occasion of the ultimate performance of this scene was to be a gala celebration in honour of Dame Sybil Thorndike, who was then arriving at one of the major mileposts in her long and distinguished career.

The screen scene was to be performed by Guinness,

Paul Scofield, James Donald, Paul Hardwicke and Vivien Leigh. I was being asked to take part because Scofield, who was to play Charles Surface, could not attend the initial rehearsal and the director, John Gielgud, needed a body to move around the stage in his place. Mine was the body chosen. The only problem was — the body had lines to speak.

"You can carry the book, of course," Guinness had said at his invitation. "We'll all be carrying the book — so there's nothing you have to learn. Just read the words and walk the moves. . . ."

Hah!

I wore my blue "audition" suit and looked okay — but I was dreadfully nervous. John Gielgud — Vivien Leigh! To say nothing of Guinness. He took me to lunch at Prunier's to soothe my nerves. It didn't work. Sir John was a god — Miss Leigh a goddess. So there I was, standing in for Paul Scolfield (another god) and very much a mortal.

The gist of what Charles Surface has to do in the scene revolves around why it is called "the screen scene" in the first place. Lady Teazle (Leigh) has been caught in Joseph Surface's (Donald) rooms by the sudden arrival of her husband, Sir Peter (Guinness) and she seeks a hiding place behind an ornate Chinese screen. Once Sir Peter is onstage, *he* is surprised by the sudden arrival of Charles Surface (Scofield — me) — whom he does not wish to see. Sir Peter hides in a closet. On comes Charles — slightly hung over — to castigate his immoral and conniving brother, Joseph — catches the sound of a cough from Sir Peter — reveals him by throwing open the closet door — and then catches the sound of movement elsewhere and throws over the screen to reveal Lady Teazle. Woe! Disaster! Humiliation! Charles then throws down the gauntlet in a rather wonderful speech (he is in love with Lady T., himself) and sweeps off. That's it.

Now, all you need to add is that we were to rehearse this scene on the set of *The Big Knife*, because they had no matinee that day and the stage was "free." The modern furniture was pushed back against the set's walls and room made for the screen.

Hearing my cue, on I came. Guinness was "hiding" in his "closet" — watching me closely. I was his protege and must do him honour. Miss Leigh was ensconced with a crossword puzzle behind the screen — but watching, I was aware, what I was up to.

I did my initial number — quaking, book shaking, voice hoarse — and castigated James Donald, who was singularly unmoved and unperturbed. I then revealed Guinness — (who muttered: "you're reading too fast! Don't garble the words!") and moved upstage to throw down the screen.

Terrified of maiming Miss Leigh for life, I somehow managed to avoid her — and down went the screen with a satisfying *crash*! There I was, face to face with Scarlett O'Hara. . . .

Oh god.

I worshipped her. She was lovely, she was kind. She *touched me*. Her fingers gripped my arm.

I finished the wonderful speech — addressing it to Vivien Leigh and Guinness — beginning to have the faintest sense of triumph. I hadn't bumped into Guinness — I hadn't crippled James Donald by walking on his toes — but, above all, I hadn't killed Vivien Leigh with the screen. In fact, at one moment I think I saw her mouth her approval to Guinness: *he's very good!*

I finished my speech and turned to "sweep off". . . .

Disaster.

There was the yellow chair.

How big it was. How well made — formidable — and

present it was. As if it had made an entrance especially to block my way.

How successful it was.

I went into it — *bam!* — and tipped it over, sending both it and a nearby table crashing to the floor. And me, of course. I went crashing, too.

I lay there in ruins. My humiliation was absolute. Done in forever by a yellow chair.

Scarlett O'Hara turned to the masterbuilder of the *Bridge on the River Kwai* and smiled her enigmatic smile. "Who was it who said: *just learn your lines and don't bump into the furniture?*"

"Spencer Tracy," said Guinness, as he offered to help me to my feet. "And worth remembering," he added, laughing kindly. "You did very well, till then," he muttered.

I looked at Viven Leigh.

"Don't worry," she said. "One day you'll play Charles Surface — and you'll tell this story to break the ice."

She was more than kind.

I never did play Charles Surface. But now, I have told the story. And I can only add: *beware of yellow chairs.* For myself, I won't allow them anywhere near me.

Stone Orchard
February 1990
Radio

My memory keeps delivering the past in brown-paper parcels done up with string and marked "address of sender unknown." One such parcel arrived the other day. Winter. Early evening. Not quite dark, but dark enough to turn on lights.

I had gone upstairs. The parcel was in my bedroom — waiting to surprise me. Not by saying "boo" and flinging itself at my feet in order to trip me up. Nothing like that. No *bangs*. No lurching shapes. It was a gentle, undemonstrative surprise.

I don't know how it arrived — I don't know why. But slowly, as I moved about the room adjusting lamps and thermostats, I was gradually overwhelmed by a certainty that someone was about to speak.

The noise, my dear. And the people. . . .

The words were only in my mind, but the voice was very clear — distinct as any living voice.

Ernest Thesiger — wraithlike enough while still alive — pulled in and out of focus as I closed my eyes and tried to conjure him. *Ernest, tied with string and wrapped in brown paper.* Where was he coming from? Why was he being delivered now?

The noise, my dear — and the people.

This was Ernest's best known pronouncement, his reply when — returning from Flanders in 1917 with his hands so badly mangled it was thought they must soon be amputated — he was asked to describe the horrors of the battlefield.

The noise, my dear.

And the people, he said.

But why had I thought of that now?

I hadn't seen Ernest Thesiger for over thirty-five years — and he'd been dead since 1961.

Ernest Thesiger. Actor. Eccentric. Friend.

Well. What else was in the package? I sat on the bed and lighted a cigarette. Outside, the sky had almost completely blackened. A wind had risen — cold and menacing, promising snow. The world was disappearing, whiting-out in the dark.

Moscow. That was it. Part of it.

I had gone to Moscow with Ernest Thesiger in 1955. We had arrived there long after nightfall, in a blizzard. The storm had been so bad and our landing had been delayed so long that the plane was running out of fuel.

We thought for certain we would be killed. And out of the silence created by our fearfulness, Ernest had asked in an offhand manner: *does anyone remember the Russian word for ambulance?*

He made us all laugh.

He always could — if he wanted to.

Christmas was not far off, that winter afternoon, and I realized with pleasure that Ernest would soon begin turning up again on the television screen, making his annual appearance in *Scrooge*. I mean in the best of all possible versions of *A Christmas Carol* — the one with Alastair Sim. Thesiger plays the conniving undertaker plotting the acquisition of Scrooge's possessions after Ebenezer "dies" in one of his nightmares. It is delightful. The undertaker's role gives him an opportunity to put on display what might be called "the essential Thesiger." Swathed in scarves and dressed in black, with his hands in fingerless gloves, he gives the impression of a cadaver's cadaver, just as, in life, he was an actor's actor.

I hadn't thought of Ernest Thesiger in such a long while. It was a comfort, sitting there in the lamplight, bringing him back into focus. I had been aware of him long before we met — aware of him even before I knew his name. He was the man whose appearance always made you smile with anticipation: something interesting was bound to happen if he turned up. His appearance had the same effect as a music cue.

Often, what happened was sinister. For instance, if it was a "costume film," the minute Ernest turned up, you knew the hero was about to be caught in a diabolical trap. Whereas, if the setting was contemporary, the presence of Ernest Thesiger signalled comic complications. He was rarely sinister in modern dress — and I've no idea what that meant, except to say it must have had to do with his physical appearance. Robes and ruffles gave him somewhere to hide — a business suit could not begin to hide him. Hidden, he could be frightening — but revealed, he caused a riot. Ernest Thesiger was a *provocateur* — in life as well as his career.

Tucked in the parcel of memories beside him, there was a ring, an autograph, a sewing needle and a bicycle.

I recognized them instantly. These were Ernest's signs and symbols: his accumulation, over time, of the keys to his personality; his signature.

The bicycle on which, in his youth, he had ridden to Tite Street and tea with Oscar Wilde had become the symbol of his destiny. The sewing needle was a sign of patience. The autograph was his signature imposed on yours. The ring was his symbol of disguise.

There was always a sense, in Ernest's company, of being drawn into a charming conspiracy. The autograph game was his way of introducing himself.

"Give me your signature," he would say. "Put it on a large sheet of paper."

Once you had complied, Ernest would stare at your name for a moment, in much the same way a medium would stare at whatever talisman you might have handed her in order to acquaint her with your karma. He would turn the autograph upside down and sideways — hold it up against the light and run his eye up and down its shape. Then he would say: *most interesting* . . . as if your name had spoken.

You would watch all this with growing fascination. His own concentration augmented yours and, this way, he could create an alarming sense of tension. *What was he going to find in what you had written?*

Then, with pursed lips, he would say to you: *give me your pen.* And he would begin to mark your autograph with what, at first, appeared to be hieroglyphs and runes. But they were not.

When he was finished, he would hand you back your pen and the sheet of paper on which *you* had written and *he* had drawn — and, instead of your signature, there would be a human figure or a tree — a vase of flowers or a gargoyle. Mine was a young Edwardian dandy — wearing a boater and sporting a walking stick. *That's you*, he said. *Or one of you. . . .*

He had not known that I had played such a character on Canadian television long before I had gone to England and longer still before I had met him.

I have said that Ernest's hands were all but destroyed in the First World War. They were crushed when a building he was hiding in was blown to pieces during a bombardment. A whole wall fell on Ernest, smashing his hands and almost tearing his arms from his body. "I lay there, waiting for rescue, almost all of one day," he said. "I could not see my arms or my hands — and the only thing that informed me I had not lost them was the pain. I was almost reassured by this, until I dimly remembered what friends had said to me when they had lost their legs and arms — which was that you go on feeling as if they were still with you — long, long after they have gone. *Ghost pains*, they call this. I got in a dreadful panic then, and prayed that I would die. I could not imagine, you see, my life without arms. I had wanted to be an artist and an actor — and how could I be either one without my arms?"

The noise, my dear, and the people.

His arms and his hands were saved — but it took a great long while for Ernest Thesiger to recover their use. This is where needlework entered his life — as a therapeutic activity by which he could regain control of his dexterity. It is also where the ring, as a symbol of disguise, took its place in Ernest's consciousness.

His hands, as he found them even after two or three

years of therapy, had not recovered their "beauty."

"Very ugly they were," he said — and held them out for me to see. "Worse than you see them, now. I could not bear to look at them. They made me weep."

Until the day of his death, it is true, his hands — in repose and stripped of gloves and other masquerades — were not the best a person could hope for. The fingers were delicate and bent and the knuckles as bony as those of any victim of arthritis. Still, he had beautiful fingernails and skin and he hid what he could of the wounds with rings.

Silver rings were his favourites. Never gaudy and always intriguing, each ring had a story. One I remember in particular. It was shown to me on a winter evening in 1955 — much like the evening thirty-five years later on which I had been ambushed so unexpectedly by Ernest's ghost in its brown-paper wrappings. The ring was one of the many Ernest wore — a heavy silver ring with an opal set in lion's claws. He showed it to me at his flat in London, after we had returned from Moscow. He was giving a cocktail party on a Sunday afternoon — the favoured day for actors' parties — and we sat on a blue velvet sofa under lamplight.

Ernest's voice, as I remember it, crackled and wavered somewhere between his nose and the back of his throat. He always seemed to be about to expire. It was a quavering voice with amazing strength. . . .

"This ring," he said — and he held it under the lamplight — "belonged to Lucretia Borgia. . . ."

I asked if I could touch it and he said: "you may, but not before I show you something. Here — look at this. . . ."

He placed the ring on the little finger of his left hand, removing another ring in order to do so.

"Give me your drink," he said.

I gave him my martini.

He placed the glass on a small round table between our knees and waved both hands above it — the right hand touching the left hand for the briefest moment.

"There," said Ernest, sitting back and smiling invitingly. "Take it now and see what you think."

I lifted the glass and drank. My martini was suddenly inexplicably sweet. I made a face.

Ernest laughed.

"You're dead," he said. "I've poisoned you!"

"You've also ruined my drink," I said.

"It's only sugar," Ernest explained. He removed the ring and showed it to me again — giving the opal a gentle tap with his fingernail. "The poison goes in here, beneath the stone, you see." He pushed against the opal, revealing a tiny compartment underneath. "I fill it with sugar from time to time, for amusement's sake," he said. His eyes were shining. "I poisoned the Prince of Wales with it, once," he told me. "It was quite a triumph!"

Ernest lifted another martini from a passing tray and gave it to me. "Whenever I dined with the Prince of Wales after that, he used to inspect my rings before we sat down. It became our joke. He asked me, once, if I would lend it to him, but I told him: *not, sir, unless you tell me who the intended victim is going to be.* My brother George, he said — meaning the late Duke of Kent — and I said: *oh, sir, you cannot want to kill the Duke of Kent!* And he said, yes, because he has more fun than I do. . . ."

Ernest became quite suddenly serious.

"You know," he said, "the strangest expression came into the Prince's eyes when he told me that. He was joking. Of course, he was joking. But . . . a look of anguish — of *sadness* overcame him — just for a moment — and he could not prevent it. Poor man. Deep inside, he really did feel trapped, I think. And the Duke of Kent — *well, he,* . . ." Ernest laughed, . . . "*was another story!* The

Prince of Wales was right. Quite right! His brother George had a great, *great* deal more fun than *any*one!"

We looked again at Lucretia Borgia's ring.

"Put it on," he said. "Go ahead."

But I had lost — I don't know why — my desire to wear it.

"No," I said. "Thank you."

Ernest looked at me.

He could see that his story had sobered me, as perhaps he had intended. Hidden inside what appeared to be a harmless anecdote about regal foibles, there had been a tender message of sympathy. He had seen in me a young man who shared the same crises and misgivings that he had endured when he was young. Ernest had found his courage long before Flanders, when his mentor, Oscar Wilde, had been humiliated, arrested and sent to gaol — losing everything in one rash gesture. We never spoke of these things in so many words. But much was implicit through various other words and gestures. Ernest, in spite of public mockery, had gone on to become, most emphatically and fearlessly, himself — and he was always urging me to do the same.

It wasn't easy.

Nonetheless, when he heard me say that I no longer wanted to wear Lucretia Borgia's ring, he looked at me carefully before he spoke — and then he said: "never mind, never mind."

Then he put the ring away.

"But I was so looking forward to hearing about your intended victim!" he said.

His empathy could be wicked.

Ernest was not alone in the package I received that late afternoon. Perhaps in some ways it was inevitable that in my memory, especially, he should always keep the company of another with whom, in real life, I doubt very much he would have kept company at all.

This is one of the better tricks that memory plays. The crowd inside is made of disparate players whose swords may have crossed more often than their lives. I find it very hard to imagine Ernest in possession of a sword — but I think he might have armed himself with one if he had known who would share the package with him that day. . . .

It was another British actor and quite an unlikely one, at that. His name was Wilfrid Lawson and my first memory of him was when he played Alfred Doolittle — Eliza's father — the dustman, in the 1938 film of George Bernard Shaw's *Pygmalion*.

As implied by his name, Doolittle's constant excuse for not getting very far in life was that he was always being thwarted by *middle-class morality*. Doolittle's complaint is fairly descriptive of any actor's life — certainly of Wilfrid Lawson's life, though for quite different reasons. And of Ernest Thesiger's life — and my own — though again, for entirely different reasons.

Middle-class morality has probably driven more actors into the theatre than it ever reached in and pulled out. But that's another story, too, and not what this is about — though middle-class morality would not have approved of Wilfrid Lawson any more than it approved of Alfred Doolittle.

Wilfrid Lawson — flailing and wiry — driven by an excess of bottled energy — dances into view. His voice, which always faltered, was like a singer's voice gone mad. He pitched his words up high and tried to catch them when they fell. His speech was made of glottal stops and choking — undelivered roaring — endless lapses into tenderness. He never spoke — like Molière's Bourgeois

47

Gentilhomme — in prose. It was always some kind of poetry.

I made a journey with Wilfrid Lawson, too — not so great a journey as with Ernest in terms of miles, but greater in terms of intimacy. I was Wilfrid Lawson's keeper, in a way. It was my responsibility, on tour, to share his digs and get him to the theatre on time.

Of course, one immediately thinks of Alfred Doolittle's song in *My Fair Lady* — the musical based on *Pygmalion*. But, getting Alfred to the *church* on time was done with a band of a dozen burly dancers. I had to do it without a band and I was decidedly un-burly. A flyweight, you might say, pitted against the heavyweight champion of the world.

Wilfrid Lawson's drinking was legendary. I knew all about it long before I knew him. But he had good reason to drink — if such a thing can be said — and I guess, in Wilfrid Lawson's case, it *must* be said. He did not drink for the fun of it. Nor because he wanted to drown his sorrows. None of the classic reasons fitted Wilfrid Lawson's relationship with alcohol. He drank to stifle pain. Real pain — not imagined. Not occasional pain — but constant.

He took to drink with cold deliberation. He knew very well that, in the end, it would kill him. Perhaps, because of the pain, a part of him wanted that. I cannot say. But in the meantime, waiting for his death — drink would enable him to function.

The pain was caused by a metal plate in his skull. Like Ernest, Mister Lawson had been dreadfully wounded in the First World War and the plate had been placed in his skull in an effort to save his life. His life *had* been saved — the surgery had done that — but life itself had been made intolerable. The plate did that. He was crippled forever after.

Given that, at the time the surgery was performed, the techniques were primitive — and given that science had not yet provided the sophisticated painkillers we have today, Wilfrid Lawson had little choice in the matter of whether or not he could deal with the pain. We are not talking here of something that fortitude and aspirin — in whatever combinations — would ameliorate. Morphine and alcohol were all that would help.

Wilfrid Lawson chose alcohol because he knew that if he had chosen the more desirable morphine to deaden his pain, he would also be choosing a drug that would prevent him utterly from pursuing his career as an actor.

Later, as he himself often said, other drugs presented themselves from time to time — especially during and after the Second World War — that might have helped. He did, in fact, try some of these — in tandem with attempts to withdraw from his regimen of drink. But by then, the drink itself had become a kind of food to him — a habit to his system from which there could be no permanent recovery. He began to go on and off the wagon like a mechanical toy that had been doomed to repeat the same process forever, until it burned out and dropped. Doomed and damned.

We were in a play called *The Prisoner*. It had been written by Bridget Boland and was loosely based on the brain-washing torture suffered at the hands of Hungarian Communists by Cardinal Mindszenty. Alec Guinness played the Cardinal. Wilfrid Lawson played his keeper — his jailer. I played a clerk in the office of The Prosecutor who succeeded in turning the Cardinal's mind.

We went on a lengthy tour in the winter of 1954, prior to opening in London early that spring. Edinburgh, Liverpool, Manchester, Leeds and Cambridge. I was not put in charge of Mister Lawson until we got to Liverpool.

The rehearsal period prior to the tour had gone quite well. It was a tough, unrelenting and exhausting play to rehearse — let alone to play. Alec Guinness had alternate scenes with Wilfrid Lawson and The Prosecutor, played by the late Noel Willman. Guinness, once on, was virtually never off again until the final curtain. It was a punishing role and it took every ounce of daring and concentration to pull it off.

Everyone was nervous of Mister Lawson.

Would he — *could* he — sustain his current regimen of sobriety and pills for the run of the play? Everyone hoped so — and everyone wanted it to be so, not only for their own sake, but for Mister Lawson's sake. He was such a splendid actor — greatly admired and loved — and he needed a success. His last performances, in the title role of Strindberg's *The Father*, had been a triumph for him — but a triumph that ended badly when he started to drink again.

At any rate, there were only one or two incidents during rehearsal — a missed afternoon when Mister Lawson returned late from lunch and his lunch had been mostly liquid. That was difficult. Guinness — who adored Mister Lawson and gave him total respect — was nervous, nonetheless. So much of his on-stage time was spent with Lawson as the jailer — and, in bad rehearsals, the outcome could be a nightmare of undelivered cues and rambling speeches, barely audible, stringing Mister Lawson's performance together.

Serious consideration was given, at one point, to hiring a replacement. But Lawson came through — and off we set.

By the time we got to Liverpool and I was living in digs with Mister Lawson, the drinking was on its way to becoming chronic. The bottle of ale was never far from his hand.

We had the loveliest landlady there. I can see her still: tiny — sweet — and very old. She adored Mister Lawson — and he had been her house guest for thirty years or more — whenever his plays had brought him to Liverpool. She always provided his favourite jams and jellies — she knew exactly how to cook his eggs — and she was expert at stashing the great green bottles of Bass on which he thrived between his rounds of hard liquor.

We did not share a room. It would have been intolerable. Mister Lawson always went to bed sodden and all night long he would be dragged from one nightmare to another — often yelling — more often screaming — very often struggling physically to free himself of impeding bedclothes and threatening shapes in the shadows.

His voice had a liquid quality at times — as if his vocal chords were being stewed — and he would sound as if he were drowning.

"Help! Help! Help!" he would shout — and sometimes, he would pound against the walls. "Help! Help!"

The noise, my dear — and the people.

It wasn't funny.

It was a horror story.

I would have to rise and go to his room and Mrs Whatever would beg me to go in and save him.

"A *man* has to do it," she would say. "He will not tolerate a woman being his saviour."

So, I would go in.

To darkness.

I was always afraid. He could be so violent.

He didn't mean to be.

I felt so helpless with him — knowing that, from his point of view, I was always coming for him out of flames and battle-sounds and the cries of other people dying. What did it mean that a crazy young man in pyjamas was coming to save him from his fallen aeroplane and the hor-

51

rors of the mud?

And so, in spite of calling *help! help! help!* he would then do battle with me — trying to beat me off. *Don't! Don't!* he would say. *Don't! Don't! I cannot bear it!*

Neither could I.

Often, I would have to lead him away — at last — from his wrecked and ruined bed — his aeroplane — and get him from that wreckage, down the hall through no-man's-land — first to the WC and then to the bathroom, where, in the dreadful light of naked bulbs, he would let me wash his face and hands and adjust his uniform.

Mrs Whatever, by then, would have a tea-tray in his room and I would sit and watch from near the doorway, while Mister Lawson topped up his tea with something from a bottle.

Next day — every day — he would call me into the parlour on the first floor and he would be sitting in the corner — lit with delicate, forgiving light, and he would say to me: *all right, Findley, stand at attention and give me your report.*

I stood — like a soldier — looking over his head, and — arms pressed in against my sides and thumbs facing forwards — I would tell him that nothing untoward had happened in the night.

Going to the theatre, we always walked — unless it was a great way off — and Mister Lawson wore a tweed deer-stalker and an Inverness overcoat with a cape.

We more or less marched. It was supposed to be good for our lungs. *Take in lots of air, Findley. Take in lots of air!*

My nightmare was that he would spot a pub and want to go in. That never happened. I guess it didn't need to. Primed before he left the digs — his dressing-room was pub enough to welcome him upon arrival.

When Mister Lawson dried on stage, he would put a matchstick into his mouth and chew on that to force his concentration. Alec Guinness used to count the matches.

On a bad night, he would say, as he made his way to his dressing room: *Wilfrid ate two dozen matches tonight.*

The record was thirty-five.

They came — already old — into my young life. They left an indelible and wondrous impression — and they gave me the gift of their company whether for good or ill.

I never lost respect for Mister Lawson. He was — and he remains in memories — a superb performer — a giant among the actors of his time.

He worked to the very last year of his life — when, in 1966, he appeared in a glorious farce on film: Bryan Forbes's production of *The Wrong Box*. See it, for heaven's sake, if you can. Besides its other joys and delights — the masterful comedy of Ralph Richardson being chief among them — there is also the wonder of Wilfrid Lawson's bug-eyed scarecrow of a butler — with his collar askew and his white gloves torn with his nervous chewing on the finger ends — brushing other visions away with an impatient hand — pointing at a packing crate lodged, immobilized, in a doorway and pronouncing with infinite wisdom: "That is stuck. That is what that is."

His voice alone is worth the price of admission.

The only time I worked with Ernest Thesiger was in a production of *Hamlet* in which I played Osric. All through rehearsals, I was tormented by the director, Peter Brook, who had decided — for reasons of his own I will not go into — that I was this year's whipping boy. He would simply not let me rehearse. Every time we came to Osric's entrance, he would say: *stop! May we have the next scene, please.*

53

It all began about one week in, when, moments after I had made my first entrance, Peter Brook called from the darkness: "Mister Findley — what do you think you are doing?"

These words were said with a chilling glaze of illogical anger. Hearing them, you might have thought I had come on riding a bicycle and juggling oranges.

Well — it got worse. Since I really hadn't done anything other than what we had so far decided I should be doing, both I and everyone else on stage knew perfectly well what was happening. I had been chosen. The knife had fallen and it was lodged in me.

I had seen this happen to other actors in other productions. It is just the way some directors are. Even the greatest of them — as with Peter Brook — may need, for whatever reason, to put someone away. They never fire you, under these circumstances. And your resignation would not be accepted. The whipping boy must stand his ground and make his way alone.

In the long run, the other actors and I worked out our own blocking and simply got on with the scene by rehearsing it, during breaks, in dressing-rooms and corridors. Peter Brook didn't even let us do the scene at the cue-to-cue rehearsal when we first got onto the set — nor at the dress rehearsal. The first time I actually played it on the set was opening night in Brighton.

Some weeks later, we all flew to Moscow — where the production was a huge success. This was in 1955 and it was an auspicious occasion. Stalin had only been dead for two years — Burgess and Maclean had defected in the relatively recent past — and the Cold War was at its height.

Ours was the very first visit of any British company of actors since the Revolution of 1917. Hamlet was played by Paul Scofield, Gertrude by Diana Wynyard, Claudius by Alec Clunes and Ophelia by Mary Ure. Ernest played Polonius. All these actors, excepting Paul Scofield, are now dead — wrapped in their own brown-paper parcels — but Ernest was my favourite. When we got, at last, to Moscow, he had to be restrained. He was determined that he was going to sneak out one night from our hotel across the road from the Kremlin and write — in chalk — on its historic walls: BURGESS LOVES MACLEAN*!!!*

I wish he had.

Kenneth Tynan once described Ernest Thesiger as a "praying mantis." It was an apt description. He often held his hands before his breast with just the fingertips touching and all the rings showing nicely. He marcelled his hair and tinted it. The length of his nose, which was immense, was often powdered to hide its redness. He was something of a fashion-plate. His clothes were always impeccably cut and he wore them always with a sense of style. He favoured Prussian blue ties with polka dots — and sometimes wore a handkerchief neatly tucked into his sleeve. . . .

The brown-paper package is nearly completely undone — its string is lying untied on the floor. Wilfrid Lawson makes one final appearance — dressed in the Inverness coat and with flying wisps of hair. He has been on a binge and we have got the understudy into costume and ready to go on. Where is Wilfrid? Where? Where? Where? We are playing in London now — at the Globe on Shaftesbury Avenue — backing into twisting alleys — the alleys filled with Soho pubs and restaurants.

Suddenly, the doors of the scene dock — enormous doors on pulleys — fly up to heaven and there is Wilfrid Lawson — roaring — literally. . . .

WHERE IS MY THEATRE? WHERE IS MY STAGE?

He is clothed in coat and hair — and little else. The overcoat flies open revealing Mister Lawson's long johns and boots.

I WANT MY THEATRE! I WANT MY STAGE!

The understudy went on.

Mister Lawson went to sleep.

It was, for a change, a sleep without nightmares.

Ernest's final symbol was a sewing needle. Under the tutelage of his therapists, he had become so proficient in needlepoint that, less than twenty years later, he was one of Queen Mary's favourite sewing partners. She and Ernest would sit at either end of the carpet she was making and stitch away whole afternoons and mornings. Ernest, by the way, began to dye his hair around the time of the carpet — a time when he was also severely depressed and it turned, in Oscar Wilde's words, *quite gold with grief!* In the long run, Ernest Thesiger and Queen Mary began to look like one another — and, over the years, as the aging dowager explored other colours, other rinses, so likewise did Ernest. By the time I knew him in the mid-1950s, soon after Queen Mary's death, his "grief" was tinted blue. "She was, in many ways, my dearest friend," he told me. "I sensed that her silence was made of the same ingredients as mine. She endured a kind of private mourning, from time to time. And so did I. It had to do with the lives we would have preferred to live but could not because of who we were." He thought about this for a moment — then he added: "I do not mean who we were when we were born. I mean the people we became by necessity, rather than by desire. . . ."

The wind blows now — the sky is black — the snow arrives. My windows — unshaded — are filled with reflections of the lamplit room. I think of Ernest's wondrous, crazy face and his broken hands and I think: *it is true that beauty is only skin deep.* But Ernest's lack of it cut to the marrow of his heart. Not, of course, that he ever said so. It was just the way he survived it: smiling.

He used to come, every night, dressed as Polonius, his needlework held in his hands, and he would stand in the wings and watch as I went out to play Osric. All through the sequence, he would stand there — every night for weeks, in all the towns we played in England — and in Moscow — and, finally, in London. Watching — just watching — saying nothing.

At last, the scene began to play and, in spite of all the problems it had presented, it became a joy to go on stage. One night, just as I made my exit, there came a round of applause. That had never happened to me before, under any circumstance. I was stunned.

Ernest, in the wings, was beaming.

He put out one hand and took my arm.

He didn't say a word. When we came to his dressing-room, he went inside, turned around and said: *"thank you."*

Upstairs, in my own dressing-room, I cried. Not because there had been applause — but because I was overwhelmed all at once with the knowledge that Ernest had stood in the wings all those weeks to show me that in spite of Peter Brook he had believed in me. And he stayed there until I got it right. Until I believed in myself. After that, he never appeared in the wings again.

The package is now completely undone — and I am left with its fragmented contents — Ernest and his symbols — Mister Lawson and his icons: sewing needles, rings and autographs — dark green bottles of Bass — beds wrecked as aeroplanes — Inverness coats and thirty-five matchsticks, chewed and ruined — thirty-five fires that Wilfrid Lawson never got to start.

As I go to the window, it seems that all I can see is the darkness outside and a few reflections. But way off — out beyond the reach of any normal light that any normal lamp can throw — I can just discern the shape of Ernest on his bicycle — making his way, aged seventeen, along the Chelsea Embankment until he comes to Tite Street, where Oscar Wilde has invited him to tea.

Ernest is about to discover the importance of being oneself — no matter what.

He arrives at Oscar's door on a day long before my parents are born — before Mister Lawson is born — before I am even thought of. And yet, I see him standing there. And, in between that day and this. . . .

The noise, my dear. . . .

And. . . .

The people.

I wave — and he is gone.

But not forever. Other parcels will arrive, in time. In time, I will remember more.

Stone Orchard
January 1971
Radio

I can remember, some years ago, walking down a particularly arid city street, making my way from the apartment where I lived to the office where I worked. This was in Los Angeles, and out there, the smog makes your eyes water so that you can barely keep them open to see where you are going. After you've been there awhile, you realize that Angelenos don't wear sunglasses to avoid the glare of the sun but the plague of the smog.

Anyway, there I was walking along whatever street it

was, having just come out of one concrete monstrosity, passing by others and heading for the one I worked in. Little plastic trees had been set up in tubs at intervals along the sidewalk. And as I made my way, I looked down at my feet and then up at the invisible sky, and was aware of the concrete that hedged me in — and I thought: but I wasn't born into *this*. My *body* wasn't born into this . . . *place!* I was born *alive*; yet this is where I'm asking my body to function. What is the matter with me?

And I looked at all the people going past. And I thought: I don't and will not ever know who these people are. And they do not and never *will* know me. And I thought: but when I go up in the elevator in the building where I work, then I'll be able to nod at the elevator operator. Yes. And I will say "good-morning" to Miss Gregson, who sits at the front desk. And when I get into the executive section, then I'll be able to see one or two movie stars, perhaps, discussing contracts — and even if I don't know them personally, at least I'll know their *faces* from the silver screen. Then, getting further into the bowels of the building, I will come upon the writers' section and in there I'm allowed to nod at Rod Serling, who is not allowed to nod back because I'm a junior, junior dialogue writer and such people do not get nodded at by senior, senior superstar writers like Rod Serling. And so I anticipated my daily ration of contacts in the city and this was the highlight.

I can nod and be nodded at by Miss Queeg, and I can even go so far as to ask her to type a few pages for me, which means we will have the following "conversation."

"Miss Queeg?"

"Yes, Mister Findley?"

"I have these few pages here — not very many. . . ."

"Thank you, Mister Findley."

"Thank you, Miss Queeg."

Bang.

The bang is my little door, shutting. Shutting me into my four-by-four euphemism for an office. And there I would stay until my agent called — an event that took place every day at 12:15. Stanley and I really did know each other, to the full extension of the telephone wire, and we even knew the intimate details of one another's lives. I knew the name of his wife and he knew that I came from Toronto, Ontario, up in Canada. Intimate details like that. Anyway, following my conversation with Stanley, which consisted of remarks about the number of pages I had managed to work, and whether I had enough money for lunch, I would go out through the bowels of the building, past Miss Queeg's desk, along about twenty-six windowless corridors, to a staircase.

Down the stairs, out into a cemented courtyard bounded on three sides by high blank walls and on the fourth side by a wire fence, through which, not too distantly, you could catch glimpses of the Farmer's Market. In the courtyard you sat on wooden benches under an occasional canopy and ate cheese sandwiches that were sprayed with plastic and drank milk that was flaked with wax. If you were tremendously lucky, as I *once* was, you got to sit down right *exactly* where Angela Lansbury had been sitting two seconds before. If you were *not* lucky, you got to sit down where Miss Queeg had just sat. And you stared at the secretaries and junior, junior directors and super-junior executive producers while they stared back — all of you wondering what you could do for each other — all of you knowing the answer was: *nothing*. Not in this place; not in this city; not in this existence.

Then back inside and more slavery until five or five-thirty, and then out through the bowels of the building, past the executive suites and the elevators and along twelve miles of totally *un*impressive "impressive driveway" to the boulevard, and blindly along the boulevard to the Plastic Food Mart where you bought the plastic pork chops and a plastic head of lettuce and went home.

In my apartment — (hah! Oh, well, it was called an apartment and I went along with the gag) — I had made a very close relationship with a fly.

No kidding. This fly and I lived together for almost three months, until one day he got drowned in the tin shower-stall — and I have often thought about that, and been reasonably certain it was suicide. I was so fond of that fly, I actually wept. And in a dream I thought I found his little towel and six neatly matched tiny slippers at the edge of the shower, and a note that read, "This is for the best, Tiff. City life is not for me. Good luck from your best friend, Buzz."

I left Los Angeles shortly after that, saying to myself, "This is for the best, Buzz — city life is not for me."

I had done forever — I swore it — with killing my feet on concrete slabs and had done forever with having to anticipate my conversation with Miss Queeg as the high point of my day. I had done forever with being stared at by the junior, junior superstar execs. And I had done forever with my best friend, Buzz — who died, to show me the way.

Now, I live on the outskirts of a town. And I can walk in on a Saturday morning at 7:30 A.M. and be the first one all the dogs bark at — and stand around under real trees eating real cheese sandwiches. I can wander in the park and see kids — little children — who know me by name just because I live close by. And I can visit several friends — if I want to. And I can buy my groceries from Mister Huyck and Mister Currie, and we *know* each other. And I can walk out under the trees and head for home along a dirt road made for human feet. And I can touch and know the reality into which I was born.

So. The towns and farms and country roads will save us. You see, I don't mind being seen as that kind of reactionary. *Let* people tell me I'm crazy and that city life's the greatest thing invented. For me, it's a hoax. Why, even a fly can tell you that. Look at Buzz. He knew. Maybe he didn't drown. Maybe he floated through the drain and is somewhere safe at sea.

· 3 ·

THE LAST OF THE CRAZY PEOPLE

Stone Orchard
November 11, 1970
Journal

Well, I have a job, now. I'm working at CFGM, the local radio station. This means that both of us at last are contributing to the coffers. We were running on what WFW (my companion, William Whitehead) has been able to make at the CBC and for a while it's been very dicey. On the other hand, we've been extraordinarily fortunate — so many things — so many elements fell into place just as we cut ourselves off from the theatre. Mom and Dad were able to let us have this house because they aren't yet ready to move up here from Toronto — and they've been considerate and generous about the rent — the absolute minimum. We have very little furniture but it hardly matters — certainly we have all the essentials — and the house is so charming it almost furnishes itself. And the garden is fabulous. Flower beds, a pear tree and a swimming pool! At the rear, there's a cottage (already rented) and the tenant is a quiet Mennonite nurse whose name is Vera Brillinger. She takes care of all the flower beds that surround the cottage, and we do the rest and cut the grass. The house was once owned by Mary Millichamp, who grew the vegetables here for her famous Toronto restaurant. Later, where her peas and carrots used to be, the owners before Mom and Dad put in the pool. The whole house is blue — inside and out — what I call "Mother blues," because they are all the different shades that Mom has favoured for our houses over time — blues with green in them and sky blue shades and shades with the barest touch of grey. We are happy here. . . .

Mouse has given birth to five kittens — Max, we think, is the father, although at the height of her heat she escaped from the house and god knows how many other male cats are out there. We have called the kittens *Phoebe, Tephnut, Gulliver, Jason* and *Moth* and they are living in an old dog-basket off to one side in the kitchen. . . .

About the jobs. WFW has been working exclusively in radio for Murray Edwards at "The Learning Stage," where he creates the science items — either from scratch or by adapting "Voice of America" Science Broadcasts for "human listeners." They tend to be presented by "V. of A." as if no one but other scientists were ever going to listen and the jargon is so convoluted and technical I get hysterics listening to it. It all sounds so pompous it seems like satire. But WFW cuts it up and puts "English" in between the sections so that listeners outside of the scientific community can understand it.

I have made, now, two presentations of possible series for "The Learning Stage" to Murray Edwards, but he's turned them both down. I could have gone out on tour with the Canadian Players at Tony van Bridge's invitation — but we are determined to make a clean break with the theatre so that we can find our way exclusively as writers. Consequently, instead of the tour, I went out and walked on Yonge Street in Richmond Hill and went from one end of the business section to the other, going into every store and office and saying: *is there work here for me?*

I almost got a job as a clerk at the Red and White groceteria — and also at the men's clothing store where the owner said: *if you can wait for Christmas . . .* But that was in October. Then I saw the sign for CFGM and I thought, well, I was a staff announcer in Kingston for a year at CKWS and maybe that will be some kind of credential. . . . *No.* They did not want announcers. But: *did you say you were also a writer? Yes. Well. . . .*

There was a position open as a copywriter and the fact that I'd written some of my own copy at CKWS was useful and, within half an hour of walking up the stairs, I had a job!!!

Gord, the man who hired me, took me in to see my "office." Two huge desks, each overflowing with paper spilling from stacks piled two feet high on every inch of free surface. Two creaky chairs on wheels. A coat rack. A dirty window and a broken blind. One neon light overhead — and over in a corner, resting upright in an umbrella stand — an artificial leg.

Behind the far desk (the near desk had no occupant) sat a man whose complexion and demeanour and overflowing ashtray informed me, in seconds, that he was riding along the edge of a nervous breakdown. His name was T—— and when we were introduced, he did not get up. The artificial leg was his.

I take it off, he explained, *when I'm working.* He had lost the leg in Holland in 1945. *Arnheim* — the nightmare battle from which, it was to become clear, T—— had never recovered. By the time I had been at the station for two weeks, he began a series of failures to deliver copy and then, with alarming regularity, to phone in sick. I felt a dreadful sense of panic for him. T—— was a gentle, industrious and friendly man who could not bear what had befallen him and, as I was to learn, the situation at CFGM drove home the final nails. . . .

Gord said: *we're altering the station's image. We're becoming exclusively Country and Western.*

Oh.

This means that virtually all the copy I write must have a C&W angle.

How do you sell tomatoes — Country-and-Western style?

Toilet paper?

Raisins?

I will go mad.

Richmond Hill
July 1963
Journal

WFW has made a circular bench that goes round the pear tree and I sit out there beneath the branches, writing. I use the draughting board as my desk, which is perfect. I can tilt it to any angle I require. . . .

I have started writing a book and I'm not sure, yet, what it's going to be. It's about a family and especially about the youngest son, whose name is *Hooker*. He's eleven years old and another of my silent, watchful children — like Harper Dewey in *Harper's Bazaar* [*Lemonade*] and Neil in the Bud and Neil stories. I've called him *Hooker* because of Tom Hooker [stage manager at the Red Barn Theatre]. Tommy's face — with its fringe of white-blond hair — and its full mouth and huge blue eyes — is almost an icon of innocence. Beautiful, of course — and always seen by me in silence. Tom was inevitably the last person you saw before you left the darkness of the wings and walked out into the lights on stage. His face would hover in the blue work-light above his clipboard and he looked like a disembodied spirit. And the person behind that face — or inside of it — the one who informed its expressions and clothed himself in dark clothing — is, without being secretive, a secret. Nothing can be told of what is really happening deep inside Tom simply by looking at his face — except that, whatever is in there, is the stuff of troubled, inarticulate innocence — and this is the perfect description of Hooker Winslow, the boy who is emerging at the centre of this novel.

I have no notion, yet, what will become of Hooker and the Winslow family. What I do know is that there are moments when he and the others almost fall from the end of the pen — as if I know them better than I think I do. . . .

Gilbert, Hook's older brother, and Iris, the maid Hooker spends so much time with out in the kitchen, have undeniable ties with Michael (my brother) and with Olive, who was our beloved maid — but as soon as I think it is them, they veer off into "themselves" — into Gilbert and into Iris who are not like Mike and Olive at all. . . . The curious, curious touchstone quality of real life touching fiction. *Reverberations* is a good word, here. Echoes. But not hard facts. I couldn't write about Mike. His mystery defies me. But Gilbert I can grasp, because a part of him is me and I can get him all the way to the page intact.

Richmond Hill
October 1963
Journal

. . .Dear God. I know what Hooker is going to do. He is going to kill his family. And I cannot bring myself to write it. How do I do this? How do you write such a terrible thing? Writing a killing feels like squeezing a trigger — not like writing any other kind of death. I've put it away, although I know it must be done. Stories have their own conclusions. Sure, you can cheat them — but if you deny a story its integrity it loses all its validity and the reader can tell.

I didn't know it would end this way when I started. It just swept over me, sitting — writing — thinking: *now, he will kill his cats to save them from Gilbert — and there it was. No, he won't. He will kill his family to save them from themselves.*

This is the logic of innocence, not yet familiar with poise, battered by too much reality.

Richmond Hill
November 1963
Journal

Crazy, that what you do at the desk can precede what happens beyond the windows. Someone has killed John Kennedy. A man called Oswald — and no one knows why. All we do is stare at television. Everything has been stripped of colour and all we see is a black-and-white world that keeps being repeated over and over and over again, until you know it all by heart — except that it has no meaning.

Richmond Hill
June 1964
Journal

The final rewrite of *Crazy People* went to Grace Bechtold at Bantam about four weeks ago. We arranged to meet in New York — on the afternoon of June 5th — at 4:00 o'clock. Meanwhile, I had arranged to meet also with Alec [McCowen], who was in New York in the Scofield *Lear* — playing the Fool. WFW, Janet [Baldwin] and I drove down — WFW driving all the way. We left on Thursday, the 4th, at about 7:30. We stopped overnight in Utica, and started off again the next morning, WFW and I in our new Harry Rosen suits, looking super, and Janet in a lovely one-piece, sort of tailored dress she made herself — all very elegant for our arrival. Lovely country — much excitement. Arrived at 3:00 as WFW had said we would. He's a wizard about hours and schedules. Went to Alec's hotel [the Ruxton — West 72nd] and I went up alone. After our first shock of seeing each other we were fine. So we all went up then as we were to stay there. Then I phoned Grace Bechtold. "Come down," she said. "Lovely to hear your voice at last." Fear and trembling. Got there alone in a taxi. She came out. Marvellous! Absolutely a marvellous woman. As Horace Vandergelder would say: "*Wonder*-ful *wo*-man!" She wears blue. Greying brown hair. Intelligent — humorous gaze. Excitable (good sign) but incredibly businesslike. "Can't see you now. Disaster has struck. Wait for me round the corner — Tuscany Bar. Don't get drunk. I'll be there when I can!" (She knew about my drinking problems.) Off I went. Phoned Janet. Janet: "Now *promise*. *Promise* me here and now — don't take a drink." "I promise." "All right, then. Alec and WFW are out with your prescription, searching for Antabuse pills. I'll send them down the minute they return." "Fine. Good. Right." "Are you okay?" "No."

So I sat at the bar and drank three bottles of tonic water. WFW phoned. He would come at once. He did. Minutes later Grace arrived — hatted now and in the blue jacket, as well, of her suit. Ordered drinks. "Manhattan — Scotch on rocks — TONIC WATER." Looks — words — and then: "Well — here we are. At last!" She would not talk about the book — or whether or not she was going to buy it. [Grace was then Senior Editor at Bantam.] Instead, she asked about our trip and concentrated on WFW. A polite tactic — more than likely to do with her need to get rid of whatever had been going on with the "disaster" she had mentioned earlier. I took a deep breath and wanted a drink — but dismissed that thought. WFW had brought the Antabuse pills and he slipped them to me unobtrusively. I took one and nearly spilled the rest. Grace said: "Antabuse?" I said: "yes." "Yes," she said, "I have at least two other friends who take it. A great invention." That was the end of it — but I thought it was good of her to put me at my ease about it. Now I wished she would put me at my ease about the book!

Janet and Alec arrived — but they didn't come over to be introduced. Instead, they took a table across the room. WFW stood up and excused himself and went to join them. I could see all three of them smiling and laughing — looking as if they had lived in NYC all their lives — and drank at the Tuscany every afternoon.

Grace opened her purse and took out a long white business envelope. My heart sank.

"This is for you," she said.

Oh, dear, I thought. It's a list of the reasons she isn't going to buy the book. Or a list of editorial problems she wants me to address before she will even consider it. *One more draft!* I didn't know whether I could do that, there had been so many drafts already.

"What's this?" I asked. I hadn't even opened the envelope.

"The conditions," she said, "of the purchase."

"The purchase?"

"Open it."

I opened it. There was a letter — yes — but folded inside the letter there was a cheque.

One thousand dollars!

"I don't understand," I said.

"We're buying *The Last of the Crazy People*," said Grace Bechtold. Just like that!

I literally began to shake. It had been such a long haul.

"The conditions have to do with my being able to find a hardcover publisher. What I'm doing is buying the paperback rights and committing myself to finding the hardcover publisher for you — and I'm sure I will," she added. "It will just take time."

"My god," I said.

"You thought I wasn't going to buy it?" she said — laughing.

I nodded.

"Oh," she said. "I knew I was going to buy it the minute I finished reading it. It was just that I hoped I could meet you today with the other publisher all lined up."

Then she said it would be nice to meet my other friends, now — unless I had any questions I wanted to ask before they came over.

But I had no questions I could articulate — and so the others came over and I handed WFW the cheque and WFW said: "what is this?" just the way I had — and I said: "it's for this book Miss Bechtold is going to publish. . . ."

Everyone burst out laughing. Janet and Alec wanted to see the cheque — "and *touch* it!" Alec said. We ordered more drinks and I toasted the sale of *Crazy People* in tonic water. My eighty-fifth of the day — or so it felt. Later, we all went out into the street and there was a lovely stationery shop. WFW went in and bought me a fountain pen. "To write the next book," he said.

I'M GOING TO BE PUBLISHED!!!!!!!!!!!

Richmond Hill
May 1964
Journal

The essence of *Crazy People* is a distilled and bottled fear of life. It is the journey of a child through a nightmare that is not ever garish but which is dim and peculiar. It is a nightmare because the people who are in the dream with him all seem to accept the conditions of their lives so easily and with such natural calm. The dream is the approach to maturity, along which the boy, Hooker, is walking. The nightmare is the ultimate arrival at adult life — which he knows is coming and which he tries to fend off — but which is absolutely inevitable. He does not want to go — but he is wearing wheels and all directions and roads are downhill. *Crazy People* must be a short, swift plunge through the fog and terror of people who do *not* cry out when they should or move when they should.

Richmond Hill
December 1963
Journal

Isn't it odd? Quite without any intention or foreknowledge of what would happen, each of the three cats given major prominence in the book — Gulliver (himself), — Tephy ("Little Bones") and Benjamin ("Frobisher") — have all come to unhappy partings. Gully and Teph died on the road — and Benjy by not being able to adapt to life with other cats. I feel so guilty about him, but I honestly think we have done all possible. We have been kind — solicitous — strict to the right degree — and provided everything he would seem to need. I think the problem really is that he needs to be the *only* cat in the household — I think he is not happy being one of a group. It is terrible how much we miss the others. Teph and Gulliver were truly supreme cats — and wonderfully individual. Short of my dog, Danny, and Max (the very best cat), no animal in my life has ever given me such pleasure and affection as Tephnut did. At least I will always be able to remember her — and that is good.

Gulliver was WFW's favourite — even above Max. It is that, about life, that can never be answered for me. In all early death — even animal deaths — there is that incredible quality of "first affection" or "special character." Now

74

I make certain every day that I never take anyone close to me for granted. No amount of time is long enough. I suppose that when it is someone you love very deeply, it would be reasonable to say that they "died young" at ninety-two.

How stupid it is to try to get through life alone. Because you can't.

· 4 ·

STONE ORCHARD

In the summer of 1964, WFW and I had saved enough money for the down payment on a house in the country. We started our search north-east of Toronto, where the prices were not so steep as those to the north-west. Luck was with us. Within days, we discovered an old, Ontario farm-house on fifty acres of land we knew we could afford.

The house had been vacant for over five years. The windows were broken; the ceilings were falling down and the paper hung in shreds from the walls. Raccoons and mice had taken up residence. The gardens had run amok with tiger lilies, poppies and roses. The grass was over two feet tall. A laneway bisected the property north to south, from end to end, and it was lined on either side with apple trees and mountain ash and elm. The fields behind the house led up, though gently, to a vantage point from which could be seen a host of valleys — a river — a railway track and the silver ribbons of dusty roads

79

that led the eye beyond the horizon, whichever way we looked. It took about as long as it takes to blink before we realized we had fallen in love with where we stood — and we have been here ever since.

To the north is the town of Cannington, just beyond the river — just beyond the hill. Though not incorporated till 1878, Cannington has been there — one way or another — since the 1820s, established by Brandons and Sproules from Ireland but populated, mostly during the 1830s, by the families of British Army officers whose military lives had ended with the Napoleonic Wars.

The river, called the Beaver, empties into Lake Simcoe at Beaverton, roughly ten miles north and east. As with all such rural centres early in our history, our town began with a mill — McCaskill's Mill, in this case — and that was how Cannington was known at first. Though the flour mill itself is gone, the mill pond is still there and the Beaver River backs up above it, deep and wide and slow — not big enough for commerce, but perfect, in the pastoral sense; a place for cattle to drink and for ducks and geese and for heron — and even, still, for the beaver from which it gets its name — and for muskrat — for turtles and frogs the size of your hand. The turtles are mostly snappers, very old and slow and covered with long, green veils of water-moss.

There are smaller, Painted Turtles, too, and summer afternoons you can go and watch them clambering up to sun themselves on the rocks and the dead-heads out beyond the current, where the wood ducks swim and the dragonflies skim the water. We have a wood beside the river — and that is one of my favourite places on the planet. You can sit there, ten to fifteen feet above the water, and watch all this and be part of it. The birds — besides the ducks and geese — are owls and bittern, snipe, killdeer and swallows of every kind — jays and chickadees and grosbeaks in winter and, every spring, a bird whose call — for me — is one of the most mysterious and haunting sounds in all of nature — the veery.

Cannington. Make a cross in your mind — and turn that image into two straight roads that intersect. East to west runs Cameron Street — and Laidlaw, north to south. Both streets are lined with maple and linden trees, creating with their shapes and shade the perfect image of a Southern Ontario town. At either end of these two streets, the town begins to dwindle, house by house and lawn by lawn, into the countryside.

They call this town "The Heart Of Ontario" and though once it was an important, thriving crossroads — with seven hotels, no less — and the site of a carriage factory, a sawmill, a flour mill, a foundry, two breweries, a furniture factory and a distillery — Cannington is now a town with three small industries, no hotels, a single grocery store and four churches. We all fill our cars at the same Esso Station — and there is no other — of any breed.

A large percentage of the population is made up of farmers — honourably retired — of both sexes. It is not, by any means, a "sleepy" town, however. One of its greatest assets is its population of children; one of its greatest successes lies in the fact that its young have not all disappeared into the cities to the south. As a town, it has a remarkable supply of citizens of every age. As a place, it has a remarkable supply of loyalties. For myself, I cannot think of anywhere that I would rather be. Though I live beyond the town, it has been my town for over twenty years. And, if I still have twenty years to go — it will remain that town until I die.

WFW and I had been ensconced in our house for only about two weeks, when there was a knock at the door and there stood a young, pretty girl — perhaps fourteen years old — whose opening words were: "my name is Emma. Are you an artist?"

Are you an artist?

What might have made her think so?

Two of her young friends and Emma had been walking along the road in front of our house and Emma had noticed wine bottles — Chianti bottles — sitting in the upstairs windows. Well, according to Emma, if you have wine bottles sitting in your window — and if one of those bottles holds a red candle — then you have to be an artist. What else can you be?

In the long run, we discovered that Emma herself was an artist, and, over the next five years or so — before she went on to study painting in Toronto — Emma became a part of our lives at Cannington.

Saturday morning — whenever the weather allowed us — Emma and I played tennis. *Early.* Early, because — according to Em — "you only get the public courts before breakfast. After breakfast the whole world turns up." The truth was, Emma was lying — but lying with some justification. She didn't want her mother to know that she was "seeing an older man. . . ." And so we played our innocent tennis games in the covert hour that followed dawn.

I learned a lot about my town — about where I live — on those early morning walks. To the edge of town it was about a mile. The dogs got up from where they'd slept and sent the message down the line that a man was coming — and one, and then another, would come to the end of its lane and I would offer each the palm of my hand to sniff — the Smallwoods' dog; the Griffins' dog; the Warlows' dog. And, in time, the tone of their barking altered from alarm to greeting; from "who is this?" to "here he comes!"

Saturday mornings, I got to know the town from its outskirts to its heart — walking in the dust and the dew up the road, turning down Griffin's Hill — with its ditches deep on either side — into Griffin's Valley and up to the crest at the other side where the road slides down towards the town across the railroad tracks and under the trees.

To the east, back then, as you crossed the tracks there was a railroad station. Just beyond the tracks, and beyond what was then a meadow, you came to the first of the houses whose lawns went down to the edge of the burgeoning mill-pond. This house belonged to the Misses Faed — a pair of sisters whose lives, as it turned out, were to be inextricably entangled in the railroad track and the Cannington Railway Station. To begin with, the lives of the Sisters Faed went all the way back to the edge of the twentieth century — back where it broached the nineteenth century, and to where the town began.

When I saw them first, the Sisters Faed appeared to be the town eccentrics, but nothing could be further from the truth. As characters, they might have been written by Alice Munro or by Robertson Davies — or, indeed, by Timothy Findley — given what Margaret Atwood has already called the "unity of Southern Ontario Gothic." Miss Daisy and Miss Emily had all the requisite characteristics, too, of women who — in another culture — might have been written by Chekhov or Tennessee Williams. So — their eccentricity only had to do with the fact that writers could not keep their hands off the image they presented. The fact is, they were simply true to themselves. Their integrity held to the end of their days — and, if that is "eccentric," then I fear for the rest of us.

They chose to continue their lives as if it was still and always the time of their heyday — from the turn of the century into the 1920s. When I saw them first, what I saw were two figures dressed in shin-length chiffon and silk, wearing cloche hats and walking arm-in-arm into the drugstore. It so happened their father had been a druggist and that was the source of their fortune — such as it was. As I saw them then, on a late September morning, their cheeks were daubed with rouge and their bee-stung lips with brilliant red. Much white powder gave their faces a soft patina. Miss Emily approached the counter and shyly asked for a single packet of Players Cigarettes. In the meantime, Miss Daisy hung about the door as if she had come to the drugstore against her will. Out on the sidewalk, Miss Emily passed the Players to her sister, saying — rather curtly — "one day, you'll have to do your own dirty work."

Both had been teachers — one of art, the other of music. They were — of course — a classic example of two inseparable human beings. And the trouble with all such relationships is that — one day — there must be a death. And one day, that day came.

But not before another death.

When the fire siren goes in Cannington, it wails and wails and wails from the top of the tower on the old Town Hall. As in all small communities, the Fire Brigade is made up of volunteers — and the volunteers must be called to duty from miles and miles around. On this particular occasion, the fire was large — and not only large in scope, but large in meaning. History was burning. The railroad station, whose presence went all the way back to the 1870s, was razed to the ground. It had stood there for almost a hundred years.

Out on our road — a mile from the town — the cars and trucks, the tractors and the hayricks all lined up along the heights, and people stood on the tops of their vehicles — while others of us stood on the roofs of our houses to watch the Fire Brigade fight their hopeless battle.

When it was over, no one spoke. We had lost a part of the past that could never be reclaimed. And the loss of our station was the precursor of the inevitable loss of our trains, now gone — forever.

About a year later, Miss Daisy Faed died. She was old — and there was nothing to be done. On the day she died, Miss Emily sat on the steps of their house — the house where they had lived for the whole of their lives — and she would not be moved from her place. Neighbours, loving and caring, tried with great tenderness to lift her and make her go inside. It was cold — and Miss Emily was very old and frail. She wore no make-up now, and her long white hair was in disarray.

"Get up! Get up!"

But she would not. She sat there all that day till evening came.

It was time for the great migrations. The geese were flocking down the flyway which passes over our town. Miss Emily shaded her eyes against the fading light and muttered something. At last, she stood. Someone had put a cardigan around her shoulders and she drew this close — and smoothed her hair. She stood as she must have stood as a girl: very tall and straight. And then she started to move. Not turning back inside — but stepping down the walk towards the street. Everyone held their breath and watched. No one dared touch her; no one wanted to interrupt whatever mysterious communication was taking place.

Miss Emily headed towards the railroad track — walking with almost alarming energy towards the site of the burnt-out railroad station. And then we heard her calling.

"Daisy . . . Daisy?"

And after a moment: "Daisy? Dear?"

Miss Emily never recovered. She tried living alone in their house, but she was old; the years were passing and she — at last — passed with them, into time.

The town's historian was Islay Lambert. She wrote — for publication in 1971 — the story of Cannington and its environs — *Call Them Blessed*. It is better by far than most such books. Islay Lambert was a professional writer and journalist — and her book is exemplary. WFW and I became close friends to Islay, and in the years before her death — in 1976 — we spent each Saturday afternoon in her company, arriving at her house on Laidlaw Street in time for tea.

Islay Lambert lived in one of Cannington's older houses and came from one of its older families. In her time, she had been a teacher, a journalist and — in between — she had served as treasurer for the local Hydro office.

We — WFW and I — were known to be "writers," but people who write novels and television documentaries can be unknown quantities in a small town. We came — after all — from the beguiling, mysterious and perhaps even decadent world of artists — that world that Emma had defined by its bohemian wine bottles in the window. Consequently, when Islay Lambert — one of the community pillars — took up with these two young men, it caused a little more than a "stir." Our Saturday visits were the subject of much curiosity. Did we carry our wine-imbibing habits with us into Miss Lambert's sanctum? Were we undermining the morals of the God-fearing element of this community by striking at its very heart, in the person of its valued historian? To be brief, Miss Lambert's neighbours stood beyond their windows, got out their binoculars and gave a new definition to the phrase, *Neighbourhood Watch,* as WFW and I arrived for our innocent afternoon teas. From time to time, we would defy them — turning to wave our greetings from Islay's steps before we entered her "den of iniquity." But they were not placated; nor could they be shamed into putting their binoculars aside.

At last — I hit upon a solution. Why not give them something to *really* talk about?

I had purchased, in the early seventies, a Honda motor bike. Its top speed was only fifty miles per hour. I am not a driver. Cars defy me. Tractors thwart me. Trucks are anathema. But motor bikes were just my style. I was known — in local parlance — as *Hell's Elf.*

One Saturday afternoon — having already arranged that tea that week would be had in our house — I arrived at Islay Lambert's front walk on the Honda. All the binoculars across the street were in hand — and now, they were raised. I felt the eyes of the entire neighbourhood on my back as I went inside. Islay was ready and waiting. When we emerged, she wore a crash helmet, trailing scarf and leather gloves — as well as a hefty woollen windbreaker. This time, we did not wave. We had no need. The telephones were already ringing up and down the street. "Get to your windows! Fast!"

Islay clambered into place behind me on the seat. I revved the motor — and we sped away. The curtains fell. It was a stunning exit.

She died the next year. But when Islay Lambert had ridden away on the back of my Honda, she had been seventy-four years old.

Cannington. I could not have found a better place to live. I revere my town — I respect and I revel in its people. I do not, however, live inside its gates. I live a mile away on the farm that WFW and I have called "Stone Orchard." We called it that in perfect innocence — thinking to pay some tribute to my favourite writer, Anton Chekhov, whose play *The Cherry Orchard* might be performed in its rooms and in its gardens — and taking into account the only true crop we have — namely, stones. It was only later that someone told us a "stone orchard," in local terms, means graveyard.

Well, it couldn't matter less. We both want our ashes scattered here — where the ashes of Bill's parents and some of my father's ashes already rest. All our animals are buried here: Maggie the dog and Mottle the old blind cat — and Maggie's offspring, Hooker — and Boy, the cat who sang before he died, whose song I have used in one of my plays and one of my novels.

A fiction writer is just that. But much that is real provides his impetus; perhaps the whispers in the ear that turn realities into fictions. Living here, I am always in the presence of the stuff of which I write.

I truly believe that each of us has a natural home. It may or may not be where we are born. We make it — yes. But we cannot make it perfect unless we discover where it belongs. My home is here. I'm lucky — and I know that. And this is what I have that feeds me — both as a person and as a writer: the curve of these hills, the lines of these horizons, the shapes and the smells of these trees, the hardness of these stones, the ghosts within these walls, the harshness of this climate — and all its weathers — and the sounds which fill my ears.

Sound is a story teller's mode.

Every day begins with the sound of young Len Collins — who runs our lives and makes it possible for us to function — as he arrives in the truck. The dogs — Belle and Berton, both Malamutes — greet him. I hear the sound of the screen door as Len comes through into the kitchen . . . the sound of WFW's greeting. I hear the sounds as twenty-seven cats are fed. I hear the telephone . . . the clocks that tick in every room, some of the clocks as old as this house . . . the sound of farm traffic out on the road . . .

the sound of the music I play as I write . . . the sound of church bells and the old hymns wavering across the valley from beyond the river.

If every day begins with sound, it also ends with sound — then silence. The last sound I usually hear is not "good-night" — but Belle, the dog, as she tells the story of the day just past to whatever ears are listening out in the dark. She tells this tale in a series of long, rhythmic sentences somewhere between a howling and a moan. All the other dogs up and down the line seem to hear her; and, very often, they tell their own day's stories back.

I have no notion, really, what it is Belle tells; but I sense that what she tells has meaning. Perhaps she tells, as I just have, of where she lives — and of who is there and of why it matters that someone else be told.

Cannington
October 1964
Journal

This evening I went for a walk down the lane. It was cold and clear and one of those rare and beautiful times when something from the mind becomes reality. It was the air — so clear, so cold — full of flocking birds against pale blue, violet-shaded sky — a white sunset — and all away from where I walked or stood — gold, orange, pink and yellow leaves — cresting hills — or shadowed and dark in the valleys.

I had not taken in that this country was so hilly, but once you begin to live in it and see it every day, it becomes clear that it is. To the west, it is chimney-plumed with transparent smoke; the Purvis house is actually in a sort of dale, surrounded by trees. I had the glasses and to the south from the top of the lane — by the old roller with the seat quite high (where I like to sit for the added view) I could see the fields below me filled with Holstein, Jersey and Guernsey cattle — a farm cluster of buildings, much like our own but in a better state of repair. This farm is owned, we understand, by a Toronto lawyer, and it is most charming. It has a house with a porch on the north side and a green barn or drive-shed — I can't tell which. It has a long drive, being set further back from the road than we are.

Our own place is becoming home. It is not so easy to adapt to it as I thought it would be. I keep saying to myself — "this is *our* house — it belongs to *us* — that field is ours — those trees — that barn — this lane — they are all *ours*" — but it does not seem real. It is not just its beauty — or its quiet — or any of its unique qualities — so much as the concrete fact that it *exists*. It is not possible — or so it seems — that we walk in and out of our own doors and drive up beside our own garden and see the trees and the buildings and then say: "well, we're home."

Our walks are quite funny because we are always accompanied by a convoy of cats. Max, Mouse, Barney, Jason, Moth, Mole, Trout — even Smoky and especially the kittens — Cindy and Figaro — love to walk down with us, sometimes five or six of them at once. Now, we miss Benjamin, and Cleo and Tephy and Gully and my lovely little Phoebe. I guess I miss them all equally — but Phoebe is more telling in my mind. I miss her and I miss Teph just as you would miss two people.

Found this written on a napkin:

> The Sadness of Incapacity
>
> Mole beyond the door
> guessing at the handle's use
> leaps for it
> but has no hand to turn it.

Stone Orchard
April 1976
Journal

Sitting at the kitchen table — 11:30 A.M. Just fed the animals — cats on the porch — survivors on a raft. Cold, dark wind, lacking nuance — bearing portents: frozen kernels of rain. Everything bending — all shapes bent — my own included — as if to be a part of the landscape, everything must assume the same angle of flight — the trees, the grass, the reeds all trying to get away — to flee. And the dogs' tails, held between their legs — their ears laid back for fear of catching rain — every hair assumes a protective posture. The rain beats down at the same (the universal) angle of this storm that is not a storm, but a new condition under which we live. And the kitchen table, massed with the colour of broken flowers and plants. I have brought in many broken tulips — geraniums (off the porch) — paperwhites — violets — strands of periwinkle — herbs and avocados in pots — ferns and apple blossoms. The house is like a green and flowering clearing in the wind — blown round with darkness and with rain.

The vapour from the kettles and pots draws the scent of the flowers.

The veery is back in the woods beyond the railroad track.

Stone Orchard
September 1970
Journal

Bicycle: I go to the rock pile between the Joyces and the Grills and visit with the cows in Grills' field — one particular beauty has rust-red markings on snow-white hide. I pause to take in the view to the north where I can see the town in all its nineteenth-century splendour — set in its valley, all the green, blue and tin-coloured roofs rising (just) above the trees and the trees now brilliant with reds and oranges — flecks of yellow (less yellow now because the elms are nearly all dead) and the roofs make boat-images — raft-images — in the smoky mist of leaf-lakes. Spires — three of them on churches and a fourth not a spire but a bell tower — white and green on the Town Hall — and in the foreground, next to the railroad track, the white houses and the one yellow house and the green of the factory — inoffensive, which surprises me.

And all the autumn smells — of fire and leaf-mould and damp earth and pleasant manure piles steaming into cool air. Way, way beyond — birds flying, and the hope of geese — and then directly before me, the silver shining road where it rises and falls, rises and falls until it rises so high — it is gone.

Caterpillars — rusty red and black — crawling from this to that side of the road and me trying very hard to avoid them — always wondering of each: "will it get across before a car comes?" And nearly home, a strange cat — one I've never seen before — was startled by my suddenly being there on my whizzing wheels. It made deer-leaps all the way over the road and into the ditch — and into the undergrowth and the safety of the fence rails where I saw it pause and turn and stare at me and wonder what I was. Its eyes were strange.

[This turned out to be Mottle — the blind cat, who finally wandered into the yard about a week later, starving, she lived with us for twelve years and, with a slight change in spelling, became a leading character in *Not Wanted on the Voyage*.]

For some reason, I've lost a day this week — and can't for the life of me tell why. Today has seemed to be Wednesday from the moment I woke up and I have to keep realigning myself. But the odd thing is, it's not so much that I think today is Wednesday as that I am completely convinced *tomorrow* will be Thursday.

I spent the morning working, then fed animals, did a bit of housework and even went outside with Mottle, who was afraid to go out alone because of the high wind, which must sound extraordinary to her and feel like the end of the world. She turned her back on it, dug a very quick pit, did her job and rushed back to be let inside. Once inside again, she had a lot to say and "talked" for about fifteen minutes.

Stone Orchard
Autumn 1980
Journal

The leaves here are beginning to go now in earnest. Lots of orange, yellow, red. (On our Ottawa trip we kept driving into Tom Thompson's paintings. The car is covered with tatters of torn canvas and splinters of the old boards he painted on.) I walk the dogs down into our woods around evening — and the look of it all gives me a great sense of safety. Crossing the slope of the ploughed field — the smells rise of earth and the ruffled alfalfa roots. Almost unbearably reminiscent of our old life in the cave by the field where we ploughed with the pointed stick. Glutted with overwhelming sensuality. The earth voice is very strong. Seven hawks the other day on one draught. The trees alive with leaping and the chatter of new squirrels afraid of the axe I never carry. It is a wild place — and I am tamed by it.

There was a full moon tonight — and a stark, silver sky — everything a winter etching — like a silverpoint drawing — nothing moving — not a single breath of movement — looking out and seeing all the rabbits and raccoons have paused halfway across the field.

93

Stone Orchard
January 1981
Journal

Got up at six. Drank thermos tea — boiled kettle — made WFW's breakfast (egg, milk, Sweet-10, nutmeg and hot water — *beaten*) — made tea. Fixed WFW's thermos. Went out 6:30 A.M. — still dark — very cold (-17 C.) — swept car. It had continued to snow in night — though wind has switched from south to north-west and colder than yesterday. Finished car and went round and swept feeding table and shelves — one hanging feeder broken.

Still dark — came in — started greenhouse fire. WFW left (6:50) — barely light — sun still not risen. Went out and put down feed — millet, corn, sunflower seed, etc. Also some on ground for dove. First to arrive (mere shadows in dark) *sparrows*. Then the *mourning dove* — the *one* grosbeak. By now, light. Then flock of grosbeaks. (7:30 A.M.) Grosbeaks and sparrows and dove will feed together — though dove will not (yet) feed on table. When she flies she goes to the hawthorn tree in front of porch — sitting at its centre. I think she must live quite close by. The *junco* (female) feeds with the sparrows — and you miss her if you don't search for her. Quite small — size of largest sparrows. By 7:45 there is also *one chickadee*. Sun fully up. Bright, golden light in frigid pale sky — no clouds except on horizon. *Blue jays* (3) arrive by 8:00 A.M. Other birds fly up at their approach. *Blue jays* feed alone and then other birds sift back through branches to feeder and gourd. *Dove* remains seated in her tree. Now *8 more blue jays* (8:15 A.M.)

Stone Orchard
May 1976
Journal

Mottle, Ceilidh and I played silver-paper hockey tonight at 2:00 A.M. A super game on the kitchen floor and Mottle won. Now — content with having eaten and played and having had her tail rubbed, she is snoring at the foot of the bed.

Smell of wood smoke — maple — applewood — cedar — locust — elm. Aromatic — pervasive — and the smell of cut, wet grass — cow manure — wet screens — the damp pine planks of the new porch. The drip of water onto stone — into rain barrels — into the wet grass — onto the earth from leaves — onto the leaves from branches. Not a breath of wind. Bird song at every distance — one far dog — and someone chopping wood — the sight of wet, ploughed earth and the pale froth of budding tree lines — with cherries in blossom, the dark cones of lilac waiting to burst next week — the orange cast of the new leaves not yet fully grown on the maples — the piping voices, like mice, of the newborn starlings under the north-east eaves by WFW's open window — the distant, tunnelled sound of wind that hasn't touched us yet. The whirr of a car on the wet road — and the crisp tat-tat-tat as it races through puddles — and the wren is the loudest bird in the garden. The male chickadee has just brought the female food — but she has decided to join him outside the nest and now they're feeding in the brush by the side of the road. A mourning dove (turtle dove) cooing, but it's impossible to tell where — impossible even to tell from which direction the sound is coming.

Looking into the house from the porch, red light and brass light and copper reflections — stone with fireglow — orange shapes in a picture whose glass looks black from here — reflecting the room and its lamps. One scarlet geranium set against the rich, wet green of the yard outside, beyond it. Killdeer screaming over the field across the road. Someone's screen door slams way up the road and the hummingbird buzzes through the garden, looking for food. Rain dripping into each barrel — one at either end of the porch — each rhythm different from the other — "Stravinsky for rain barrels" and a bird whistling out of tune. (Is that *possible?*)

Sounds and voices carry in this wet stillness as if over a calm lake. Only absence is insect sound. I can even catch the smell of cut wood — someone still chopping way up at the corner. Turned wet earth is beautiful. Even the stillness of stones is alive. A mere pause, now. Hiatus. Then there is an insect. One huge bee. The hiss of wet wood that won't burn yet. Wren flight — sudden — with songs at either end.

Curvature of land. Not a rolling sequence of humps and valleys — but a sloping-off — a gentle, lovely falling into secret corners filled with crowds of trees, as if the land had spilled them — tipped them into the corners of a wet, warped box. Black-wet trees — each with one green-fronted aspect (facet?) — lichens, not moss.

Islay Lambert was moved to the grave on Thursday last. She died in February, but with the ground frozen, couldn't be buried. Now, there is no room and she has to buried in the plot her brother is supposed to have. Louise Hewlett and I went out Friday evening and I took a dozen red tulips from the garden. I hunkered down — in a cloud of blackflies — and touched the ground with the palm of my right hand. Gone — but the elements are the same. I can still hear her voice — see her fingernails — smell her hair — feel her weight exactly and the way she balanced it, using my arm as she walked — taste the flavour of her house, made up of tea and lemon smells and nutbread with dates in it — smells of paper napkins — the particular puff of these odours when you rounded out of the hall into the living-room and she was lying on the sofa, already rising, or seated in her chair, waiting. And that one, treacherous rug between the living-room and kitchen. And the unique tremble in her whole presence — voice — hands — the head on its wavering neck. Turning the corner onto Laidlaw street, I get in a panic, now. No one is waiting — and we never think of the silence or the empty space where a person stood and waved. We think we know what absence means. We don't. It is weight and space and silence — and an endlessly uncertain pause.

Stone Orchard
June 1984
Journal

Think of what the town was like in those days — say, from 1912 to 1922. Think of all the men going home in the evenings, smelling of the workplace — and the women, waiting, smelling of cats and children and lunch and supper and hands burned white with naphtha soap and lemons. Think of the butcher's wife who must overcome her natural fear of the smell of blood — who must sleep with someone soaked in blood — someone whose fingernails and toes are caked with it. Think of other fingers that smell of gas and oil — of straw smells and granary smells — and the smells of merchandise — books, scribblers, ink and vegetables — the smells of candy, cotton goods and shoe leather. Think of these embraces, the mingling of the florist's arms with the sweat of the nursery; of the brewer's apron pressed against the floured apron of the pastry cook; think of the gardener embracing the druggist's daughter who serves behind the counter. Think of the baker embracing the telephone operator and the teacher embracing the cat. Think of the naked foundry workers showering under pumps until they smell like husbands — and the mothers, waiting until the evening meal has been eaten before they slowly begin to smell like wives. Think of all this and *breathe!* It is a wondrous thing — to think of all these glorious odours mingling somewhere over the town, declaring: this is a human habitation — just as, high above the prairie, the scent declares that "here, there are buffalo!"

Stone Orchard
January 1969
Journal

Yesterday we had a marvellous experience — an expedition down the river on skates. Jimmy Roots came up and said: "the river's frozen" and since it's rare to have it clear of snow, we decided to seize the opportunity and skate right away.

Very cold. We took the dogs and it was supremely beautiful.

First, we skated towards the town and got as far as the old Griffin bridge. After that, the ice was too rough and so we skated back to our own bridge and went the other way — after a pause in the car to smoke a cigarette and get warm.

I fell twice! Terrible. Those sudden, complete falls — without warning — and my knees and elbows are still aching.

The first way had been interesting and fun. The second, heading south, was an adventure. On other occasions I had walked as far on the track as we went on the river, but the track loses the river after a while and you get a good view, but not this opening of vistas that the river route affords. There is a lot of twisting — many bends in the river — so that you are doubling and tripling the distance of the track's straight line. WFW wore his orange sweater, and the sight of him skating ahead, with all the grey-brown, black and peroxide colouring of the river and the reeds and the forest was unforgettable.

Every once in a while the dogs would cut across our path so that the whole journey was like being in a marvellous maze, with everything in motion — criss-crossing back and forth between the dark trees on either shore and the reeds between each bend in the river — and far off and away, a great, low opening of pure Northland vista — a cloud-barren sky — and long filigreed cut-outs of row on row of tamarack interspersed with the solid black/greens of the cedars and pines.

All along there were muskrat houses and the tracks of rabbits — foxes and dogs (maybe brush wolves) and just the three of us and the two dogs, sometimes very suddenly dashing across the river-line to intersect us — all going fast and gliding — and then the great, wide curves — Jim and then WFW rounding them ahead of me — and following their coloured clothes in all that massive distance in its muted shades of gold and brown — the steel-blue ice — the white snow, utterly white — and the black hordes of trees on either bank.

Something in that landscape always makes me think of *Maria Chapdelaine* — of being alone in nature and lost on railroad tracks.

Then back home to fire and coffee — the safety symbols of all Canadians.

Stone Orchard
February 1971
Radio

You realize, of course, that dogs lead private lives. You can't entirely own one; they belong to themselves.

We have two dogs — mother and son — about the size of German Shepherds. We think of them as being the classic farm-dog breed.

Because we live in sheep country, we aren't allowed to let them roam free and this means that they have to live in a pen. The pen is about the size of the average city backyard.

Pretty nearly every day — although some weeks, I

99

must confess, this doesn't hold true — they get out for a long walk, which means that I get out for a long walk, too. By "long walk" I mean we're away for an hour or more. In the winter we walk along the railroad tracks — or on the river — and, sometimes, down in the woods.

But — I wanted to tell you about their *private* lives, because I don't think we give enough thought to what our dogs are doing when they're not with us.

I used to be afraid they would suffer from boredom, having to be in their pen so much of the day and all night. But nothing could be further from the truth.

Their day is just as rich and varied as ours can be — right down to the playing of games. I know this, not only because I have watched them from the window, but because — overcome with curiosity on the subject — I went out and spent a night and part of a day with them — laying out my sleeping bag inside their hutch. This hutch was once a goose-house, and consequently, it had a sloping roof and a thick mesh window which we boarded over in winter.

I swear the dogs behaved exactly as if they had invited me for the weekend. There was a great deal of fussing over where I'd sleep — about where the sleeping bag would go and about how much straw I got to lie on. They were very kind and let me have the place near the screening — and since this was in the summer and it was very hot, I'm certain this was a great privilege. I've seen them sleeping when I wasn't being the house guest — and the older dog is the one who gets the window. That makes me certain it was a privilege.

Settling down for dogs is a little different than our way of settling down. When we go to bed, we stay there — except perhaps for a midnight ramble. But the dogs get all settled (sort of "nested" is what it's like) and then immediately abandon the nest to go out and look at the moon. So. Out I went to moon-watch with them. We simply sat there on our haunches and gazed at the moon. Also a few stars. And a few lighted windows. And a few bats. And then, we went back into the hutch and settled down again. But not for long.

Then we had to go out (that is, the male and I had to go out) and let that bitch (who was in heat down the line a few miles) know that we were there and if only we could get out of the pen, we'd be glad to meet up with her. This took about half an hour — and we were joined in our salutations by several other dogs over a five- or six-mile radius.

(This is not the same as the "Great Bitch in the Sky" — which is the train that goes by every day. And when it hoots, our dog hollers. He's quite convinced the train is calling to him and he's developed a special song for her that almost matches her own. Then, too, the Great Bitch in the Sky has a sister. This is the fire siren in town — and I'm very glad it doesn't call him too often, because when it does, all hell breaks loose. *That* song is something to hear, believe me.)

Anyway, after we've gone through our mating call repertory, we go for a little walk around the periphery of the pen and leave a few marks in case any marauders come in the night. Then we head back to the hutch. The male now goes to sleep — or "snoozes" — and this is the female's cue to tiptoe out and dig up a very special bone she's had hidden from him, buried near the tree. We get this dug up and I test her, just to see if she'll share with me — and she will. I'm allowed to hold the bone in my hand — and even to raise it to my mouth. Naturally, I didn't actually put it in my mouth, but I'm sure she'd have let me. By this time, I'm beginning to wonder whether I'm going to get any sleep at all — so I leave her there, lying under the tree chewing on the bone, and I go in and join the male in a snooze. About an hour later, the female comes in and lies down. And it is at this point that I begin to discern the *pattern*. They never go *sound* asleep in the night together. One of them is always up and prowling, one way or another. I don't know why — and I won't conjecture. But it's an interesting fact — if a sleepless one, for me.

Finally, it gets light. By this time, they're both in the hutch, but only resting. They seem to be waiting for something — for some moment — or for some event. I don't know what it is, so I wait with them to get the cue.

It comes — and you might already have guessed what it is — but I hadn't, that morning in the pen with them. What happens is this. Simultaneously, they lift their heads and look at each other. Then she gets up and makes for the door. He rises and follows. I do likewise — on all fours — because the door of their hutch is dog-size — not man-size. We crawl out (they walk out) and then we take a few steps towards the east. Then — we bow.

That's it. We bow.

But my amazement is not yet complete.

What we are bowing at is not just the new day and the east and the sun.

We are bowing at its precise and exact moment of emergence over the horizon.

I have never forgotten that. That sensation. And I've checked on it often from the window of the house. They know — I swear it — they know when the sun is going to appear — to a second.

Well. I could tell you a lot more — about the games they play and the rules they live by — but that's another story. For now, I can't top that thing about the sun.

And — well — I don't want to.

That's what I mean about their leading *private* lives.

London, Ontario
January 1979
Journal

(Here for rehearsals of *John A.,
Himself* [at the Grand Thea-
tre]. Getting away was not easy.
The whole week leading up to
this moment of separation — and then the leaving —
driving away with, as always, that dreadful sense that I
won't come back — that I've said goodbye forever to the
animals — the house — the land. I might as well be
asked if I can give up breathing. "Breathe what — if I'm
not there?" Odd, but not odd at all, given that it's me I'm
talking about — that Stone Orchard has become my life.
Not the concrete place, but the "place." The air of where
I live. The magic of its rooms — the pervasive presence
of its ghosts — the whole conglomeration of animal life
— paintings — books — music — its flowers — the light
that illuminates the way in which I see — and what I see.
I live, I guess, a stained-glass life, defined by icons —
shapes — noises — smells — the mathematics of movement, etc. And when I'm broken off and swept away in
the car, the fragmentation is terrible. I fear it when I
leave.

·5·

THE BUTTERFLY
PLAGUE

Stone Orchard
March 1967
Notebook

Just beginning to be able to concern myself with the new novel, now that *Crazy People* is about to appear. I have not entirely shaken myself free of it — and I guess, until Hooker is out there on his own, I am bound to be worried about the reception he gets. But I do have to come to grips with the new people and put the *Crazy* Winslow family behind me. I must concentrate on Davis, Octavius and Selena. [These were names I had given characters in an early version of *The Butterfly Plague.*]

This will be the first time I have written exclusively about adults — no child's-eye view of things to fall back on. The innocent watcher in *The Butterfly Plague* will have to come from another quarter.

Why am I so concerned about the innocent watcher here? I guess the answer has to be that I want to show the evil aspect of this story without the sophisticated overlay of people's excuses for doing what they do.

An exploration of evil being invoked for its own sake?

To do this, I must create a character whose innocence — or do I mean naïveté? — can cut through the red tape of psychology. A child can do that. But what adult can do it, who has not preserved his innocence by some trick of circumstance? An illness that has kept him from the world? A mental deficiency that has kept him cloistered? An internment of some kind? I don't know. It will be fascinating to discover who this person is. I only know I haven't found him, yet — though I sense he will come all at once — quite whole — the way that all the interesting characters do. Not "made up" — but encountered, hidden in the mind. . . .

Stone Orchard
January 1990
Journal

Having scanned so many pieces of paper from so many sources in search of material for *Inside Memory*, it came as something of a shock last Wednesday when I found the notes from March 1967 — the passage just quoted. Finding them has been almost alarmingly coincidental with other events.

In the notes, I am looking for one of the leading characters in *The Butterfly Plague* and I write: *it will be fascinating to discover who this person is.* . . . Ruth Damarosch, of course, turned out to be that person — and Ruth was very largely based on my friend, Janet Baldwin. Janet's profound naïveté, her marriage to Boris, her presence at the 1936 Olympics and the fact that she is a carrier of haemophilia all contributed to Ruth as I wrote her — and on the very day I found the *Butterfly Plague* notes, Bill Bryan telephoned to say that Janet Baldwin was in Room 837 of the South Wing at the Wellesley Hospital. . . .

Aside from emphysema, she is suffering now from

dementia brought on by lack of blood in the brain. WFW and I went to see her on Thursday before going on to the opening night of *Breaking the Code.*

Janet was sitting up in a chair in the hallway outside her room. She was dressed in a hospital gown and a sort of apron that acts as a bib. Like a child, she must be fed by one of the nurses. Pretty well everything must be done for her. Although she can move her arms and legs, she is both weak and somewhat unco-ordinated. A blanket kept her warm as she sat there, but I could see her arms and they were thin to the point of emaciation.

Apparently, she had all but completely stopped eating when she was at home. Her friend from Meals on Wheels, who went in daily with Janet's supper, wondered why Janet was getting so thin in spite of the fact that she was receiving food every day. At some point, the friend went to get some juice from the fridge and she discovered all the meals from the previous week, stacked up on top of one another — entirely untouched.

The theory is that, given the way her system is slowly breaking down, the messages sent to Janet's brain about the need to eat are not being translated into action. She may very well have thought she'd already eaten and put the food away accordingly. Whatever the problem was, she was basically starving herself while remaining unaware that she was hungry. Her arms and legs are matchsticks now, and her face is gaunt and haunted by confusion.

As WFW and I came off the elevator, we could hear her calling out.

"Hello? Hello? Hello? Is someone there?"

She speaks in a monotone — but very loud and the monotone has an edge to it. Her back was to us and she couldn't see us as we approached. She was calling out her words without any sense of direction — simply staring ahead of her like someone in the dark or someone who is blind.

"Hello! Hello! Hello! Is someone there?"

We stopped at the nursing station and were told that Janet is sitting in the corridor because, if she can see activity around her, she is not so agitated. She had begun, they said, to fight off the nurses with her fists. I saw one episode of this and was surprised at how much strength Janet can still muster, in spite of her apparent weakness.

She looked at us with a mixture of alarm and chagrin. Who might we be — and why did we call her by her name?

"Hello, Janet."

"Yes," she said — as if acknowledging the fact that Janet was her name and we had got that much right.

"What are you doing here?"

"We've come to see you."

"You know me?"

"Yes."

She thought about this. She struggled with it. She looked away. Perhaps the wall would tell her our names. I sat down beside her in a chair. WFW still stood facing her.

"Who," she said, "are you?"

"Tiff, Janet. Tiff and Bill. . . ."

She narrowed her eyes.

Perhaps I was lying.

The eyes moved back and forth as she tried to conjure the names I had spoken.

"Tiff and Bill," I repeated. "I've known you all my life," I said. I was smiling. Smiling seemed the most reassuring thing I could do.

Slowly, a kind of recognition began to play on her face. She didn't speak our names — but clearly she had begun,

110

to whatever degree, to decipher who we were.

"Would you like to take her for a walk?" one of the nurses asked. "She loves to go to the end of the corridor. "

I said: "sure" and then to Janet: "would you like to go for a walk?"

She smiled.

"Oh, yes," she said. "Please, yes."

I put my overcoat on the chair I'd been sitting in and turned Janet's wheelchair so that it faced the most distant end of the hall. There was a window there, very brightly lit with sunlight, showing the buildings on Sherbourne Street and, way beyond them, something of the lake — just a flat, blue shimmer stretching towards the horizon. Frozen.

WFW stayed and talked to one of Janet's nurses while I pushed the chair towards the far end.

Looking down, I could only see Janet's knees and the top of her head. Her knees were tucked over sideways beneath her blanket and the top of her head was crowned with pure white hair that looked surprisingly healthy for someone who had been starved of nourishment. Janet's hair has always been one of her greatest assets — pure white — cut short — almost a costume piece. I don't remember when it wasn't white, though I met her first when I was six or seven, which means that she must have been in her teens. I remember, then, that she wore it long with a braid that she sometimes coiled at the back of her head or wound over one of her ears — like a hat worn sideways. Janet's hair and her great blue stare — the eyes very widely set and pale like ice — were the trademarks of her appearance. That, and the way she stood.

I guess I have never seen anyone who stood so well as Janet did — so completely at ease inside her body — straight without stiffness — poised without intensity. Her eyes, when she moved, were always fixed on where she was going and she always gave the impression of having a destination somewhere out of sight. I guess this was due in part to her peculiar "blindness" and her absolute refusal to wear her glasses in a public place. Janet also gave the impression of being in another dimension. Space accrued around her as she went her way. . . .

Once, in a long grey gown with silver threads, she came into the dining-room at the Atlantic House Hotel in Maine and brought all conversation to a halt. Around her neck she wore a chain of African medallions and as Janet moved towards her table, the chain and its ornaments made a tinkling, silver sound, as if an act of magic was in progress. No one spoke until she was seated and when, at last, the silence was broken, the first thing heard was a collective sigh.

If Janet knew how to make an entrance, she also knew how to make an exit.

She came to Stone Orchard shortly after the death of Boris Volkoff, her ex-husband, and the whole weekend she didn't utter a word of detail or of comment on his dying. Nothing. We spoke of a hundred other things and she drank a fair amount of rye, which she always provided herself — the bottle in her satchel, the satchel loosely hanging from her shoulder.

WFW was living then in Ottawa, working at the National Arts Centre. Consequently, I was living at the farm alone when Janet came.

We ate our meals and took our walks and sat in front of the fire. Nothing. I dared not mention Boris by name, for fear it might start a flood of recriminations. All the bad, sad memories, the old wars between them that had been so harsh and the dreadful, unforgiving silences that had lasted for years — these might all rise up again and damage her as they had when Boris had gone off with his other women.

His presence sat there with us — glowering at us, stick in hand — the whole two days. I kept remembering the way, in ballet class, he would strike us with that walking stick. It had a silver handle — round. The stick was black. *Boris, the Ballet Master.* His nineteenth-century ballet master's sense of discipline was governed by his passionate sense of line and any deviation from that line would bring the stick down, rapping out a warning on the floor. Then he would crack you with it across the wrist or behind the knee or right in the small of the back — wherever your sense of line offended his. This, while you worked at the barre.

All your offences would catch his attention — even the very least of them: a misplaced finger, a turn-out that missed perfection, a foot that rolled from its balance for half a second — and Boris would strike. We came away from classes blue with Volkoff-tattoos! Over time, these bruises became the marks of our transition from novice to serious student.

Boris Volkoff was a martinet — but the result of his training could be spectacular — viz. Melissa Hayden, Lillian Jarvis, Natalia Butko. Viz. Janet Baldwin. . . . I do not regret the time I spent in his classes — though I readily admit that when Janet left him and I went on to study with her, I was greatly relieved. The stick with the silver handle and the stinging voice were happily relegated to the past. In time, it became clear that I was not a dancer but an actor. But the actor had the benefit of knowing how to move.

Now, Boris was dead, and Janet had been with him when he died — but that was all I knew.

Our weekend drew to a close. Janet went upstairs to

pack and to change for her drive back into the city. I went into the kitchen and fed the cats.

Ten minutes later, Janet came downstairs and set her suitcase somewhere near the centre of the kitchen floor. She was wearing a suit and shoes with heels. She was also wearing a hat. The hat was small and it sat on the back of her head — like a bird that had tagged along for the ride.

Janet was smoking a cigarette and drinking the last of her rye. I swear I remember her wearing gloves. She was poised, in a sense, for flight. She said: "sit down."

I sat at the kitchen table.

Now, it was late in the afternoon and darkening. Janet said: "don't turn on the lights."

I didn't.

Janet said: "just be quiet. . . ."

I hadn't said a word.

She walked up and down. She crossed from the kitchen door to the study door and back again — once — twice — three times — four — always avoiding the suitcase placed, it seemed, so deliberately in her chosen path.

Then she said, still walking, pacing — saying it not to me but to the air around us both: "he was in great pain, you know. . . ."

"Yes."

"Be quiet."

She paced.

"He was in great pain — he was alone — but he needed someone with him all the time. His wife had left him — *kaput* — that happened long before he was ill, and. . . ."

I waited.

"I started going to see him every day. Mostly, he was bedridden. Sometimes not — but mostly. His bed was in a room that had a fireplace. . . ."

The fire in the living-room was crackling somewhere

behind her — picking up its cue from her story. Cars went by on the road. The sky got darker — the garden was more and more in shadow.

"Boris never lit the fire in his room because he said a *raccoon is living there*. The raccoon came down to visit him. He fed it bread. The raccoon would sit on the mantelpiece and climb around the tops of all the bookshelves. Boris didn't know what to do. His big concern was *what will happen to my raccoon when I have died?* I said: it will find another house and go and live there. But he said *no, it will die without me. What can we do?* We, he said. What can *we* do? I said: we can have them come from the Humane Society. *No,* said Boris, *they will kill it.* No, I said, they won't. They'll take it and set it free in one of the ravines. . . ."

And so this is what was done. Janet telephoned the Humane Society and a woman came with a cage and Boris called the raccoon and the raccoon came down the chimney.

"Boris said *bring her to me.* So — I took her to him. Boris sat in the bed and gave the raccoon the last of her bread and he said *goodbye.* He spoke to her in Russian. Watching them together — she was so trusting — he was so gentle. It reminded me. . . ."

Janet had been little more than a girl when Boris had come into her life. Memory tells me she was barely eighteen when they were married. Maybe it was just that she was barely eighteen when they fell in love. At any rate, Boris was a good deal older than Janet — freshly arrived from San Francisco via Shanghai. He had gone to Shanghai from Russia after the death of Lenin. That would have been in 1924. When he and Janet first came together was in 1936.

They had gone together, as participants, to the Berlin Olympics. Dance was still an Olympic event in 1936 —

and they were on the Canadian team. It was a momentous time for Janet — the whole world suddenly opened up before her with all its adult responsibilities and involvements and with all its political complexities begging for her attention. And there had been the matter of what she must tell Boris, now that it was definite she was to be his wife.

He had wanted children. But Janet could not, in her own words, "provide him with children." She could not because she would not. Janet was a carrier of haemophilia — and any male child to whom she gave birth would possibly — the odds are hazardous — suffer consequences Janet was not prepared to take responsibility for. "He would bleed to death. The pain of it would be intolerable. Nothing could persuade me to chance it."

Nothing but Boris's determination to have a child.

In the 1930's and 1940's, Janet underwent multiple episodes of conception — anguish — and, finally, abortion. She travelled again and again to Buffalo, New York or Chicago, Illinois in order to have these operations — always in the worst of appalling circumstances. Drunken doctors, quacks or so-called midwives whose Dickensian ministrations cost the earth would butcher Janet's beloved fetuses — the victims of her own despair, of Boris's punishing determination, and the victims, too, of inhuman laws that failed to provide a haven for women in need of safe abortions performed in clinics or in hospitals by qualified surgeons.

Under these circumstances — and because of the added pressure of their professional lives — Janet's marriage to Boris began to tear at the seams — and bleed. Janet became, in essence, a permanently wounded animal. Boris took up, over time, with various other women — many of them as young as Janet had been — and so, in the late 1940s, their life together ended.

Boris and Janet — Janet and her father . . . the question must be posed.

Mister Baldwin was still alive, though very old, in the 1960s. By then, he was living in New York City — somewhere in the East 60s — high up over the Park — strangely, seductively appealing. He had long ago left his wife, Janet's mother, and — being a romantic figure with a romantic view of passion — had gone off to live where galleries and theatres, restaurants and Bonwit-Teller were available to cater to his taste for beauty.

Women came first on his list — but what he wanted was what the kings of France had wanted — a highly educated, witty, beautiful and devoted "courtesan." He found such a woman — an actress — who, not incidentally, was also a walking advertisement for class. Beautiful in the patrician sense — a sensualist in the cultural sense — this prize of a woman had brought Janet's father all the happiness a man of his tastes could want.

There he sat, the King of France, with his abandoned wife at a convenient distance and his rebellious daughter held at bay. His relationship with Janet was that of the quavering, Lear-like parent who nonetheless kept her mesmerized by his power.

How much of this overbearing father had Janet been seeking in Boris — the older man who would tell her what to do and who she was, but who, at the same time, would love her?

There was a lot of the unbroken child in Janet. But a part of her never matured beyond that. Helpless, while refusing the only true help there was — growing up.

On the other hand — "growing up" had been made to seem like the worst thing that could happen to a person in Janet's time. Especially a girl. The first thing they told you was that you were worthless as who you were — and the second thing they told you was that, once you had stopped belonging to your parents, you would belong to someone else. Of course, such people are prone to being damaged. If you rebelled, you were doomed to be broken.

Janet maintained this childlike quality up until the day her mind gave over. She would virtually stand before you, wide-eyed with wonder. *You look like such a nice man,* this look conveyed. *Can you tell me where I am?* . . .

Where am I? Who am I? How do I survive? This was the essence of Janet's persona. How deep the innocence actually ran was quite impossible to tell. She made, after all, a greatly successful life for herself after the separation from Boris. She created and ran a thriving school of ballet with highly respected standards and a large body of students, all of whom adored her to the point of reverence. A "fool" cannot accomplish such things. In the cut-throat world of running a business, a helpless innocent would not survive five minutes. Janet survived it — with notable success — for over twenty- five years.

On the other hand! . . .

She would arrive at Stone Orchard twice a year with her accounts. She would lay out her ledgers and all her carefully assembled chits and cancelled cheques and she would say to WFW: *now what do I do?*

WFW would sit with her for hours, poring over the books, explaining how every item complemented another item somewhere in the mass of papers. Sometimes I would hear him telling her how to add and subtract!

But Janet had — surely — perfect understanding of her ledgers. After all, she had created them from scratch. WFW may have found frustration in the process — but he never encountered blunders. The point was — Janet required the given hours of patient schooling. She remained the perfect child, who put up her hand in class and said *please explain it all again.* Perhaps she needed this explanation of what she already knew in order to recall the innocence she had lost — and endlessly mourned.

Sometime after Janet first became ill with what had still not been diagnosed as emphysema, she went through moments of childlike behaviour that verged on "crazy." But she was not alone in this particular craziness. Burt and Margot Clarkson shared it with her.

There is something odd about the children of the rich who have been abandoned, one way or another, by their parents. Perhaps it has something to do with receiving all your money through the mail — and all your direction through a surrogate. *I'm waiting to be told what I'm to do* these children will tell you, in so many words. *My trust officer — my bank manager — my estate agent — my keeper has not yet informed me if I am free to marry you. . . .* Also — or so it seems, no matter what age these abandoned children achieve, they give the impression they are waiting for their Nanny to come and whip them into shape.

When Janet was at the Atlantic House Hotel with Burt and Margot Clarkson, they behaved like children who have escaped from the nursery in adult clothes.

Burt and Margot's parents had deserted them by dying. The children were left an immense old house in Toronto and a good deal of money — carefully administered — to run the house and pay for their lives. They would arrive, with Janet in tow, in the dining-room at suppertime, drunk with freedom.

Margot, who was a hypochondriac and thin as a rail, with bony arms and a wide, painted mouth, affected English seaside clothes — a cloche hat and a foot-long cigarette holder. Burt, her younger brother, was pale, ambivalent about his wish to be seen in public and wore a bright red baseball cap, grey flannel shorts and a loose cloth jacket. Burt and Margot would bicker — mostly about the menu, sometimes about who got to be first to write their order on the chit — their voices rising higher and higher as they drank their wine. Janet — who tended to weave back and forth very slightly if she was drunk — would sit quite silent — seemingly stupefied — staring at everyone else in the room. The scene could be both wildly funny and oddly horrifying. I wish it was not a memory I had.

On the other hand, it marked the dividing line between her active life and her decline.

By the mid-1970s, when Boris was dying, time had been less kind to him than to Janet. He had failed in his great ambition to be the first Artistic Director of Canada's National Ballet. His school began to falter and ultimately to fail. His health began to fade. He accepted more and more work as a walk-on player in film and television; his distinctly Russian features and his small, taut body made him very useful in these media. And, of course, as a walk-on, he had no lines to speak. The thick, persevering accent of his mother tongue did not hamper him in acquiring work as it might have if Boris had been less impressive to behold. His presence was that of The Master to the end.

Boris said: bring her to me. So I took her to him. . . .

"When the raccoon had finished eating," Janet continued, "we put her in the cage and the woman from the Humane Society took her away."

Janet had not paused once in pacing. As the story unfolded that darkening afternoon in the kitchen, it was told as much in footsteps as it was in words.

"We had suffered all those years of battering one another — yelling at one another — hating one another

— seeking revenge and taking it at every opportunity. He had been monstrous to me and I had been deceitful, jealous, spiteful and hateful to him. But I loved him."

Yes.

"And something, then, of his forgotten love for me — the old, old love from all those years before — began to return, I guess, in Boris and it was just as if all the time and tragedy fell away from who we were and we were young again — whatever that meant — untouched by the awfulness — as if the awfulness had never happened and I said to him *yes, I love you* and he said, in Russian, *yes, I love you, too. . . .*"

And they were married.

Again.

Janet laughed when she told this.

"We had the priest from the Orthodox Church and all the words were said and all the vows were taken. All the sentiments were duly expressed and all the proper gestures were made, Boris sitting up in the bed and me standing there beside him. The only thing we didn't do was get a marriage licence!"

Janet finished her rye.

"But in every other sense, we were married," she said.

"The day before he died. And I cannot tell you how at peace I am."

That was the end of it.

The pacing stopped.

She put down the glass. She put out her cigarette.

She kissed me on the cheek. She picked up the suitcase. She walked away.

She didn't even say goodbye.

Still sitting at the kitchen table — I heard her car depart.

A lesson in perfect timing.

Once a week, now, on the days we go to Casey House, we stop for a while at the Wellesley, South Wing, eighth floor.

Hello? Hello? Is someone there?

WFW talks to the nurses. I take Janet down the hall in her chair.

It seems unbearable. Simply unbearable.

But, I guess, as final exits go, it's not. Janet has already left us. All that remains, for her body's sake, is the dignity of our attentions until it, too, departs. I wish I knew where she keeps the African medallions. They should be hung in a tree nearby when she is buried.

She will go on living for me — it is purely private — in *The Butterfly Plague* — trying to give birth to her children — trying to understand the world she lived in and why it was the way it was.

Hotel Meurice
New York
April 1968
Journal

This whole journey has been a disaster. Arrived early morning by train from Toronto day before yesterday. Border crossing okay, although Customs officers never seem to be able to deal with the idea that publishing a book has anything to do with business. They seem to think it is something people do *for fun*. "You mean you're going to New York for a vacation?" she said, when I had explained that I was delivering the manuscript of a book to Bantam. "No," I said, "I will be paid for this. It's my job." "Oh," she said — blank-faced. "Gee."

What can you do?

. . .at Buffalo got off and went to bar with humming neon Genesee sign near station. [Train stops for about two hours.] Ghastly, depressing bar full of argumentative men who were all yelling at each other about baseball. Since the season hasn't opened yet, don't know why all the yelling. Anyway — unpleasant, typical locker-room atmosphere. Women sat alone — three of them — each obviously rooting for her husband's or boyfriend's point of view. "Charlie's right about this. . . ."·"Fuck you, Evelyn!" "Charlie's an asshole! *Frank* is right!" Etc. What the crux of the matter was, was never made clear the whole time I sat there.

Drank only beer — after one double rye. Bartender sold me a six-pack to go with me on the train. . . .

. . .arrived so early I was still asleep as we came along the river. Only woke as we were crossing over bridge. Rushed to dress. No time to shave. Hateful arrival.

. . .ordered breakfast in room at the Meurice. Thank God for sanity of room service. Ran bath. Felt a bit better. Shaved. Went out and bought papers — roses for Grace [Bechtold] and two bottles of gin, promising self I would not open them until I had been to Bantam. . . .

. . .opened gin at 11:45 A.M. Telephoned WFW, quite convinced I could pull this off. Have feeling, nonetheless, he could tell. He has the ears of a longtime listener. I could tell by his reaction that he "knew." On the other hand, he said nothing overt. When I hung up the 'phone, I felt a sense of relief. *I will be okay.* . . .

. . .not okay. On basis of positive phone call, I drank a whole tumbler of Gordon's straight — with a second tumbler of tepid water as a chaser. I began to think I should eat. . . .

. . .suddenly it was after 2:00 P.M. and I was due with Grace at 3:00. Looked at self in mirror. Thought — *take a shower* — showered — came out looking pale, tired, vaguely sober. . . .

. . .bolstered self with a second tumbler of gin — adding water as I drank. . . .

. . .went down to street [just south of the Park] and hailed a cab. . . .

. . .cabby turned out to be Irish. I was sure he'd just emerged from the nearest bar — screamingly funny — yelling jokes at the top of his voice. I sat — bewildered by my inability to pull myself together — in the back seat. Grace's roses sat beside me and I had the final draft of *Butterfly Plague* on my lap in a soft-cardboard box. Manuscript printed on yellow copy paper — all we could afford — but also a boon because its colour set it aside from other drafts. I removed the lid to make sure the pages were in correct order. . . .

. . .suddenly arrived at Bantam — quite unprepared to have got there so fast. Thinking — *well, here I am in New York City and about to take the world by storm!*

Masterpiece in hand, I got out of cab and turned to pay the driver. Finding wallet was difficult, given box of manuscript — and sudden discovery that, because we had arrived so quickly, I had not returned cover to box — set box on top of cab and began a one-handed search of body for wallet. . . .

Whole of Madison Avenue is, of course, a canyon. This creates wind and updraughts — lifting women's skirts and blowing away men's hats . . . and yellow manuscript pages from the tops of cars . . . A nightmare ensued. . . .

Tiddly Irish cabby and drunk Timothy Findley and half a dozen wind-blown passers-by all rushed after yellow pages — leaping — running — falling down. Looking up, all I could see was a whirlwind of yellow — giving way, as one draught fought against another over Madison Avenue — so that pages rose on one side and fell on the other. Traffic was halted. People, being kind, went through balletic exertions — and, at last, the manuscript was retrieved entirely and the lid clamped down on the box.

. . .going up in the elevator, the cabby carried most of the pages in their box, while I — attempting the impossible performance of sobriety — rode beside him, clutching in one hand roses and in the other, a bouquet of yellow copy paper. . . .

The doors opened. There was BANTAM BOOKS, INC. — EDITORIAL OFFICES — and a smiling, baffled woman stepping forward to say: "Mister Findley, how lovely to see you again. . . ."

I said: "can someone pay the driver? He's been most helpful and I have lost my wallet. . . ."

"Yes, of course," said the smiling, baffled woman — who then proceeded to get a bill from her purse — and to pay the cabby. "Would you like some coffee, Mister Findley?"

She, like WFW, had some sense of discretion at least. But now it was too late.

Grace came round the corner.

Death.

She took one look at me and guessed at once.

She was dressed in grey and brown and seemed to have been prepared to greet me with a hug. Seconds later, she was red — then white — then red again with fury. Totally enraged, she pointed at me: "Out! Out! Out!" she said. "Just get the fuck out of here and don't come back!"

Get the fuck out of here and don't come back.

. . .I gave her the roses. She threw them on the floor. I offered the yellow-paper bouquet to the woman who had paid the cabby. I retrieved the box and set it down on someone's desk. Grace was over by the elevator, pushing buttons.

"I never want to see you again," she said. "This is worse than disgraceful — it is a horror story. Why didn't someone warn me you were drinking again? I hate you. . . ."

The elevator finally came.

I had already turned my back on everyone and was trying to run — but, in fact, I was standing perfectly still.

The dull metal doors stood open. The cabby — sheepish — got in. I got in, too.

Grace again pressed buttons.

"The elevator has arrived, Grace," I said — with all the dignity I could muster. "In case you hadn't noticed, I'm *in* it, now, and already leaving. . . ."

The doors were closing.

I was completely sober.

Grace said: "you bastard! You will never know what you've done!"

The doors — by the time she had finished — closed and she was gone.

The cabby drove me back to 58th Street, parked his car and said: "I'm buying."

That was yesterday. I can't remember the rest. We went, I suppose, to a bar — and with his help, I suppose, I got back up to this room. Today, I am supposed to go to William Morris — bearing the news of my triumph. I will go tomorrow and lie.

Train enroute to Toronto
April 1968
Journal

. . .Elizabeth — the woman who had paid for the cab and accepted the yellow-page bouquet without a hint of embarrassment — telephoned and explained why Grace had been in such a state.

"It wasn't just the fact that you were under the weather, Mister Findley. It was because she has just been having a very bad time with Mister [naming another writer]."

"Oh?" I said — pretending I didn't know what she was saying. The writer in question, who happens — next to Thornton — to be the greatest living American writer so far as I am concerned — is also a notorious drinker.

"Yes," said Elizabeth. "Miss Bechtold has been editorially involved with him recently and — well — to put it mildly, Mister ———— has been a wild man."

Elizabeth laughed. But lightly.

"The thing is," she said, "Miss Bechtold has been put through the wringer with Mister ————'s antics and her attitude, now, to any writer who. . . ."

". . .drinks too much," I offered.

Elizabeth paused. Then: "yes," she said. "I guess that's what I mean. Anyway — Miss Bechtold can't cope with it just now. I told her I would be phoning you, and she said. . ."

"Yes?"

"She said to say *goodbye*."

There was then a very long pause.

"Mister Findley?"

"Yes?"

Elizabeth's tone was even and unreadable.

"I'm sure she only meant goodbye for now."

Finally — after leaving Elizabeth in limbo for a moment — I said to her: "thank you. Tell her I said the same."

Now — I'm going home to face WFW. Maybe he will say goodbye, like Grace. I hope not — but — I would understand if he did. The thing is — what do *I* say?

Salisbury Hotel
New York
June 1968
Journal

Arrived here on Wednesday the 5th — late and lost. The drive had been hard on WFW since we did the whole trip in one day. The Meurice, our favourite hotel, is now being turned into apartments so we've come here to the Salisbury, which is okay, but somewhat off the beaten track. WFW had a bad time with the one-way streets and it took a long while to find the right route.

Finally, fell into bed long after midnight. . . .

Awakened from a dead sleep by Gary [Cosay] phoning at 7:00 A.M. to tell us that our appointment at William Morris would be delayed because of "this Kennedy thing." . . .

"What Kennedy thing?"

"Robert Kennedy was shot last night in L.A."

"Dear God."

"He's still alive, but they don't expect him to survive it. Frankly, Tiff, I just can't pull myself together. This news is devastating, through and through. Do you mind if we meet after lunch?"

"Not at all, Gary. I'm terribly sorry. . . ."

The fact is, his grief was like a remonstrance — surely the whole of America will feel tomorrow as he does today. Two assassinations in a row — King in April, Kennedy in June . . . the two great hopes that wars would end and people could come together.

"Why don't we meet tomorrow?" I said.

For a moment, Gary was silent — and then he said: "yes," and "thank you," and hung up. He was weeping.

. . .When we finally heard that Kennedy had died, WFW and I went over to the Bronx and went to the zoo. I don't know why we decided we would do this. Maybe something about the presence of animals — the need for behaviour that wasn't grotesque. I don't know. I don't know. It just seemed the only proper thing to do. In me there is always the impetus to apologize to animals for what we do to them — and today, perhaps, for what we do to our own kind.

Out at the zoo, we discovered we were not alone in our decision. Hundreds and hundreds of schoolchildren were also there. Their teachers have decided to remove them from their classrooms on a day when mayhem might result from too much enforced stillness. The undercurrent everywhere is dangerous — held in place by shock. The awfulness of what has happened has left most people blank with confusion and sorrow.

. . .In the Monkey House, we came upon a scene that I will never forget as long as I live. . . .

The gorilla — a female — was seated in her cage behind glass. I suppose the glass was to protect her from dangerous offers of inappropriate food. And from — it became all too evident — the laughter of children.

Rows and rows of little boys in purple T-shirts and little girls in pink jeans paused before the glass and pointed and screamed and yelled with deafening delight at the great black beast who was seated on a chair. . . .

Why was she given the stupid chair? To make her look funny? Human pretensions? "This is just an animal, folks! Look at her trying to be like us! WHO THE HELL DO ANIMALS THINK THEY ARE? DON'T THEY KNOW THAT WE ARE KINGS OF THE JUNGLE!!!!?"

The pointing and the laughing and the screaming, yelling and jumping up and down nearly drove me mad. "Why don't you tell them to stop?" I asked one of the teachers in charge of these kids. "Oh," she said, "they're only children. They don't mean no harm. . . ."

Like fucking hell they don't.

Their grown-up counterparts just killed Robert Kennedy.

. . .and all the while we stood there, the great black beast just sat and watched us.

Bewilderment — sadness and dignity shine from her eyes — and they leave an indelible mark on me. I will never, never, never forget her. She was the embodiment of all the grace and poise and splendour we have abandoned.

They brought Robert Kennedy here to St. Patrick's Cathedral today, because he was the Senator from New York. All day long, thousands of people have gone to see him lying there in state.

WFW and I passed by down the Avenue. We had considered going in to pay our respects, but it seemed, in the event, inappropriate. So many people to whom he truly belonged had come to see him that we felt it was enough for us to pause by the Cathedral, think our thoughts and go our way.

Later, we took a taxi to the Village where we were having supper with Grace and going on to see *Jacques Brel is Alive and Well and Living in Paris*. We are attempting a reconciliation with Grace following the disaster of my last visit here. This is really the principal reason we have come to New York — though Owen [Laster] and Gary want me to meet Mister [Harvey] Ginsberg at Viking, who is going to publish the hardcover edition of *The Butterfly Plague*. Grace will still publish the paperback at Bantam.

She lives at the corner of 12th and Christopher — in an apartment above a store. The whole place reeks of the 1930s. Charm and atmosphere. You feel as if, turning on the radio, you will hear Mister Roosevelt speaking or Billie Holliday singing. Grace is a rabid New Deal Democrat and her photographs and mementoes all reflect this — Madison Square Rally, 1937 — Washington Square orators in black suspenders, shirt-sleeves and straw boaters — pals with Grace at Reno's, standing in the sawdust, raising their glasses to Roosevelt's third term win in 1940. . . .

There was tension, yes. I am back on the pill — the way I was when first we met — but I know that, once a negative image is in place, it's hard to wipe it away. In the restaurant, she hesitated before she ordered a drink for herself — and only did so when WFW ordered his

Manhattan. I wish she realized it couldn't matter less what other people drink. The only drink that matters is your own! Tonic water for me — which I'm getting heartily sick of — too bitter.

Anyway — we set off to see the Brel revue at the Village Gate — walking through the old, beloved streets that have seemed like a second home to me ever since I first encountered them in 1951. The shock and sorrow of Kennedy's assassination seemed even to have touched the leaves of all the trees as we passed along our way. People sat staring out of windows, looking pensively — it seemed — for any other time but this. The people walking with us moved, as we did, slowly and without deliberation. Grace was still in a tentative mode — still performing charm instead of being charming — cool but not cold — distanced but not completely aloof. I was beginning to think we would never recover our friendship.

In the theatre, we sat at tables. The place was packed. Four singers sang Brel songs — two men — two women. It was electrifying. Somehow, everyone needed this — performers as well as audience — the reaffirmation of what is better in the human spirit than what we have been witnessing and sharing through this past week.

There is something about the human voice — the yearning to articulate whatever it is that will not come through words alone. Or gestures. Music drives away the sense of panic that you cannot explain how you feel — it releases all the desperation — all the baffled weeping *(why am I crying)* — all the pent-up laughter that makes no sense. It gives you back the hope, I guess, that all is not lost when silence descends and people can no longer speak.

One of the women sang a song called "Sons Of" — which tells of all the children lost in the wars. The room was utterly stilled. The heat was stifling — yet no one

131

moved a muscle — while this woman stood there in the light and sang.

Towards the end she almost broke — but she didn't. She concluded it triumphantly, but there was no applause. How could there be?

He is dead — and we have watched him die — and some of us have killed him. That is what she said for us — though little enough of this was actually in the words. It was in the singing. In the music. In the need — and its fulfilment.

After the whole revue was over — we came out into the streets. We were reconciled. I guess it must have been the song. Grace took my arm and the three of us walked back over to 12th Street — silent.

. . .Now I have written this — and tomorrow we go home. As we are heading north and west by car, Robert Kennedy's body will be taken south and east by train to Arlington, Virginia. We will all go with him, in our minds. This is a new America — lost and cut off from the one that was. It is a desperate America — waving its flags and sinking into chaos. It is hard to know if there can be recovery. In *The Butterfly Plague* it is 1938. A train runs down and kills an American hero. People stand there watching and cheering. The train, of course, is America itself.

And I thought I was writing about the past.

·6·

THE WARS

Stone Orchard
April 1987

Every writer goes through bad times; for me, it was after the publication of my first two novels — *The Last of the Crazy People* and *The Butterfly Plague*. Once they were in print, I found that most critics greeted them lukewarmly or completely ignored them. What followed was a period of seven or eight years in which I wrote almost exclusively in television and radio. I also wrote two novels — dark, depressed, depressing and totally unpublishable. Finally, in 1976, I wrote a play — *Can You See Me Yet?* — which went into rehearsal at the National Arts Centre in Ottawa, where WFW was then working.

This is how WFW tells about what followed:

"One morning, shortly before the play opened, Tiff emerged from his room in our downtown apartment in Ottawa and was wreathed in happy smiles. *I've got it!* he shouted. *I've got the next book! It came to me last night when I was sitting up in bed, making notes.* Being all too aware of the bitterness and pessimism in most of Tiff's writing in the years since *The Butterfly Plague,* I made some enthusiastic noises and I cautiously asked what his new book was about. *Oh,* said Tiff, *it's great! And guess what — it's* positive! *No more doom and gloom. This book says* yes!

"I relaxed and repeated my question: *what was the book about?*

"This was Tiff's answer: *Well, it's about a young man from Toronto who goes off to fight in World War I, and he falls in love with an English girl, only she turns out to be unfaithful, and then he does something that everyone thinks is insane, and after that he's horribly maimed in a fire and finally he dies!*

"It wasn't until the following year, when I first read the manuscript of *The Wars,* that I had to agree that Tiff was correct on all counts. Dreadful things happened to Robert Ross, the hero of *The Wars* — but still, the book did end up saying *yes.*"

Ottawa
January 1976
Notebook

Wars . . . you walk through rain and mud with horses and ammunition carts to a village. You eat. *Everything glass has been destroyed.* There are no reflections anywhere. This frightens you. You pray for someone to look at you and say your name with a sense of immediate recognition. No one does. You need sleep. You want a bath. You bathe with the inmates of an asylum — though you don't know who or what they are. Someone feeds you while you sit wrapped in a white sheet. You are mistaken for an inmate of asylum — you want sleep, but feel unsafe. An inmate steals your sheet while you are walking down a corridor — you can't get it back — naked — no cover — you hear people coming — go into a semi-dark room. People stop in hallway. You wait. Gradually aware there are others in room with you. Someone reaches out and strokes your genitals. Then someone else. You try to break away, but someone puts hand over your mouth. There are four or five men with you. They fondle you like a doll. You try to cry out — and your struggles are heard in the hallway — you think you'll be saved — but realize those in hallway are "inmates," too. They gather in the doorway to watch. You are stroked and fondled like a toy — softly and slowly — so the "violence" and violation are drawn out — like rape in double-slow-motion — by children. They "feed" from your body. You are made to pass out by someone who puts his hand over your mouth and nose. You wake in empty room. Find your way to "safety." Deep night. You can't find your clothes — nothing that belongs to you. Then suddenly — someone appears and calls you by a name not your own. You don't know who he is. Can't remember. He is fully dressed — a fellow officer. Jovial — friendly — disregarding your nakedness — talking about a party in London. He inadvertently leads you to your clothes, etc. — all the time insisting he knows you (but has your name wrong) and proves he knows you by remarking on event you know yourself you've shared with *someone* not unlike this person. He takes you to a pension where you will sleep. In the Asylum Courtyard, by lamp-light, you see a group of Canadian nurses and you are overwhelmed by fear they will recognize you — and will know by some sixth sense what has happened to you . . . .

Ottawa
February 1976
Notebook

I have no photographs of this in the concrete sense, but the pictures in my mind are much more like photographs than remembered images from life. This has to do with Juliet [Mannock] and the particular way in which she comes

137

into focus inside memory. I see her so vividly — I can even turn the pages on which she appears in these imagined photographs. Juliet offers an album: *here — this is me* . . . .

She sits beside a table, looking away from the camera, turned in profile towards a window. An ashtray, a book laid open — lying face down — and a glass of sherry occupy the table top. Juliet wears a wide blue skirt and a shirt I can only describe as being the colour of water. She is smoking a cigarette and every few moments she lifts the glass of sherry and drinks from it briefly — always returning the glass to the table — both hands shaking, each hand trembling very slightly as she lifts the glass or turns the cigarette. The shaking isn't because of nervousness but, rather, because of some interior impulse she cannot control. It is simply part of her signature.

Juliet makes a garden everywhere she lives. Most of her gardens are in pots and she always has at least one plant in bloom. Cut flowers and dried flowers often augment this garden — and whatever else is set about in Juliet's rooms — from china plates to pictures, books and velvet pillows — all the colours complement the colours in the garden. Violet, mauve and blue predominate — many shades of green and always something red or yellow tucked in a corner.

She lives mostly in flats inside of sub-divided houses. The streets on which these houses can be found are always treelined. Often, there is a park nearby and neighbourhood shopping, which Juliet prefers, as opposed to gigantic supermarkets and department stores. All of this — the shops, the parks and the trees — are a part of her English past and — I assume — prerequisites. Juliet's Englishness is the governor of all her tastes.

It isn't always easy to imagine everyone you meet in

terms of what they might have been like as a child — but Juliet I can imagine. Juliet and Caroline [her sister] have remained remarkably loyal to one another, which means they must have depended to some degree on one another as children. I think it was probably an intriguing rather than a happy childhood they shared. Which is not to say they were made appallingly unhappy by what they encountered there. But I'm sure they had to work at survival.

Both the parents were writers — father a critic, mother a novelist — and, as I gather, both had very strong personalities and rather devastating private lives. The view of life they provided for their children was filtered through fascinating people who, it seems, were always engaged in something that set them apart from the adults who populated the lives of Juliet and Caroline's contemporaries. Parents who worked intensely at home in a house that was full of books and of telephones that rang at midnight and whose open doors might offer, at any moment, Harold Hobson, Virginia Woolf or Malcolm Muggeridge were hardly what anyone would call your average middle-class couple. Darby and Joan they were not.

Independence of outlook was encouraged early — if, indeed, it needed to be encouraged at all. I suspect that Juliet had few problems deciding who she was. She verged, perhaps — from time to time — on making naïve assumptions about the willingness of the rest of the world to accept her as she was — and I dare say this had disappointing consequences. But I also suspect that — given the milieu — Juliet had incipient savvy. She learned very quickly how to cope with idiot contempt. Her smile — both wise and mischievous — informs me of this.

A world that does not universally put its hand out to strangers is bound to baffle a child who is unafraid. One of the Juliet stories I love is the one where, having learned to read at a precocious age, she began to scan the papers with an adult's eye. If *The Times* were dull that day, she would gravitate — aged six or seven — to the *News of the World*. The stories there were so intriguing — and such exciting, death-defying — or deadly — things could happen to you in its ultra-adult world, that Juliet could not contain her impatience to get out into the streets and experience it all!

"Mummy?" she said one day, "do you think that Caroline and I could go to the park?"

"Whatever for?" said Mother Mannock. "It's pouring rain."

"There's someone there I want to meet," said the child — Juliet — biting her lip in anticipation.

"Someone I know?" asked Mother Mannock.

"No, I don't think so," said Juliet.

"Who is it, then?"

"The Child Mole Man."

"The Child Mole Man? . . ."

"Yes," said Juliet. "He always wears a mackintosh and he hides behind the trees in the park and, when the moles come out, he offers them sweets and takes them back to his flat."

"Really, Juliet! Where did you hear about this person?"

"I read about him in the paper." Juliet thrust the *News of the World* at her mother. "There he is there," she said — and jabbed her finger at a headline.

ARREST OF CHILD MOLE. . . .

Mrs Mannock went pale.

Juliet repeated the headline aloud. "Arrest of Child Mole-ster in Green Park, . . ." she said.

Her mother had to explain that Child Molesters were *not in the least bit interested in moles, dear.*

Juliet survived to tell the tale.

Juliet has a way of finding light that any actor would kill for. I don't know what this talent is, but I know it is a native thing and not a thing that can be learned. You have it or you don't. Blessed by whatever gods of theatre there are that govern such gifts, I know about light myself and have that same mothlike propensity that Juliet has — and others. Light has a way of "seeing" and the secret has to do with meeting it eye to eye.

Juliet's capacity for finding light is more than likely why she appears in the mind as an image on film. She is also, like most of the subjects of successful photographs, one of those people whose beauty or handsomeness cannot be analyzed. There is nothing perfect about such people except their whole appearance. The elements rarely have classical values and, taken one by one, would be dismissed as in: *nose too long — mouth too wide* and *chin too pointed — ears too small.*

I have always believed that *concentration* lies behind the images we remember — a concentration of energies or of focus or of space. Tension. The tension in what we see is what forces us to look again. Juliet has that kind of concentration in repose. She is never vague or vacuous. She is always completely *there.*

This has to do, of course, with why I am drawn to her as a person — the person beyond or inside the image. She can be wicked at times — and maddening — but never less than caring, in the widest sense of that word. Her wickedness can be a riot and whatever drives you mad in the moment is gone in the very next moment, because the endearing qualities in Juliet are greater by far then the maddening ones.

Juliet is also brave. She has survived — since leaving home — a multitude of sorrows and disappointments — and has made her way alone with the kind of angry good humour that only survivors are blessed with. Juliet, pursued by an over-persistent irritant, will turn and say to it: *piss off!* She never pleads with trouble — and she makes no bargains. Who has time for that? And on she goes.

Some of these qualities in Juliet have begun to filter onto the page in the sketch of a woman who perhaps will play an important part in what I am now exploring — namely, one of those people who remembers Robert Ross [in *The Wars*]. I don't know who she is, yet, but I do know her name is Juliet. That much is unavoidable. You can't put even the smallest portion of Juliet Mannock onto the page and call it *Betty* or *Lucille*. The spirit of Juliet refuses any name but her own.

Stone Orchard
May 1976
Journal

I have been making notes in preparation — while the thing gels in me. Reading Uncle Tif's letters — looking at photographs — steeping myself (but lightly) in the times. By "lightly" I mean cautiously — lest I get over-burdened with detail and lose touch with imagination. Light browsing and grazing — like a deer eating: slowly, he is filled and can rest. Reading the chapter notes already made — there is a sense of real excitement — that I've caught something this time that is communicable . . . things I don't know yet are *names* — and I am going to wait until these are answered in the usual way. Applied names never work for me. Characters have their own names and will tell you, if you wait. . . .

Stone Orchard
August 1976
Notebook

Wars: Chapter One.
    Begin with his being awakened by the valet. Tea by the bed. Sound of water being

drawn for a bath. Lies in the bed letting himself awaken slowly — half-dream — half-life. Clothes on the chair. Rising. Being bathed by the valet. *Wanting* the valet there — *needing* someone to see him — see his beauty and see his vulnerability. Someone to touch him (one last time).

Include memories of the previous night. Dancing — food — the girl — the drive — the park. Animals at dawn.

Home on leave — wounded hand — no sense of touch in fingertips.

Begin:

He had only slept two hours when the man came in to wake him. . . .

Stone Orchard
October 1976
Journal

Stanley [Colbert] was here this afternoon. He came for lunch and stayed till four. I was, admittedly, absolutely terrified. All I could think was: do not ask me to burn this book . . . . This stems, of course, from that other winter day in Westwood Village, L.A., when Stan, who was then my agent, had said: *well, Tiff, what are we going to do about this?* . . .

I was living with them, then — with Stan and Nancy — and they had that crazy, wondrous, joyful, disastrous and immensely creative household of crippled, recovering actors and writers — of whom I was one — and we all drove Stan and Nancy mad as we rode our way back towards stability and usefulness. There was Jim, who was writing the television series based on *Pete Kelly's Blues* and who played the blues from dawn to dawn — there was Vanessa, whose marriage and career were being driven with a kind of manic fury onto the rocks — there was Jan, the Colbert's daughter, who had just been born and was trying to decipher what it meant to be alive — and there was me.

I had been writing a novel — living in Santa Monica with three inverted artists (one of whom painted in the nude) and I had been making my living working as a model in the life class at U.C.L.A.

My food had consisted of dried Lipton's soup, from which — if you used a strainer to contain the solids in the mix — you could get about three tasteless meals of coloured water. I also collected ripe avocados from the front yards of other houses on the street, and revelled in the sense of utter nourishment they gave. My other food was cigarettes and bottles of Thunderbird wine, which you could buy for seventy-five cents apiece.

Every Friday, the inverted artists would take me out for *filet mignon,* baked potato and multiple Gibsons at a steak house along the Pacific Highway heading north to Malibu. Afterwards, every Friday, one of them would bed me — not as payment, but as experiment. If all three had sex, taking turns on consecutive Fridays, with the same "body" — it was supposed to give them insight into one another's work. It made them, I guess, a kind of "school" and I — or rather, my body — was the touchstone through which they found their common voice. Madness and glory!

Meanwhile — labouring down in my pure white room with the pure white Japanese papers pasted to the window-panes and the pure white Japanese lanterns shading all the lamps — I was creating my masterpiece. . . .

When Stanley "rescued" me from this, his only concern was for what he had discerned through other, already finished writing — a talent worth paying attention to — if only he could persuade the person in charge of the talent to pay attention, too.

This was in the autumn of 1957. I had been in California then, about five months. My novel told the story of three inverted artists who. . . .

I had written it not only under the influence of what was passing, then, as my life — but also under what I believed to be the influence of *Ulysses,* by James Joyce. I had read this book in a single sitting (it took me just over twenty-four hours) and I guess, for whatever reason, I had decided I was destined to be the second coming . . . Ulysses II.

Well, Tiff, Stanley said, as we faced the collected pages of my work, *what are we going to do about this?*

I knew it could never be finished. There was nothing there to proceed with. Not that it was necessarily garbage — but its pretensions would have embarrassed even Edgar A. Guest.

There really isn't any point going into why we did what we did. The conversation did not, in fact, last all that long — and it mostly had to do with making up my mind that I was going to turn my back — not on the writing, but on its *perpetrator.*

Stan said: "you see, these pages here are not creative — not a legitimate exploration of style — not a declaration of purpose — and not the transcription of any true voice. These pages . . ." he poked them with his finger — ". . . are a crime. And you are the perpetrator of that crime. You have wasted what is good in you and best in your talent on a play for meaningless notoriety, Findley. And, though I can't tell you what to do about this — I am going to ask you whether or not you want to strive for meaningless notoriety — *or do you want to be a writer?*

I can hear him still — and see him, as he said that.

"I want to be a writer," I said.

"Okay, then — what do we do about this?"

I looked at the manuscript. Sixty — a hundred pages. White on white — or so it now seemed.

"Burn it," I said.

"Okay," he said. "We'll burn it."

Then he said: "do you want to do it alone — or do you want me to be there with you?"

It was like a death. Not a murder — not by a long shot. But a death, nonetheless. It was like people who split because a love affair is over. The death is not whole. It is just a part of you.

"You, too," I said. I guess I was afraid I wouldn't burn it all.

So, we burned it together.

Margaret Laurence burned a manuscript once, in her backyard incinerator.

No one else should burn a writer's book.

The only books you can burn are your own. And you have to know why. It is really not so that no one else can read them. It is so they will be gone from who you are. I mean, who you are as a writer.

So, when Stanley arrived this morning and we had our lunch, I was thinking all of the above and already feeling protective of what I have so far written of *The Wars*. I guess that one of the things that made me nervous most was the fact that what I have here now is just about fifty pages — fifty pages vulnerable as the other, 1957 pages had been.

Stan sat alone in the living-room and read. I should have lighted him a fire — because it was cold — but I wasn't able even to strike a match in the presence of my pages.

He read and read.

I sat in the kitchen and stared out the window. Mottle sat with me. I wished that WFW were not in Ottawa — I wished devoutly that I had never given up acting.

Stan, at last, appeared in the doorway.

"Okay," he said. "This is possible. We can fix it."

This is possible. We can fix it.

Stanley doesn't pussy-foot.

We sat and drank tea. He spread the pages on the table.

"What we have here is a book you are calling *The Wars*," he said. "So far, I have read about Robert Ross and Rowena Ross and Mrs Ross, their mother. I have read about Rosedale, Toronto and South Drive. I have read about the factory downtown. I have read about Mrs Ross's companion who is a woman called Davenport. . . ."

Stan sighed.

I waited.

"This is a book about the wars," he said. "And I have read, now, about fifty pages. . . ." He pointed at them. "Where are the wars you have promised me?" he said.

"Promised you?"

"*Me — the reader.* Where is what you promised me? Where are the wars, here, Tiff?"

He was smiling.

I didn't answer because I couldn't.

"Okay," he said. "Here's what I'm saying. . . ." He settled back. "You have promised to tell me the story of *Goldilocks and the Three Bears.* . . . I am your trusting child — and you have *promised* me. . . . Do you see?"

He patted the air with the palm of his hand extended over my collected pages. "Goldilocks — Goldilocks - Goldilocks — Goldilocks."

He paused.

"You promised me bears, Tiff. . . ."

He hit the table with his hand.

"BRING ON THE BEARS!"

Tonight, I printed a sign and pinned it to the shelf above

the typewriter: *Bring On The Bears,* it tells me.

Now, I can breathe again.

The fires have been avoided.

I am writing, already, about the wars.

Stone Orchard
November 1976
Journal

Did people really do this? Survive this? I mean the freezing rain, the wind and the mud. I went down yesterday to the foot of the lane where the fence gives way to the lower fields. There was a good deal of puddling there and everywhere the cattle have walked, they have churned up the earth, creating a kind of stew made of stones and clods of weed and mud. In the lane, I had already lost a boot and fallen on my knees so that now my trousers were soaked and one of my socks was sodden and the bottoms of both my sleeves were freezing against my wrists.

This is the mud experienced by Uncle Tif [*Thomas Irving Findley — my godfather, for whom I was named Timothy Irving Frederick Findley*]. This is the mud that he and all those men in that Flanders campaign had to live in every hour of every day for weeks and months on end.

My determination was that I would go down the lane and stay there twenty-four hours. I would do all the things that they had had to do and I would do them — as best as I could — in weather and conditions matching theirs. This, of course, was impossible. No one was firing at me — I was not being shelled. The mud was only ankle deep and, at its worst, it rose to halfway up my shin — which is to say — I sank down halfway up to my knees.

I stayed there long enough to do the following — all of it in the freezing rain and wind — and I used, I must admit, the shelter of the tree-line — though not the abso-

148

lute shelter of the grove of apple trees:
- — shaved in cold water
- — I tried (and failed) to light a fire for boiling water
- — I ate cold beans from a tin
- — I emptied my bowels, using newsprint for my toilet paper. Oddly enough, taking a crap was not as bad as peeing. Crouching, at least one part of your body covers another. Also — crouching, you manufacture body heat. But peeing, I could hardly undo my zipper, my fingers were so cold. You cannot perform this act in gloves. My penis had retracted deep inside my underwear and, with gloves, I couldn't find it! Peeing — in itself — was agony. All your muscles are telling you not to let in the cold and are pulling against you. . . .

I lay down on the tarp I'd brought as a groundsheet — and tried to sleep in my sleeping bag. This was utterly impossible.

There is nothing for the mind to do but feed on present circumstances. You cannot speak — you cannot sing — you cannot "shiver out loud" (these were rules I had set, in the pretense that somewhere there was an enemy) — you cannot pretend it isn't raining — you cannot pretend you are not wet — you cannot walk away from where you are — and all you have to look forward to is the allotted "pleasure" of turning in a new direction, drinking another cup of tea from your thermos — which has much too quickly been depleted — and the impending defeat of your spirit.

I don't know when it was that I decided I could not stay down all night. But sanity at some point said: *you don't have to die for this.* . . .

So I knew I would come back here to the house before my allotted time and this was my defeat.

Worst of all:
- — shaving in cold water is virtually agony

— peeing is a mix of comedy and pain

— having to discipline your natural fury that *nothing* functions

— *being alone* — which I suspect I would have been, even if two hundred other men had stood beside me. This aloneness is unique. I guess it is because you know that being "saved" has nothing to do with other people — but only to do with chance. . . .

— being out of doors in a freezing, driving rain, when you cannot hide from it, reminds you very quickly how vulnerable your face is. . . .

— it is light — but you cannot see.

Stone Orchard
July 1977
Journal

We are now locked in to the printer's schedule and all the final decisions must be made in the next two days. People have been asking me to cut the rape scene and I can't.

They don't want it cut because they are squeamish. At least, I trust that isn't why they're concerned. They're concerned, I assume, because they think it will get the book in trouble.

So many books have been banned by school boards and libraries; I think that, in the so-called Western world, we have one of the top five records for this. Margaret [Laurence] has had such troubles only recently — and Alice [Munro] the same. So I think that Pearce [John Pearce, the editor) and Ellen [Powers, the typist] are thinking about that. Ellen said the scene *had rung a warning bell* — and Pearce has attempted a diplomatic, roundabout route, whereby I will come to the decision to cut the scene myself. I respect their concern — and I certainly respect the fact that nobody has overtly attempted to twist my arm. It is just a campaign of quiet but urgent persuasion.

Margaret [Laurence] phoned just yesterday and said: "it would be tragic if something went wrong because you're being pig-headed. . . ." She was smiling — laughing — when she said it, but she meant it. "Tell me why it has to be there," she said.

"It has to be there because it is my belief that Robert Ross and his generation of young men were raped, in effect, by the people who made that war. Basically, their fathers did it to them."

Margaret said: "yes, I agree with you. But surely that's implicit in the book already. You don't have to *say* so."

This is what someone else had said. *It's there already*.

But I cannot remove it. As a scene, it is intrinsic — deeply meshed in the fabric of the book as I first conceived it. I cannot cut away its arms and legs — no matter how convinced other people are that the book will stand and function without them.

In the Wilfred Owen poem that Britten uses in the *War Requiem,* the tenor and the baritone sing together — Abraham and Isaac . . .

Lay not thy hand upon the lad,
Neither do anything to him, the Angel of God commands.
But the old man would not so — and slew his son. . . .
And half the seed of Europe, one by one . . . .

And slew his son and half the seed of Europe, one by one.

It *was* rape.

The scene stays.

Cannington
January 1988

In 1980, Beth Appledoorn of the Longhouse Bookstore in Toronto was asked to select the "Ten Most Popular Canadian Novels" for the soon-to-be published *Canadian Book of Lists*. As co-founder and co-owner (with Susan Sandler) of one of the country's busiest book emporiums, Ms Appledoorn — due to her heavy workload — was understandably late in submitting her list. Consequently, some days after her deadline had come and gone, she received a panic call from the publisher asking her to dictate her selections over the telephone. This, Ms Appledoorn proceeded to do — out of breath from having just run up the stairs — and using her characteristic Dutch accent. The combination of her breathlessness and her linguistic style more than likely accounts for the fact that, when the first edition of the *Canadian Book Of Lists* was published, it contained among the "Ten Most Popular Canadian Novels," one that had not yet been written: *Divorce*, by Timothy Findley — a writer better known, perhaps, as the author of *The Wars*.

· 7 ·

ALICE DROPS HER CIGARETTE ON THE FLOOR

Stone Orchard
July 1989
Journal

On being a writer: there are so many fascinating things the human race doesn't want to know about itself — and what it *does* want to know bores the shit out of me.

Life isn't hell — hell is.

Stone Orchard
November 1965
Journal

I begin to think that some writing is like talking to yourself. That is why, so often, I fail to get my points across. Like Jo [Diblee] said about my piano playing: "it doesn't matter, dear. I know *you* hear the rest of it in your mind." Perhaps that is what a first draft is: the unaccompanied piano — and the other drafts are the orchestration. Ultimately, it is all one concerto — but the *reader* plays the solo part — which, in the beginning, the writer played.

Stone Orchard
August 1975
Journal

Remember Wilder's dictum: in a play, the characters don't know what's going to happen next. Remember, too, that in one respect, the difference between a play and a novel is boldness of presentation. Plays happen. Novels unfold. In a play, there is no place — no room — no time for explanation. The *doing* must explain.

Stone Orchard
August 1970
Radio

Last year, I spent two months in the wilderness of the Northwest Territories. And there was a journey down a great wide river, with dark forests crowding either side. Sometimes, these forests fell back to make way for the entrance of some other river which came pushing and panic-stricken out of the dark — tumbling helter-skelter over rocks and fallen trees, as if pursued by beasts and spirits — as if terrified by the darkness itself. And I was caught by this sensation of terror and by the enormous loneliness that made this terror possible. And I thought — if the rivers are afraid — what should I be?

And when I came home and it was all behind me — something had formed in me: a feeling about what a man might become in that context if he took the wrong turning and got lost. What becomes of his mind at the mercy of such absolute forces? Would he go mad?

And I became intrigued with the idea of a man to whom this might happen and I thought — there's a novel in this — perfect — perhaps a short, incisive horror-story about the spirit of man broken by the spirit of nature — a sick, ambitious man perhaps, and a wilderness unwilling to give up its sovereignty after his intrusion.

A week or so later, I became ill and had to go to bed. This gave me a chance to catch up on my reading. And one of the books that came to hand was *Heart of Darkness* by Joseph Conrad.

Heart of Darkness is the story of a sick, ambitious man and of a wilderness that breaks him. There it was — and there it is: Joseph Conrad's masterpiece. So I put away even the thought that I might write my story — not out of any sense of self-denigration or anger that the subject had been dealt with. After all, there isn't a subject in the world that someone hasn't put in a book. No — I set it aside because whatever I wanted to say had been so *perfectly* said.

There was nothing left to add — except my appreciation of what Joseph Conrad had done. And I thought that what I should do is publish a one-page book, between neat blue covers. And on that single page it would say: "In lieu of writing his own book, the would-be author respectfully draws your attention to *Heart of Darkness* by Joseph Conrad. In it, all that the would-be author would say — is said. The End."

Stone Orchard
January 1988

In 1973, WFW and I were hired to adapt Pierre Berton's railroad classics *The National Dream* and *The Last Spike* for television. WFW was to write the documentary segments while I would attempt the dramatized segments. The combination was apparently propitious — the series was a grand success and WFW and I went on to win an ACTRA Award for our adaptation. Not that problems didn't occur along the way. On one occasion the writing process was stopped dead in its tracks; Berton and I were at loggerheads.

It was a well-established fact that Berton's books had been meticulously researched. Consequently, Pierre was conscientious to a fault when it came to the dramatic interpretation of people and events. Unless it had historical documentation to back it up, nothing could be introduced in the television series merely for the sake of "dramatic effect." As dramatist, I'm afraid I was not so scrupulous. Needing a piece of comic business for a scene involving Sir John A. Macdonald and his wife, Agnes, I invented a pair of white kid gloves which Sir John refuses to wear on a formal occasion. Lady Macdonald insists the gloves be worn. Sir John is adamant and manages, several times, to "lose" them: in his pockets, in a desk drawer, behind the drapes, etc. Every time the PM thinks he has succeeded in ridding himself of "the damned wee things," his wife uncovers them.

All this was intended only as business with which the actors could occupy themselves during an extended scene of expository dialogue. It was not intended to stop production. Pierre, however, saw the whole episode of the gloves as an attack on history — and he refused to allow the scene to be shot as written. I received a note to the following effect:

> Nothing in all my research informs me that Sir
> John A. Macdonald had an aversion to white kid
> gloves. Please remove all references to same.
>
> P. Berton

I was flabbergasted and made the mistake at first of thinking Pierre was kidding — no pun intended. WFW assured me he was serious. But I wanted — I needed — those gloves. Without them, the scene would die. Consequently, I made an appointment to visit historian Donald Creighton, who had written the definitive biography of Macdonald.

The upshot of our meeting was fairly straightforward — but also wonderful. A precedent was established for

Sir John's presumed "aversion to white kid gloves" and I returned to Berton, triumphant.

In the meantime, however, Pierre had outfoxed me. He greeted me with the news that he was withdrawing his objection after a talk with William Hutt, the actor who was playing Sir John. Hutt had managed to convince him the gloves were both useful and historically inconsequential.

This somewhat took the wind from my sails. I would now not have the opportunity to confront Pierre with the ingenious "precedent" concocted by Donald Creighton: a photograph of Sir John A. Macdonald, showing him impeccable in formal evening dress — and not a white kid glove in sight. *If that,* the famous historian had told me, *is not the very picture of a man with an aversion to white kid gloves — then I ask you, what is?"*

Stone Orchard
May 1985
Speech

In a television series based on Stephen Leacock's *Sunshine Sketches of a Little Town,* I played the role of Peter Pupkin. This was back in the 1950s — and I thought I might say a few words about that — about what it's like to be inside a Leacock character. Also what it's like to have a Leacockian character inside of you — because it works both ways.

This is true of all good characters, of course. The universal aspects have to be found inside the actor: the touchstones by which he recognizes and understands the person he's going to play. The other part — the pulling on — the getting inside of the character can only happen once you've made the basic connections between the character and what you know of yourself.

I guess what I understood first about Peter Pupkin was the quality of his shyness. It was a seething kind of shyness that was kindred to my own: an actor's shyness. He could play all kinds of wonders to the audience in his mind — or the audience out in the dark, where he didn't have to see them — but he was absolutely mortified when made to confront real people. He blushed — he stammered — did everything wrong. He'd confess to things he hadn't done, because it was too embarrassing to admit he hadn't done them.

He was also a *klutz*. It was typical of Peter that, when he went out to save the people on the stranded pleasure steamer, *The Mariposa Belle,* he found himself in the middle of the lake — with a single oar — in the dark — in a sinking rowboat. This was very *me*. I understood Peter Pupkin at once.

Peter's greatest embarrassment was his father's enormous wealth. This was not, it so happened, a problem of my own — but it was still a problem that was fun to play. The images Leacock provides of Peter's terror that his father will arrive unannounced in Mariposa — chauffeur driven in a mammoth touring car — trailing truckloads of servants and tossing huge sums of money into the streets — are wonderfully evoked. *Money, money, money* — all it does is get in the way! It gets in the way of your natural sense of decorum. It makes you seem brash and vulgar, as if you could buy your way through life. It also gets in the way of tragic and romantic love affairs. It was this latter aspect of his father's money that troubled Peter the most, since Peter was overwhelmingly in love — both tragically and romantically — with Zena Pepperleigh. If Zena were to discover that Peter had wealth in his background, how could he possibly ask her to marry him? . . . She would only think that he wanted her because of his money.

With a stroke of genius, Leacock gives Peter Pupkin a job as a bank clerk. He forces him into a situation where he is surrounded by money day and night, because Peter not only works in the Exchange Bank — he lives there. Or, rather, he lives in rooms upstairs — above the bank. Now, the thing is, all that money surrounding Peter Pupkin is not his own. It is money he can regard objectively: money he must protect — and, therefore, money he can regard with greed and parsimony in behalf of others. In this way, he has control — so to speak — of the kind he cannot exert in his father's case — the control over everyone's natural inclination to take their money out of the bank and throw it around the streets as so much largesse. Peter worries about the human race: he hates to see it embarrass itself. But, above all, he hates to see it embarrass him.

Sunshine Sketches of a Little Town isn't noted for its dialogue. The book is narrated by a character — presumably Leacock himself — who knows all and tells all — but who takes no part in the lives and events he describes. In the television series — written, incidentally, by Don Harron — the Narrator's role was played by the late John Drainie. What a pity a film was never made with Drainie playing Leacock and the town of Mariposa spread out around him. He was — and this is not hyperbole, but simple fact — a genius: and by everyone's accounting who ever worked with John Drainie, or who saw him work, he was the finest actor of his time in this country. His voice is inextricably mingled with my memories of playing Pupkin. Which brings me back to what I had started to say about Leacock and dialogue.

Leacock didn't write much dialogue — and the dialogue he did write was largely unspeakable. His *prose* was speakable but not the dialogue as such. From an actor's point of view, the dialogue Leacock wrote was inextricably tied to the prose that surrounded it — and the syntax could often be awkward if you tried to lift the words in quotes from the midst of the words that weren't to be heard. Of course, so far as Leacock himself was concerned, he had never intended the dialogue for actors.

In the long run, this couldn't have mattered less. It couldn't have mattered less, because what he gave you — as an actor — was an absolutely clear-cut, fully rounded and marvellous character to play. Though the words themselves were rarely provided, the manner in which the characters would speak — including the pitch and tones of their voices and the rhythms of their speech — was always perfectly clear. Speech, in theatrical terms, cannot exist without character. For an actor, to know the *person* is to know precisely how the person speaks.

Given Peter's character — with all the nuance laid out by Leacock on the page — it was easy enough to discern that his speech was most likely *breathless.* Consequently, Harron wrote Peter's dialogue in short, very often unconnected sentences. In between the sentences, it was obvious that Peter himself was under the impression he had voiced the missing connective tissue — and he was under this impression because the connective tissue *was* being voiced in his mind. Thus, under Don Harron's hand, Peter's stammered, staccato sentences were filled with *non sequiturs.*

Peter might say to his best friend and room-mate, Mallory Tompkins: "Mal. I love her. My father. I'm going to kill myself."

As you can imagine, the unspoken parts of these sentences were of some importance to Mallory Tompkins.

However, as Mallory came to know and understand Peter's ways, he also came to know what the missing words might be. "Her" must be Zena Pepperleigh. "My father" must refer to Peter's terror that his father would appear and throw his money between them. Therefore — Peter would "kill himself" of shame.

Peter was always "killing himself" and Mal got used to it, more or less — although as Leacock wrote of this situation: *I suppose there are few people, outside of lovers, who know what it is to commit suicide four times in five weeks.*

This was another reason Peter was always short of breath. Even when you are young, all that climbing onto roofs and steeples — all those wintry hours upon the bridge, poised above the icy waters — all those automobiles in front of which one is constantly preparing to fling oneself, can really take it out of you.

Leacock was a master at creating scenes: the stuff of scenes and the shape of scenes seemed, very much, to be the basis of how he worked his wonders. How he avoided becoming a playwright, I cannot tell — unless it was that he knew for a certainty the dialogue would elude him. Nonetheless, it hardly matters. The marvels of his comedy are there to be transcribed theatrically, whether the theatre be a stage — a television screen — or merely in the mind. His theatre is on the page and anyone can give it life.

Stone Orchard
September 1987
Speech

First, a few words about what I am going to read here tonight. I was delighted when asked to take part in this event — the launching of *The Canlit Foodbook* in aid of P.E.N. International. But what could I read that would speak both of food — and of censorship? Then I hit upon the perfect answer: namely, the recently censored *Tale of Peter Rabbit*.

The Tale of Peter Rabbit is based upon on a desire for garden vegetables that verges on the manic. It tells the story of an individual who is willing to give up his life for a carrot stick.

The Tale of Peter Rabbit is also a cautionary tale — and therefore most appropriate for this evening's gathering — especially in terms of what it has to say about violence.

All that being said, I must also tell you that, in my opinion, *The Tale of Peter Rabbit* is one of the greatest novels ever written. Its hero and his adventures are set before us with dash and style — in prose that gives weight without being weighty — lightness without being trivial — and pointedness without resorting to propaganda. . . .

Peter Rabbit comes, as we know, from the pen and paintbrush of Beatrix Potter. When the book was published first — it had such great success that Ms Potter expanded the story of Peter and his family until she had finally achieved what we now acknowledge as her masterpiece: *The Cottontail Saga.* . . .

In all these books — of which there are four in number — Beatrix Potter tells us what it is like to be a rabbit — not only in the general sense, but also in the particular. Her characters — the introspective Peter, his resourceful sister Flopsy and his daredevil cousin Benjamin — live out their lives before the reader's eyes in a series of breathtaking adventures and romantic interludes that keep the reader turning pages faster than you can say *Jack Rabbit!*

The deeper questions, such as *the truth about the death of Peter Rabbit's father* and *Josephine Rabbit's pernicious addiction to camomile tea and its effect on Peter Rabbit's psyche* have kept the critics busy for years. We all know this.

But now we are being told *The Cottontail Saga* has come under fire from the City of London Council on Education. (I refer to London, England.) Words and sentences thought to be "unsuitable for children" are to be expunged from the *Saga*. Words such as *soporific,* which occurs in Volume III, *The Tale of the Flopsy Bunnies.* And sentences such as: *don't go into Mister McGregor's garden; your father had an accident there; he was put in pie by Mrs McGregor.*

Of course the word *soporific* is notoriously connected with the drug culture. It describes the state of dreamy lassitude experienced by humans addicted to morphine and heroin — and by rabbits addicted to lettuce. (I am merely repeating the reasons given for the need to excise this word. . . .)

In the case of Peter Rabbit's father and the pie — clearly, several prejudices are being affirmed in the given example. For instance, that *gardens, as such, are dangerous.* The link here with Eden is obvious. *Don't go back there! It means certain death.* There is also the prejudice against Mister Rabbit's careless habits, which placed him in fatal jeopardy. And, finally, the anti-feminist prejudice — so evident in the reference to Mrs McGregor baking persons in pies. Clearly, Mrs McGregor — so this prejudice would have us believe — is no better than Medea!

Not a fit example for children.

And so, it is with much sadness that I stand before you tonight; much sadness and a little pride. Sadness, because this masterpiece is to be mutilated — but pride because, after all, this may well be the last time anyone, anywhere, will stand before an audience in a public forum to read aloud the *unexpurgated* version of *The Tale of Peter Rabbit.* . . .

Stone Orchard
June 1979
Journal

In the mid-1970s when both of us had work in Ottawa, WFW and I bought a postage-stamp of land on the shores of Lac

Bernard in Quebec. We built a platform and set up our tent on the side of a wooded hill overlooking the water. It was idyllic.

Every summer weekend we would drive up twenty miles or so, past Wakefield on the Gatineau and turn off the highway onto the Joyces' road. I miss it, now, already.

Joyces' road was a right-of-way that had long ago been procured from the Joyce brothers by a number of cottage owners who, otherwise, would have had to park their cars and walk in over a mile to the lake. When we were there, the brothers were already greatly old and they would sit on their farmhouse porch and wave at us as we passed.

Lying awake of an early morning, savouring the smell of trees and the bright orange canvas of our tent, WFW and I would listen to the loons who came out hunting in the pre-dawn light and who called and called to one another round the lake. It is a sound, once heard, that never leaves your memory.

Rain or shine, this early-morning chorus would happen every day. The circle of calls would proliferate until there was great crescendo — every loon singing in its turn — a silver chain of song. I have only heard its counterpart once, in the Northwest Territories.

One morning, just as the song was building to its climax — ten or a dozen loons taking part — a child's voice called out over the water from one of the cottages.

"Ah — shad-dup!" the child cried. "Shad-dup! Shad-dup!"

Instantly, the voices fell silent.

The child had won.

Lying there, both of us bemused and disappointed by what had happened, WFW said: *sort of reminds you of the critics, doesn't it. . . .*

Yes.

The critics in this country are rarely satisfied with

telling playwrights and actors merely that their work is unacceptable. They also tell them to *shut up — go away — and leave me in peace.*

On the other hand, playwrights, actors and loons have too much respect for singing to give up the song. The very next morning, the singing was doubled in its intensity. Maybe we should take all critics and expose them to the sounds at Lac Bernard. I wonder what they would say. . . .

Stone Orchard

October 1981

Article

Having been asked by Canadian Literature *to produce a piece about my own work, I found it quite impossible to do until the following format emerged:* The hardest thing of all to write about is yourself.

For one thing — if you're a fiction writer — most of you is already out there, somewhere; chopped up in little bits and hidden (or not hidden) in your books. Fragments. Not that you've put yourself there consciously. But your energy is there. Something of your own character — something of your own make-up goes into the character and make-up of everyone you write. And the rest of you is private. Mostly. So obliquely private that it's very hard to get at. Especially if you yourself are the questioner.

The thing is, everything you ask yourself — or very nearly everything — already has an answer that doesn't interest you. It would interest you about someone else — but not about yourself. "When were you born?" "1930." "Where?" "Toronto. What a stupid question . . . I mean, you already know all this." "Are you happy?" "Don't be silly. If I was happy, would I be sitting here worried to death about how to write this article? It's already two weeks overdue and you're asking me when I was born. What a twit you are."

In the end, you lose your respect: not only for yourself as a character worthy of interest but as an interviewer. And who needs that? No one. However, when I put the problem to WFW, his answer was both succinct and a godsend. "You don't know how to ask yourself the right questions," he said. "Let me do it for you."

"You mean the way Gertrude Stein wrote the *Autobiography of Alice B. Toklas?*"

"No," he said. "I mean the way you write all your books. I will be you — and ask the questions. You will be a character — and try to give the answers."

And thus — what follows.

The interview took place in a sunny room on a cold, bright autumn afternoon. The interviewer was William Whitehead — a documentary writer for television. The person being interviewed was Timothy Findley — a fiction writer and playwright. The interviewer had a touch of the flu — so the questions were interspersed with coughs and wheezes. Out in the larger world beyond the garden, the President of Egypt had just been shot by a would-be assassin. In another part of that world, the fiction writer was about to publish the fourth of his novels, *Famous Last Words*. As a consequence of both these events, there was an undercurrent of tension in the room — a sense of wonder that horror and suspense could be walking hand-in-hand through such a domestic landscape.

w.w.   Somewhere up in a cupboard, locked away, we have a number of your paintings. This is something you've dabbled with from time to time: something you seem to be drawn to. How is it, then, you've never tried to be a professional painter?

<u>T.F.</u>   Because I'm not accomplished enough to do with painting what I would like to do with painting. And I haven't the facility — even with a great deal of study — to do that.

<u>W.W.</u>   What is it you would like to do with painting?

<u>T.F.</u>   Something enormous. I have visions of huge canvases — not murals — but Stanley Spencer's type of stuff — where there are masses of people in the picture. And they're very colourful. They would be stylized. They would be recordings of events. Or of moments. The visions of my mind are very graphic in that sense. And, when I sit down to paint, I inevitably paint something that is in my mind, rather than something beyond the window. I'm not inclined to sit down and paint whatever happens to be in front of me. Maybe because what's in front of me already satisfies my curiosity; you know — satisfies my sense of wonder in itself. The only time I might paint something right in front of me would be when I wanted to catch a person in a particular *attitude.* I've tried to paint my mother — I've tried to paint my brother — I've tried to paint you. Lots of people. And each of these paintings shows the person in repose of some kind: occupied with something private. And, in each of the paintings, it was not the person's face that attracted my attention — but the attitude of the person who was sitting there. However, I'm really not accomplished in this area. Perhaps I have a talent to see — but I haven't the talent to translate what I see into something on canvas. Or whatever.

<u>W.W.</u>   Would you say it was "character" — your interest in character — that drew you to the theatre as an actor?

169

<u>T.F.</u>   Yes. Interest in *attitude*. And by that I mean the physical attitude as much as the intellectual attitude. That's why I got to the theatre through dance: through the gesture: through the way people present themselves. The thing that always moves me most — whether you see a person alone or people in huge groups — is the concentration of emotion: or lack of it. The *attitude*. And, in the theatre, that has as much to do with what you see as with what you hear. I guess that's why I like Chekhov: because of the famous *pauses* — which he provides so that people can fill out or complete what he has begun with words.

<u>W.W.</u>   Is this why you find it so hard to resist the creation of stage directions when you write a play? Because you see so vividly?

<u>T.F.</u>   Yes. Even though I know it's dangerous to write too many stage directions: because they can be very limiting so far as the director and the actors are concerned. The first thing Robin Phillips does, for instance, is remove every single stage direction. Nonetheless, I provide them. Because I am always seeing what the people are doing, when I write: as well as hearing what they're saying. I see and hear in tandem. Whereas, a lot of playwrights — and a lot of novelists, too — really only seem to hear their people. The answer, of course, with plays is to put it down for yourself — you know — put down all the stage directions as you write and then excise them from the final draft. Which leaves the movement inherent in the body of the dialogue. This way, the actors will be impelled to move, without knowing why. And, also, be impelled to the moments of stillness. But, in novels, when I'm reading — I find so often the curious sense that what is seen has been written after what has been heard, and sort of "tacked on" or pasted into the fabric of the book.

170

As if the writer couldn't see and hear at the same time.

<u>W.W.</u>   But how do you sort it out? I mean — if it's simultaneous. Come on, Tiff. You can only put one set of words on paper at a time. . . .

<u>T.F.</u>   Well. All right. Look at it this way. In a sense, the writer is a *voyeur;* while, in another sense, he's eavesdropping. He is watching with fascination and — equally — listening or overhearing with fascination. Yes? Now — imagine a scene with a number of people in it and there you are watching it unfold. Watching and listening. And your eyes are sweeping over the whole roomful of people. . . . Yes? You keep track of everyone who is in the scene. Let's say the scene is set at a table and the people are eating a meal. And — you know what it's like when you're at a dinner party and everyone leans out towards the person who is leading the conversation when suddenly . . . *(snap!)* . . . someone at the other end of the table will do something that draws your attention to them. Maybe all they've done is take a sip of wine: but you catch it and you see it from the corner of your eye and the sipping of the wine is there as part of the conversation. So this is what writing is like — for me. Your eye and your ear are always poised upon the moment. So that whenever there is speech, you hear it and whenever there is gesture, you see it: no matter where it occurs in the room: no matter who it comes from — even if it comes from the mice in the wall or the spider up in the corner over the plate rail. . . .

<u>W.W.</u>   Now there's a plate rail. Where did the plate rail come from?

<u>T.F.</u>   Well — it's in the scene. But how weird! You seize

upon the plate rail when I thought — because you're an entomologist — you'd seize upon the spider.

W.W.   What — and throw it out the window?

T.F.   No. And talk about it — the way you did in your thesis.

W.W.   Oh, I gave all that up years ago.

T.F.   Now — you see? We all know a little more about you.

W.W.   What about this scene we were in?

T.F.   What scene?

W.W.   Weren't we at a dinner party?

T.F.   Well. We were — but it's over, now. What were we talking about? Plate rails?

W.W.   You — as a writer — being able to see and hear at the same time. Be specific.

T.F.   Okay. Specifically — when I'm writing a scene in which there is more than one person — however many more there may be — I will find myself . . . let us say when George and Brenda are having a terrible argument . . . I find myself sitting there watching them: listening to them — trying not to interrupt them — fascinated . . . when, all at once, Alice drops her cigarette on the floor. But the focus of the scene — the point of the scene — is the argument between George and Brenda. Now — I don't know how it is that I witnessed Alice dropping her

cigarette on the floor. And I don't know *why* I did. I only
know I saw when she let it go — so I make a record of it:
ALICE DROPS HER CIGARETTE ON THE FLOOR. Does it matter? Is it an important gesture? Does it tell us anything?
Was it a comment on the fact that George was right in the
middle of telling Brenda about that thing he's found in
the drawer upstairs? . . . I don't know. All I know is — the
gesture was there and I saw it and I put it down on the
paper. But only time and more writing: only the continua-
tion of the writing process is going to tell me whether
Alice dropping her cigarette is meaningful. I mean — you
know — it could turn out *(laughter)* that Alice doesn't
even smoke, for God's sake. So what's she doing with this
cigarette in the first place?

W.W.   Could I ask you something?

T.F.   Fire away.

W.W.   Who the hell are George and Brenda and Alice?

T.F.   I don't know.

W.W.   *(Laughter)*

T.F.   Well, I don't. They just arrived. I don't even know
their last names. George, Brenda, Alice — this is Bill
Whitehead.

W.W.   How come you assume they don't need an introduction to you?

T.F.   Yes. A very good question. *(Silence)* Uhmmm. . . .
The only answer that occurs to me is that — they were in
my mind. Sort of like house guests. So, I assume we know

each other. Unless, of course, they're burglars. People very often are, you know — and you have to kick them out.

W.W.   Have they gone yet?

T.F.   Yes.

W.W.   May I continue?

T.F.   Yes.

W.W.   You don't want to mislead people, you know, about the process of eavesdropping. You make it all sound as if it's terribly easy. As if the process of writing fiction were nothing more than taking dictation, whereas . . .

T.F.   It's not.

W.W.   I mean: how do you explain — in terms of "eaves-dropping" and voyeurism — having to re-write scenes — having to discard chapters — having to create whole new passages? A minute ago you were talking as if all you had to do was "take notes" — and as if the characters were in control of everything. But don't you have to exert some control over *them?*

T.F.   Oh, indeed.

W.W.   Well — give me a sense of this: as effort. Because I know how hard you work — and I know how much you re-write — and I know how dissatisfied you always seem to be with what you do. So how do you account for this, in the face of the other: of the characters being in control?

<u>T.F.</u> Well — the effort: the effort on the writer's part is to fulfil the character: to fulfil the story. You know — to do it justice and to get it all right. For instance, the writing of the play *Can You See Me Yet?*, I wrote it all first as a straightforward play about a family: the family of Cassandra Wakelin. And the play all took place in the garden of the Wakelin home. And the family were all there — and the people came and went and the story unfolded and, to some degree, that play succeeded. On the other hand — in the mode of the conversation we're having — the character inside my head, to whom I had been listening — the character of Cassandra Wakelin — was unhappy with the way I'd handled her story. It was as if I had not provided the means by which she could tell it all. I had not resolved her situation. So I thought and thought and thought — and I tried this and that and the other — and, finally, I hit on the idea that Cassandra's story somehow needed to unfold *backwards*. Well . . . in the original version, Cass ends up in an insane asylum: driven there by her perception of the real world being a madhouse . . . But — what if I were to *begin* the play in the asylum? What if I were to show the "madhouse" as the world? Then the perceptions of Cassandra Wakelin would be crystal clear to everyone. Her view of the world would fall into place for the rest of us, and her story could unfold in a way that made it easier for her to tell and for us to receive. She pretended the garden of the asylum was the garden in which she had grown up; she turned the inmates of the asylum into the "inmates" of her home. Besides which, an asylum is the perfect place to act out a story whose parts are joined by emotional chronology, rather than timeology. . . .

<u>W.W.</u> There's no such word as "timeology." . . .

175

<u>T.F.</u>   There is now. Don't you see what I mean? In asylums — time flashes on and off — and, in between the flashes, there's nothing: greyness, stillness, silence. Waiting. But the things that are seen in the flashes are astonishing. Riveting: vivid and stark and absolutely unadorned with the grace of soft edges. All this, to say nothing of the fact that Cass's life needed to be set in a frame of fire. Every episode is a kind of burning. . . .

<u>W.W.</u>   She sounds like Robert Ross in *The Wars*.

<u>T.F.</u>   Well, they have a lot in common.

<u>W.W.</u>   Outside of fire?

<u>T.F.</u>   Yes. Photographs, for one thing. I think that maybe the photographs in Cass's album may have been the basis for the photographic technique of *The Wars*.

<u>W.W.</u>   Cassandra Wakelin enters the asylum with nothing but a photo-album.

<u>T.F.</u>   Yes. And *The Wars* unfolds as a series of pictures. Pictures and interviews. Anyway — I think the subject of this part of the conversation had to do with the effort involved with writing, and finding where Cass belonged was the effort in her case.

<u>W.W.</u>   And *The Wars?*

<u>T.F.</u>   The effort there was to find the right pictures and find the right characters to interview. Also — as with everything — to pay attention to what it is the character really wants to tell you. What the character requires of

you. And you don't know any of that until *after* the fact. Before the fact, you're lost. And — you know, that, too, is a good analogy for the process. Being lost. What you have to do is go with your characters into the void — and help them find their way home. Does this make you think of lost animals? It does me. And the first thing you have to do with a lost animal is discover a mutual language. After the language — the problem can be revealed — after the revelation, the search can begin and after the search: maybe a solution. Maybe. Maybe. Only maybe. But that's what it is. You try to get the character all the way home.

<u>w.w.</u>   What about your new book? *Famous Last Words.* You had so many people to get home. How many was it? Twenty? Thirty major characters?

<u>T.F.</u>   Something like that. Yes. Good heavens . . . writing *Famous Last Words* I went through five whole modes before I hit upon the character of Mauberley. Ezra Pound's Hugh Selwyn Mauberley. Five whole modes. I don't mean drafts. The draft work was endless — on each of them . . . but, in the end, I came upon the figure of Mauberley and realized I'd found the perfect voice to narrate the story. And it was really through him — through Mauberley — that all the other characters found their way home. For which I was profoundly grateful. Believe me. I never fancied myself as a Tour Guide. And I think he maybe got *me* home, too.

<u>w.w.</u>   Yes. I've noticed you've been around a little more, recently.

<u>T.F.</u>   Maybe that's where George and Brenda come from. And Alice. . . . You know: maybe they sort of tagged

along on the return trip.

<u>w.w.</u>   Well — I'm here to tell you, you'd better do something about that Alice. Dropping cigarettes on the floor . . . burning up the rugs . . . Can't she learn to use an ashtray, like anyone else?

<u>T.F.</u>   I'm sure it was an accident.

<u>w.w.</u>   Didn't sound like an accident to me. Not the way you've put it there: ALICE DROPS HER CIGARETTE ON THE FLOOR. What does she do about it? Leave it there — watching it eat its way through to the floor-boards?

<u>T.F.</u>   Maybe it's a stone floor. . . .

<u>w.w.</u>   Somehow, I doubt it. Given the fires in all your books. Oh, God — I hope that Alice leaves!

<u>T.F.</u>   Maybe in a puff of smoke?

<u>w.w.</u>   It would be a great relief.

<u>T.F.</u>   I take it you and Alice don't get along. . . .

<u>w.w.</u>   You're damned right we don't.

<u>T.F.</u>   What about George and Brenda?

<u>w.w.</u>   It remains to be seen. Are they loud? Do they argue all the time? And what are they arguing about?

<u>T.F.</u>   Something George has found in a drawer upstairs.

<u>w.w.</u>   What?

T.F.   I don't know. Something rather sinister, I should think.

W.W.   Maybe one of Alice's cigarette butts.

T.F.   Kept in an old lacquer box from Japan. . . .
*(At this moment, the telephone rings and W.W. answers. A
friend has called to tell us President Sadat has died and
perhaps we should turn on the radio. We elect not to listen. We do, however, pause for a very long while to think
about his death and the scene of his death and the world
in which it happened. Later on, W.W. starts the questions
again. Out on the lawn, one whole tree has been stripped
of its leaves and, as if its job had been done for the day,
the wind has dropped. The other trees are not yet bare.)*

W.W.   One of the themes that is threaded through your
work more than any other is a particular view of insanity
— be it insanity by itself or drugs or alcohol induced
insanity . . . You do have all these people who either see
and deal with the world as if *it* were insane, or as if *they*
were insane. Can you tell me why this is and where it
comes from?

T.F.   Yes. It comes from a perception of insanity which
was introduced to me very early on in my life through
someone close to my family — and consequently close to
me — who had to be placed in a mental institution. And
the effect that had — especially, in the long run, of
course, on the person involved — but also on all the people who surrounded her — this was the first truly profound experience of my consciousness. I was seven.
Maybe six.
    My perception of this friend was that she was brilliant
— that she had incredible insights into what was really

179

going on in the world around us: but that she was . . . *odd*. Instead of having conversations, she would deliver monologues — in which she would reveal things about reality and portray things in a way that the so-called "sane" people around her did not understand. And it struck me that I should listen. And everything I heard — all of my experience with this person went down very deep into me. And I remember that one of the most vivid things was that she saw things very sharply. She could see the heart of things. Of hurt, for instance. Of where the hurt truly lay and of what had caused the hurt. And sometimes, the hard-core hurt of an accusation might issue from her mind, you see. And once it had reached her mind — how could she prevent it from reaching her lips? And this was dangerous. Because it . . . well, it tampered with the protective walls thrown up by other people to keep the hurt of reality out. So this was dangerous. Very dangerous. How do we live with reality? Once all the walls are in place. . . . It was a matter of the truth! The truth! The truth! And, of course, the *truth! The truth! The truth!* became unendurable for other people to bear. So . . . do you see? When such people exist — then other people must look across the room and say: "that person over there is mad." You see? "That person over there is crazy." Because it is too disturbing to be told *the truth, the truth, the truth.* So — what can you do? You turn it off — like a radio.

W.W.   Yes.

T.F.   Or . . . you hide it in a drawer somewhere. In a lacquer box from Japan.

W.W.   Called "asylum?"

<u>T.F.</u>   Precisely. And also . . . one thing about the "mad," you see, is they don't like lies. So this is why I seize so often upon these people as the heroes of my work. It's only because they have this straight, flung-out connection through the mind to some kind of absolute clarity. And this is what fiction is all about: achieving the clarity obscured by facts.

<u>W.W.</u>   So what are facts?

<u>T.F.</u>   Walls.

<u>W.W.</u>   All right. Talk about the writer as "madman." And writing as therapy: something of value for the rest of us to eavesdrop on, from time to time.

<u>T.F.</u>   Writing isn't therapy. Writing may be cathartic, but it certainly isn't therapy. On the other hand, if you're talking about the reader — and only about the reader — maybe the "therapeutic" value for those of us who read lies in the fact that we don't have to pass through whatever territory it explores, except vicariously. This has been said — and best said — by Adele Wiseman. Adele Wiseman said the writer goes down into the other world of hell for a few years and comes back up and tries to articulate the experience for everyone else.

<u>W.W.</u>   It sort of saves you the busfare.

<u>T.F.</u>   Sort of. But the main thing to remember is that the writer has a round-trip ticket. The writer comes back. Do you see? And this information — the information that everyone doesn't have to perish down there is marvellous. Marvellous. And so maybe this is the therapeutic value: the therapeutic spin-off for the reader. *Hell can be sur-*

vived. And since everyone, at some point, goes through hell — this news is extremely valuable. But everyone can't articulate this news. Everyone can't tell what it is they've survived — and how it is they're still alive. But a good writer can.

<u>W.W.</u>   All right. Talk about genius, now. Is genius a kind of "madness?"

<u>T.F.</u>   No. I don't think so. No. Though I see why you're asking. People think it has to be a kind of madness the same way they think the people I talked about before are "mad." Put it this way. A genius is someone you cannot avoid seeing. I mean — how could you walk into a room and not see Margot Fonteyn? If Margot Fonteyn is there — there's no way she can hide. Is there. *(Laughter)* Even if you've never seen her before. Even if she's wearing the most ordinary, everyday dress — even if she's standing behind a man who's six feet tall: you're going to see her. And what you see is really the thing that drove her to be a genius of dance . . . the unavoidable: the ultimate. The clarity of gesture. Bam! And Mozart must have been the same. Can you hear him and avoid him? Never. . . .

<u>W.W.</u>   But you may not like him.

<u>T.F.</u>   No. But that's not the point here, is it? The point is — you cannot remain unaware that something extraordinary is happening through that person. Something that no one can explain. And yet — if you're reading Shakespeare — listening to Mozart or watching Margot Fonteyn — there doesn't have to be an "explanation." The thing is — you come away different. Changed. Put it this way: the audience that sits down to *Lear* is not the

audience that rises at the end. And that is Shakespeare's genius. If this is "madness" — more! More!

<u>w.w.</u>   All right. Here we are back, more or less where we began. In the theatre. And you've just been talking about Margot Fonteyn, and you, yourself, began as a dancer. So — what you wanted to express as a dancer — as an actor — as a painter — you now express as a writer. *Words.* Words on paper . . . which is a little different from these other forms of expression you began with. . . .

<u>T.F.</u>   Yes. Yes. Words. Well, now. . . . Take dance. What a dancer does is make a series of statements. And the statements are made up of gestures: gestures in a sequence. So words — words are the vocabulary of literate gesture. And the combinations of your words have to be as precise as the combinations of gestures used by a dancer to make an articulate statement in dance. And there's something else, I think, to be said about this. You know, when you learn to dance — when you learn to move — you learn to move, to make each gesture from the centre of your body: from the solar plexus — from the diaphragm. You learn that *everything* must originate there and grow outward towards the conclusion of the gesture: the formation of the statement. And, as an actor, when you learn how to speak — you learn to speak from there: from the centre — from the diaphragm. And, oddly enough — and here we come to writing — when a sentence *hits* — or when a paragraph *hits* — that's *where* it hits. In the solar plexus.

<u>w.w.</u>   But —

<u>T.F.</u>   Now, wait a minute. Be patient. I'm making a

point. You know how you and I, in the theatre, will so often say: "Isn't it strange. Isn't it really too bad. . . . Everything about that person is right — except: they don't know how to use their hands." Or — they carry their heads too high. Or the shoulders are stiff. Okay? *Now:* think of that marvellous, wonderful moment when Lynn Seymour dances onto the stage. Yes? Glorious. Because the whole of her presence is unfolding from the centre. Toller Cranston is the same. Every single gesture is totally fulfilled. Their fingertips — you know? they flick the last cadence from the ends of their fingers. And *you cannot breathe until it is over.* They hold you enthralled to the very last nuance. Yes?

W.W.   Yes.

T.F.   Well, words are the same. Words in a sentence are a written gesture. And if the cadence is wrong — if the rhythm is wrong — if a single syllable is out of place — the sentence fails . . . the book fails. Why? Because you have failed to impel the reader forward with every gesture . . . right to the "fingertips" — all the way from the solar plexus. That's where books are written. That's where readers read.

W.W.   You know what?

T.F.   No. What?

W.W.   I think our friend Alice just dropped another cigarette. . . .

T.F.   Aren't you going to pick it up?

W.W.   No. *(Pause)* I want to see what happens.

· 8 ·

FAMOUS
LAST WORDS

Salman Rushdie's *In Good Faith* and *Is Nothing Sacred?* were published earlier this year in the United Kingdom. The first is Rushdie's reply to those who would proscribe his novel *The Satanic Verses*. ("What is freedom of expression? Without the freedom to offend, it ceases to exist.") The second is a meditation on the act of writing and the written word itself. ("Literature is an interim report from the consciousness of the artist. . . .") Taken together, they provide an incisive and timely discourse on the place of the creative writer in modern society — a society Rushdie sees as being increasingly threatened by its own refusal to acquire less and to imagine more.

Is Nothing Sacred? opens with the words "I grew up kissing books and bread." As a child, Rushdie was taught that when a book or a piece of bread is dropped, the fallen object, having been retrieved, must be kissed — "by way of apology for the act of clumsy disrespect." He goes on to say that he and his family kissed not only bread and holy books, but dictionaries, atlases, novels and comic books as well. The image this presents is not merely charming. It also evokes the poignancy of Salman Rushdie's present situation and his tenacious respect for the integrity of the written word.

Books and bread. Bread and books. In essence, these are the subjects of both these essays, which — taken as a single meditation — can be read as a discourse on the corporeal and spiritual needs of humankind as reflected in fiction. Bread feeds the body and fires its energies. Books feed the mind and fire its visions. We persist by means of one and we survive by means of the other.

What cheers me most about *In Good Faith* and *Is Nothing Sacred?* is their relentless advocacy of books — and especially of fiction — as providing stages — perhaps the last — where the imagination can play out "all the great debates of society" in ways that society itself forbids. "A book," Salman Rushdie tells us, "is a version of the world." And it couldn't matter less, in the long run, if the version being depicted is scandalous or laudatory, nihilistic or celebratory. All that matters is the chance books give us to catch our breath and bypass the world as it really is, if only for a moment — and, in that moment, to satisfy our need for the comfort of "wonderment and understanding."

Books are mediators between our desire and our despair. They bargain for us in behalf of our sanity and our survival. Maybe "bargain" isn't quite the right word — but they set down questions and arguments that, by their very nature inside fiction, prompt us to think again about our response to being alive. It is only inside fiction, where evil is still incarnate and dragons can still be slain, that we perceive the possibility of surviving reality. Rushdie writes that "what is forged in the secret act of reading is a different kind of identity, as the reader and the writer merge through the medium of the text to become a collective being that both writes as it reads and reads as it writes — and creates, jointly, that unique work, *their* novel."

I nearly fell over when I read this. It so perfectly describes what happens when I read. And it equally describes what happens during a part of the writing process: the deliberate making of room in the text for the reader to exist inside the fiction. "This secret identity of writer and reader," Rushdie continues, "is the novel form's greatest and most subversive gift."

I like the word "subversive" in this context. It reminds me of something written by the playwright Arthur Miller in his autobiography, *Timebends*. Miller is here describing the late 1950s in America — a time when he perceived that the written word and the arts in general had lost their coinage. "The whole country seemed to be devolving," he writes, "into a mania for the distraction it called entertainment, a day and night mimicry of art that menaced nothing, redeemed nothing and meant nothing but forgetfulness."

Salman Rushdie and Arthur Miller have much in common. Both have been vilified. Both have survived the vilification. Both — in the course of that survival — have continued to give voice to all the voices in them, as writers, that speak without compromise.

"Literature," Rushdie says in *Is Nothing Sacred?*, "is made at the frontier between the self and the world." He also says, of the novel, that it is "the art involving least compromise . . . the interior space of our imaginations is a theatre that can never be closed down."

Implicitly, that space belongs to writer and reader alike. You can do no better than to go out today and bring home *In Good Faith* and *Is Nothing Sacred?* — turn

189

them loose in that inner space and rejoice that Salman Rushdie lives. Bring bread and books. Kiss them for Salman Rushdie — and for their own sakes, too.

Stone Orchard
November 11, 1970
Article

There was a famous figure whose fame, around the time I was six, became rather alarmingly personal to me. This was the woman who came and cleaned our house every Tuesday and Friday. I have never known a woman so dour and endlessly unhappy. She never smiled and was given to heaving sighs halfway up the stairs. This woman, whose name was Mrs Simpson, was tall and extremely thin and wore her hair very tightly bound underneath a net. Her skin tone was grey.

One day in December of 1936, the lady in question was standing on the landing, leaning on her mop and heaving one of her sighs, when the paper arrived. My mother unfolded it, as she did on any other day — and suddenly cried out: "My God! *The King is going marry Mrs. Simpson!*"

To me, of course, there was only one Mrs. Simpson and she was standing halfway up our stairs.

But why hadn't she told us the King was going to marry her?

Needless to say, he did — and very soon afterward she stopped coming over to clean our house. We were not — by the way — invited to the wedding.

Stone Orchard
February 1981
Notebook

I don't know why — I never have known why — but I'm impelled to lock things into place with words. Words are iny safety deposit boxes — my guarantees against the extortion of what I know. Words are the only currency I have, and without them, I might as well fill my mind with stones and swim out to sea. *I am a writer, and a writer writes* — Mauberley's creed.

Q: Why must we always disguise the truth as fiction?
A: Truth slips in through whatever door it can find.

I didn't know quite how to tell this story [*Famous Last Words*] until I realized that if I were Homer, I'd have recognized this wasn't just the story of men and women — but of men and women and the gods to whom they are obedient; of the fates that rule their lives and of the fact that history is created through the enactment of symbolic gestures — and told best through the evocation of icons. So what I must do is transpose this story, which is history, into another key — which is mythology.

Mauberley is endlessly fascinated with what he calls "the mythology of now," and because of the circle he moves in, he is able to record that mythology from a privileged vantage point. Slowly, however, the privilege will give way to nightmare. Mauberley's "icons," after all, are just real people — not the gods he imagines them to be or wants them to be. The truth about Helen and Paris, for instance, is told in every discarded condom in the gutter. Homer was able to elevate that image to the icon plane. Given *his* people, however, can Mauberley do that?

Never lose track of the devices of mythology — of its having the edge on "reality," because of the way it uses reality as an ingredient only — as the baseline upon which each of the "stories" stands. A myth is not a lie, as such, but only the truth in larger shoes. Its gestures are wider. Its voice is projected to cover distance. Its face is made up of withheld, imaginative shadows and lines and colours. It is the ultimate theatre of human intrigue. Sometimes the

191

gods are added because it is the only stage on which the humans can match them. But of course, the gods are never bested by anyone but other gods. Larger. Larger.

Stone Orchard
June 1980

The Bahamas consist almost entirely of aeolian deposits on coral reefs. The soil is therefore thin but extremely fertile. From July to October there is grave danger of hurricanes. Once, in the season of 1866, the soil and everything in it from trees to roots to animal life was lifted and all but completely blown away.

Someone says: "What's an aeolian deposit?"
Someone else: "It means the wind did it?"
Someone else: "Sounds like the Immaculate Conception."
Someone else: "Well . . . look around you."

Stone Orchard
November 1989

In every piece of writing there is an element the writer has to cut from the final draft. All too often, these elements are paragraphs or story lines the writer loves — but recognizes as weights the whole piece will not carry. This is what William Faulkner called the process of *killing all your darlings*. . . .

Such a "darling" existed in the penultimate draft of *Famous Last Words* — and the killing of it caused a good deal of pain for me — and a war with John Pearce, who was then my editor.

The element in question was the story line of Jane Porter, her vacuous husband, Judd, and their children — ten-year-old Clyde and eight-year-old Vivie. Together, the Porters played important roles in the final section of the novel — the section concerning the murder of Sir Harry Oakes in Nassau, 1943.

Pearce made a very good point about this story line —

and his editorial instincts were absolutely correct when he insisted it be cut. The point he made was this:

Famous Last Words is a book that is written on the walls of a hotel by a novelist under threat of death. The novelist — H.S. Mauberley — can only afford to put on the walls what time will allow and time will not allow him to tell Jane's story. If he paused to do so, death could overtake him before he had transcribed more vital news about the leading characters. Therefore — Jane must go.

I knew he was right — though hated the fact of it — and I set about removing her.

Nonetheless, Jane Porter is still — for me — a permanent figure in that landscape and she haunts me even now as I sit here writing this, although eight years have passed since I pulled her from the book. I have promised myself that, one day, I will complete her story.

Jane gets her name — and certain elements of her character (though none of her drinking habits!) from a woman I have loved from afar and admired ever since I first encountered her in the early 1970s. This woman is June Callwood — and before I pass on to Jane Porter, there is one swift image of June that bears telling. It was in this image that Jane Porter was born. . . .

Stone Orchard
April 1987
Article

There's a paradox in June Callwood of which nearly everyone who works with her will be aware. She has a way of turning up for riot duty looking like a million dollars. One day — I can't remember what it was we were doing, but it certainly wasn't the cocktail circuit — June turned up in one of her super-elegant outfits with a star attached to her lapel. Not just any star, mind you. It was made of tin — and I think it came from a box of Cheerios.

"I see you're looking at my star," she said.

"That's right," I said. "It's . . . interesting, to say the least."

"My daughter gave it to me," she said. And she leaned forward, showing it off. "See what it says?"

I looked more closely. Then I blinked — and sat back, chastened. Someone, at last, had done her justice.

Written on the star was a single word:

SHERIFF.

If only it were true.

Nassau, Bahamas
1941
Famous Last Words

Jane Porter was going to wear the Sheriff's badge. There was no way around it. She already wore the Mickey Mouse watch — though most of her friends forgave her for that. But a Sheriff's badge! To the Spitfire Charity Bazaar! What will the Duchess think?

"I'll tell her to shove it up her ass," said Jane to the mirror. I like it, she thought, as she pinned the badge in place above her heart. It's unique and it gives me *character.*

She sipped her Scotch. The sweet, pale smell of wisteria drifted through the screens. Mickey's little hand pointed at two and his big hand at ten. Nearly time to go. She touched her hair. Because of the humidity, it flared in an unruly halo of curls. Nevertheless, she thought; in spite of my freckles and my crimpy hair, I'm almost beautiful. Maybe I do hunch my shoulders, but so does that model in *Vogue* and even my pansy husband says I have the most gorgeous bum he's ever seen.

Judd's not a pansy. Why did I say that — think that?

Because of that McCabe man: Arnold. Damn him. He was probably downstairs right now, making up to Judd. Sinister. It was all so sinister. Arnold McCabe kept "hanging around" — watching them all from his corner — just watching. Especially watching Judd — and the children. Taking Judd aside for private little chats in the garden. Watching the children from windows — making excursions into their private lives with his eyes. Staring. It was the way he stared — unblinking. . . . He was like a snake — possibly dangerous — species unknown. And he kept making eyes — snake's eyes — at Judd. And Judd didn't seem to mind. In fact, he preened for the man. But then, Judd preened for everyone. For anyone.

But me. We haven't made love since the 29th of April.

She drank her Scotch. The glass was blue. Its base was chipped. If her mother or Mavis found it — they'd throw it away. So she kept it hidden under a cloth in the tall commode by her bed. It was her favourite glass. Sapphire. She'd had it since before her marriage. Before the invention of drink. . . .

The trouble is — I love him.

Damn it. Damn. Damn. Damn.

Perfume. What will I wear?

Which scent goes with a Sheriff's badge?

She glanced at the array of bottles: Bois des Isles, l'Air du Temps, Shalimar, Captive Heart. Hah! She seized the bottle shaped like a heart, pierced with its gold-plated arrow. Two hundred dollars an ounce.

If I spill it, then I smell of Captive Heart for a year. That's the trouble with expensive perfumes. Nothing will wash them away. *All the blood of Arabia will not wash these poor hands clean . . .* or something.

Jane stood up. Chartreuse chiffon. Emerald shoes. Blue glass. Tin-plated star. And on the bed, her wide-brimmed hat with its white velvet ribbons and her handbag made of tinted straw.

One more sip of Scotch — with a dash of *crème de menthe* so her breath would be green like her dress.

She straightened the seams of her silk hose.

195

I also have good legs.

All right. Where's the door?

She turned towards the bed and almost fell. Laughing, she steadied herself by catching at the netting overhead, and picked up her hat and her handbag. Then she faced the mirror again. Beautiful — with frightened eyes.

One more belt of Scotch. And a belt of *crème de thing*. And one more dab of Captive Heart.

I need a hankie. Two. One for the blood — and one for the perspiration. She opened the drawer. Mavis's neat little piles of lingerie sacs and sachet filters; hosiery and handkerchiefs were weighted down with half a dozen boxes of Dick Tracy bullets and the nickel-plated Dick Tracy gat. Jane selected a monogrammed handkerchief and another made entirely of lace and placed them in her handbag. She also lifted out two of the bullet boxes and shoved them down beside her compact and her lipstick. Then she took the gat — checked that it was loaded — and dropped it carefully on top of the other contents. *Two whole boxes of Dick Tracy bullets?* Well. One never knows — *do one.*

"There," she said out loud, throwing back the last of the Scotch. "Okay, Chester. Let's go save the world for Democracy."

The aeroplane had approached as far as the harbour. The sound of it grew inside the ear — swelling outward through the music and the children's voices. Somebody said: "what's that?" and a few looked up, startled that anything worth remarking on should be in the sky at four in the afternoon.

Jane was poking in her handbag. Someone jostled her.

"Excuse me."

"Not at all."

Jane went on rummaging.

Whoever had jostled her stayed close by. A stranger. She could feel the shape of his body crowding her space and she knew he was watching her. Breathing on her.

"Clyde?"

"Yes, Mother?"

"Here." She handed Clyde money. "Go and get some champagne." Then she handed him the dark glasses, too. "Wear these and tell them you're a midget."

"Yes, Mother." Clyde had played the midget game before.

"Not a dwarf, mind. A *midget*. Dwarfs are different."

"Yes, Mother."

"Don't spill. And don't sip."

"No, I won't."

The stranger pressed closer.

Jane said: "wait a minute," to Clyde. "take Vivie with you." She tried to make light of it. "That way, you can bring me four glasses."

"They'll never believe she's a midget," said Clyde. "She hasn't any breasts."

"They'll believe it if she doesn't turn around," said Jane. "Just be sure she stands with her back to the barman."

"Yes, Mother."

"Go on, now."

The children started away beneath the arms of the people in front of them.

"Wait," said Jane.

(Why?)

They stopped.

Jane leaned down as best she could in the press and smiled with her perfumed breath. She wanted to obliterate the thought of Arnold McCabe. Vivie was staring at her, slightly bewildered, having just been told to go and perform the midget routine.

Jane touched the star.

"See what I'm wearing?" She reached out and let her fingers in their gloves slide across the children's foreheads — one and then the other. "Don't go getting lost," she said.

"No, Mother."

"Bye."

Seeing the odd expression on her mother's face, Vivie said; "we're only going across the lawn to the *Café de Paris . . .*" but Clyde gave her hand a tug and shut her up.

He knows, Jane thought, *whatever it is that I know.* (She would think this afterward, too — that Clyde had been psychic.) Now, she looked straight into his eyes and he looked back. It sent a shiver through her heart. Then Clyde turned, taking Vivie in tow, and was gone — disappearing instantly into the thronging backs and craning heads — for nearly everyone was looking skyward now, wondering what was up there.

Drifting down towards the sea of parasols and up-turned faces was a large white parachute. The figure falling with it could not, as yet, be clearly seen but it appeared to be the figure of a man. It was wearing bright yellow trousers and a purple shirt. The aeroplane had ceased its ascendancy at a height of eight thousand feet, where it hovered now like Daedalus over Icarus.

Staring past the floating island of silk, the smiling man in the goggles pushed the joystick forward in the cockpit as far as it would go and the plane began to dive. In seconds, the parachute was visible behind him.

"*Now,*" the man said to himself, "or *never.*"

Someone screamed on the lawn: "IT'S GOING TO CRASH!" and everyone ran. First they ran one way — and then they ran another. Then another. But the plane kept falling. This is when — all at once — it was clear: there was no escape route from the lawns.

198

Eight hundred people were entirely hemmed in by the circle of marquees and by the Mansion at their backs. The driveway was clogged with motorcars and blocked by iron gates and barriers, the latter having been set there against the intrusion of curious natives. Now, when the plane pulled out of its dive, it passed so low above the heads of the terrified guests that every one of them fell to the earth in an attitude of prayer, as if a muezzin had suddenly called them all to their knees. Men, women and children all fell down.

The Duke of Windsor was standing on a platform, raised about three feet from the ground. He was staring, open-mouthed, at the falling figure of the parachutist and he held in his left hand a wooden spatula — and in his right hand a pancake pan. He was about to turn the auctioned *crèpe Suzette.* In fact, when the plane had begun its dive, the American beauty expert Elizabeth Greenslade had just made a bid for the *crèpe* of ten thousand dollars. She, too, was standing open-mouthed — with her hand in the air.

Behind them, the Duchess of Windsor was poised on a table top in the candy-stripe shade of the *Café de Paris.* The hem of her pearly dress was in her hand. Her toes were pointed inward like a pigeon's. She had been about to launch the Charleston contest. The band came blaring to a halt and the drummer fell to the floor with a scream of cymbals.

By now, the aeroplane had made its pass and was rising once again above the hill. The guests began to rise as well. Everyone was in a state of dreadful confusion and panic. Behind them — bayonets fixed and rifles at the ready — stood a phalanx of kilted soldiers — a thin red wall of tunics cutting off escape through the Mansion and down the drive. Everyone turned and ran, *en masse,* towards the canvas enclosures that only moments before had provided delight and music and haven from the glaring of the sun.

Some still had their eyes on the figure falling from the sky — while others were searching for their friends and loved ones. But all were running in the same direction, for it had entered everyone's mind at once that for some unimaginable reason they were all to be the sudden victims of a massacre. Why else should the troops have walled them in that way, with pointed guns? Was the Duke to be assassinated and they, in their hundreds, to become his fellow victims?

No one paused to wonder why this should be — they only *knew* it must be so. And thus they became a mob — and completely lost control of reason. No one in this universal state of panic paused to take note of the fact that the Duke of Windsor's marquee had caught on fire. No one saw the flames because the Duke was already falling — tackled by Major Bunny Gerrard in a flying leap. "HE'S DEAD!" they screamed. "THEY'VE KILLED HIM!" "RUN!" And again they wheeled, this time towards the Duchess, white and beckoning on her table top. But the flames wheeled with them — fanned by the breath of their panic. Suddenly — everywhere they turned — there was fire.

Then it was that the parachutist fell at Lana Turner's feet. Jane was a witness to this. Afterwards, she swore that the man had been dead already when he hit the ground. His legs and arms fell under him and his neck appeared to be broken, the whole disjointed figure lolling like a giant marionette entangled in its strings. Lana Turner screamed — but Jane was certain that within the scream there was a word — a name — a strangled cry of awful recognition.

The parachute, meanwhile, fell in waves of billowing silk on top of the people nearest Lana Turner, and Jane was one of those who were trapped underneath like so many netted birds. Someone raced across her shoulders — wearing boots. Others were blinded by the heels of women's shoes. There were cries of "FIRE!" and shouts of "HELP!" Jane removed one shoe and struck against the pressing backs around her, trying desperately not to suffocate in silk. The light was eerie, coral white and green, and she could see the shadows of the flames played out along the swelling waves of the parachute above her. When, at last, she had fought her way to the edge — and risen to her knees and had taken her first great gulp of air — she opened her eyes on a scene that would haunt her till the day she died.

In the cinema marquee, two hundred people had been watching the Fall of France and now, in a nightmare, they were caught themselves in the hordes of refugees who clogged the roads on the screen while the dive bombers strafed them in the ditches. Between the rows of chairs, real flames caught at their hair and their clothing. Real children screamed for their mothers and the cries on the screen were echoed in the fiery furnace that exploded now and fell across their backs.

Jane turned away, on her knees, and began to crawl across the silk that had imprisoned her. Somehow, she remembered to get to her feet and was looking for her children, even as she stooped back down and lifted the silk in her hands and began to draw it aside. Underneath, the dead already stared at the blackening sky.

Jane saw the Duke's white body in its naval uniform passing over the heads of the crowd, borne on the hands of Bunny and his agents. The Duchess, calm and courageous, had formed a sort of conga line of survivors and was leading them back towards the menace of the troops, completely unafraid. Very young children were being thrown above the crowd like parcels. Jane looked desperately for Clyde and Vivie. She saw her mother, Marian, blue and serene, stand up from the ground and begin to walk in a daze towards the fiery awnings. Jane went running then — one-shoed, limping — unaware that the earth was flesh beneath her feet. When she got as far as Marian, she still had not seen Clyde and Vivie, nor Judd nor her father. Nor anyone she loved but Marian. Her mother's face, when she reached her, was absolutely blank. Jane put her arms around her shoulders and drew her close. For a moment, they did not even try to move, but stood like rocks and let the movement of the others flow around them like a river. Then, very slowly, Jane began to push her mother backwards — both of them against the stream.

This was the longest walk that Jane had ever made. It was not unlike a dance, with her mother as her partner, catatonic in her arms. For weeks thereafter, Jane's legs and back would ache with the effort of it, and in her dreams she would go on pushing her mother around that wild, chaotic dance floor on the flaming lawns, hearing the song about the paper moon and the cardboard sea and the honky tonk parade, and the melody played in the fiery arcade. . . .

In less than half an hour, the fire had died and all that remained was the smoking, ruined shapes of the great marquees, like ships at anchor — all their ropes untied on the grass. Soldiers and firemen, doctors and nurses and mesmerized survivors, some with their clothes still smouldering, wandered over the scene, identifying — trying to identify the victims, trying to comfort, trying to save the wounded and the dying. Thirty-five dead in all, including one who had fallen from the sky and was burned beyond recognition — and also, Vivie Porter — found beneath an ice-cream table in the *Café de Paris*, where she had gone to buy her mother pink champagne because her mother was afraid.

For half an hour Jane sat on the bed, just staring. Then she rose, as the sun had done, and passed through the pallor of the shuttered light. She stood and brushed her fingers over all the familiar things that were scattered there on the tops of all her furniture. Stars and Mickey Mouse watches — bottles of perfume — photographs — the heads of dolls — and a goblet, sapphire blue. Then, without even looking, she opened the second drawer of the bureau and drew out the bottle of rum — or something; who knew what it was? Who cared? When she pulled the stopper, all she knew was that it smelled of safety — and maybe, too, of sleep.

Goodbye.

Goodbye.

Sunday, August 10th, Mavis Boodle went upstairs with the tray of avocado mash and lemon juice. When she came to the door it would not open.

Both the houseboys and even Mister Raymond had to be summoned. Clyde came, too, with a stone. It took them fifteen minutes to break down the door.

Inside, Jane was dead. She was lying in a corner on her stomach, with her face towards the wall.

Sometime in the night she had choked on her vomit.

The sapphire glass was on the floor beside her. She wore the Mickey Mouse watch and the star was pinned to her dress. In the window, she had hung a paper moon.

Jane was buried in the same grave as Vivie. There were only five people present at the graveside.

This time it didn't rain. Sunlight poured from a cloudless sky, lavishing the whole scene with brightness.

Everyone wore exactly what they'd worn the afternoon that Vivie was buried, except that Mavis "borrowed" Jane's black gloves and mourning veil. Harry and Marian Raymond and Clyde Porter represented the generations either side of Jane. Her own generation was absent entirely.

This time it was Clyde who stood alone, wearing his mother's dark glasses. But there wasn't any game this time. *Dwarfs and midgets are not the same,* she had told him. Now it was evident how true that was. They were not the same as one another and they were not the same as children. Clyde, for the first time ever, knew he was neither dwarf nor midget, nor child. He was just another abandoned doll — a remnant and repository of someone's love, as long as he should live.

Stone Orchard
June 1985
Journal

We were still sitting in front of the television set upstairs, just finishing supper, tonight, when the news came on. We didn't always watch it — it was all bad news — all the images of violence, sadness and injustice, and it was usually both depressing and frustrating — but neither of us felt like getting up and turning off the set, so we sat and watched. And that's how we got to hear about the Duchess of Windsor.

The thing is, when *Famous Last Words* was first published in 1981, WFW and I had to take out a fair amount of libel insurance because of the number of real people whom I had used as characters in the book — most notably, the Duke and Duchess of Windsor. This insurance was considered sufficient for the Canadian and American editions, but we were strongly advised not to attempt publication in Britain or France as long as the Duchess was still alive. The problem was that, according to European law, an author could be sued for a great deal of money simply for putting words into the mouth of a living person. And goodness knows — apart from the story I had chosen regarding the Windsors' involvement with fascism — I had certainly put a lot of words in the mouth of the Duchess!

When the book came out here, in 1981, she was in her eighties, living in Paris, but she had sunk into the depths of senility. This certainly did not rule out a libel suit, though, because however far out of the world the Duchess may have drifted, her lawyer, Maître Blum, was still very much *in* the world, and had shown herself to be both highly litigious and fiercely protective of the Duchess's good name. And so, while *Famous Last Words* was selling in North America, it was completely denied two of its major European markets.

This brings me back to tonight, and the newscast we watched. It was all as disturbing as usual, until Knowlton Nash came to the very last item — which is where the obituary notices of the famous are usually read.

He gave a small, slightly sad smile and his voice dropped just a bit in volume as he said: *and finally, tonight in Paris, the Duchess of Windsor quietly . . .*

WFW and I both automatically leaned forward, the word already echoing in our minds: *died* — along with the relief that at last the book could be published in Britain and France! The thought of movie sales, mass-market paperbacks and Johnny Carson danced around the ceiling.

And then, as smoothly as ever, Knowlton completed his announcement.

. . . celebrated her eighty-ninth birthday.

After a stunned moment, WFW and I looked at each other — more in shame than anything else, and then, without saying a word, we raised our glasses, with their

last few sips of wine, and offered silent tribute to a remarkable — if maddening — woman.

Dieppe
March 1987
Journal

*This visit to Dieppe gave rise
to two of the short stories that
ultimately appeared in* Stones:
After the disastrous reception
of *Famous Last Words* in the U.K. *(Who is this colonial
hack who has dared to besmirch the memory of our
beloved Duchess of Windsor!)* WFW and I retreated
here, across the Channel, to lick our wounds. The joke is,
all the furor over the book has catapulted it onto the best-
seller lists. Number six on two lists — number five on
another!

I've had bad reviews before, but never any quite so
depressing as these have been. With one, there was a car-
toon which shows the Windsors hanging from a gibbet.
Another suggests that, now that Macmillan's have published Mister Findley's attack on the Duke and Duchess,
perhaps they should hire him to do a hatchet job on their
own late publisher, Harold Macmillan. Frank Kermode
— who had already told Eileen, the publicist, that he
thought the book was great — turned around and put a
knife in me for my "unjustified" treatment of Ezra Pound.
(Kermode is a Pound scholar.) I think their idea was —
make Findley suffer the same fate as his own victims —
because it was me they were getting at more than the
book. This is not pleasant — in fact, it's lousy, as a feeling
— but what they're *not* acknowledging in their reviews is
that *FLW* is not a pack of lies. It tells the truth. Dear
God, the *Express* has a contract with Bloch — a Windsor
biographer — and it's so obvious they're upset because
FLW has covered Bloch's material before he got it into
print on their pages. They're an embarrassment. As if it
was some kind of bloody competition! *No one* wrote

about the writing or the story of Mauberley or anything but the Windsor issue.

Poor James [Hale, the publisher] is devastated. He's invested a lot of himself in this book — and the effect of the reviews is as harsh for him as it is for me. Or worse. At least I have the good reception at home and in the U.S. to fall back on — but this is *it*, for James, whom I happen to like immensely and admire. So, I'm sorry for his sake, as well as my own and the book's, that the critics have treated it so badly.

In time it will pass. But there is one thing you cannot ever forget when the reviews are negative — and that is the years of trying to get it right (in this case, *four* years) — as opposed to the week's-work dismissal by the critics. That, in itself, is fairly devastating — the sense of being brushed aside like some troublesome, vagrant fly.

. . .Dieppe is the scene of the tragic battle in August of 1942, when so many Canadians lost their lives — and so many others lost their freedom for the next three years — and some, their sanity — forever. WFW was here once before, when we were writing the CBC documentaries about the battle — but I have never been before this — and now, here I am — walking over those stones and along those streets.

. . .I think, too, constantly of Oscar Wilde, who came here after being released from gaol — and the Mayor refused to let him stay because — *you will drive away all the English tourists, Mister Wilde!*

Well, he didn't drive *us* away — dear Oscar. And here we are, enjoying splendid food and the rest we have needed now, for a year.

. . .Yesterday afternoon, while lying in a cold sweat, I had the following troubling dream:

1. *Three volumes of a book called* Hysteria — obviously

a learned work by a figure such as Freud. I had purchased them at great expense. We were staying at someone else's house (?) in another country — probably England — although in portions of the dreams that followed, it was as if "home" had been transferred there and "there" was more like France or Switzerland.

At the other person's house where we stayed there was a party. It appeared to be an all-male party, though not overtly homosexual. The three volumes were laid out, lying flat on a cushioned window-sill in a bow window. Each volume was bound in soft leather and on the spine of each one was written *Hysteria* plus a volume number — *1* and *2* and *3*. The writing was stylized script, as if a facsimile of the author's hand.

WFW came to the window with me and said; *Oh-oh, you've gone and done it again. You've bought more books we can't afford and that you'll never use.* And he opened one. I also opened one. The chapter headings — there were dozens of them — were all handwritten in the front of the books. Each chapter appeared to be a case history. Two pages of these chapter headings came away in my hands — and I thought, *oh, god — Bill will think I've been gypped — such expensive books so cheaply bound they fall apart!* So I said, *look how expensive and beautifully thought out these books are. They even have detachable pages!*

In the city beyond the window it was evening — getting dark. WFW said — very kindly and with concern — *don't be alarmed. Everything will be all right.* And we stood there with the books — me holding the pages — and it was just as if someone had died — sad and desolate, with the party in the background behind us.

2. *Scene:* a man I was attracted to — (not anyone known to me — dark hair — forties — wearing a blue suit) was entertaining *everyone* — using a book I could

not see — the book on the floor and everyone seated very close together, looking at the book and at the man. The rest of the room was empty and lonely. I came to the edge of the group and stood looking down at them all and I felt appallingly lonely — and *ill.*

3. *Scene:* I am in a clinic — feeling nervous and ill — a doctor is there with the results of a test I have already been given. He is holding a glass slide and a piece of paper. Very personable — thinning blond hair — round face — blue shirt and white lab coat. I am in shirt sleeves — *cold.* he says, *this is all right. Nothing wrong — you can have these, if you like.* I put out my hand for the slide and the paper and suddenly he is looking at me with great concern. *Just a minute,* he says. *You aren't well.*

I know that, I think. *And now he's going to prove it.*

4. *Scene:* back at the party, as if there had been no departure or interruption. There is now a dog and some children, who are in the background, only barely seen — making a fuss over the dog. I am leaving the party with WFW and some others, including women. It is daylight — beautiful. Clear, cool, crisp. This is the part where we seem to be in a familiar landscape — although in reality, it is not. But in the dream I know it well, and the people, although — again — they are all (except WFW) unknown figures in reality. I am confident, here, that I am setting out for "home" — where I will be made well. But I must get all the way home for this, or I will not get well. We are leaving a town (European) and heading into a pastoral world. We cross a very high, long bridge over a river.

As we are on the bridge, a woman's voice says, *oh look — it's Mary Graham!* (This name, in real life, means nothing to me.)

I turn and Mary Graham — middle-aged — pretty — wearing a blue (bachelor-button blue) suit — silvery hair — is coming towards me across the bridge. She has a female companion who says, *surely you want to say hello to Mary Graham.* And I say, *of course,* and go back. Mary Graham and I "know" one another. She is wearing a make-up cape and the woman with her is a make-up artist. Mary Graham is being prepared for a television appearance. Her lips are wet with fresh lipstick. She leans forward and says, *don't worry about my make-up. Kiss me.* I kiss her on the cheek. She says, with amusement, *here I am just back — and with a glorious tan — and you go and wear red!* She points at me and I am wearing a maroon sweater. Then we start to walk across the bridge to catch up with WFW and "the others."

Mary Graham is telling me about her important work — *saving people in distress.* She asks for my help. *You would be very useful.* I say that I can't help now, because I'm going home to get well. She says, *oh, what a pity.* We have finished crossing the bridge and are walking right at the edge of the road. It is all very familiar to me as a landscape. Behind Mary Graham there is a valley that is so deep the houses in the village there are like toys. There is mist there — wisps of clouds in the bright air. Mary Graham turns to look behind her. She sees the valley and says, *oh!* But she has already taken a step in its direction. I reach for her — but cannot touch her. She is gone. All "the others" rush back. I look over the edge. Mary Graham is falling in slow motion, using the make-up cape to slow her fall. She reaches out and takes hold of the eavestrough of an unseen building below us. I am in shock — and so, of course, is she. Preventing us from finding the house with the eavestrough is a lot of frothy greenery, like ferns. Mary Graham is holding on and desperate. The others look at her and turn away — retreating to where they cannot see her. One woman says, *oh, god — we can't help her. There's nothing we can do.* . . . I say, *but we must* try. I turn and blunder onto the road. A car passes and misses me and I am aware of thinking: *there will be one tragedy after another, here, because we have blundered.*

I thought it was my fault that Mary Graham had fallen. If I had not gone back to speak to her and walk with her, she might not have paused after the bridge and fallen. I started to yell, *Bring rope! Bring rope! Everyone bring rope!*

I wanted her to hear me so she would know we were *trying.*

On the other side of the road there was a farm — with a long, endless laneway. I thought: all farms have ropes — and started staggering up the lane, calling out, *Help! Help! Bring ropes!* — thinking they must keep ropes because they lived near the treacherous edge of the valley.

I was thinking this and calling out when I woke up.

I was wet with perspiration and my mouth was dry.

I lay still, thinking: *now I am awake, who will save Mary Graham?*

NOT WANTED
ON THE VOYAGE

This is from a letter to Thornton Wilder:

Nothing else I can imagine doing could have had more effect on me than our trip to the Northwest Territories this summer. I had not taken in — even living where I do — how deeply I am affected by nature. I had never thought of myself specifically as an animal before. I had lost biological touch with where I am. And I had failed to grasp that what we call *the human spirit* is absolutely rooted in the earth.

Some few things in life alter its course for us, forever. This experience was like that for me. In the most concise way — in the starkest sense — I was shaken. I lost a good deal of fear — and gained some understanding that "courage" is a form of simplicity. I gained access to my biological past and I was linked — not just to other human beings — but to life itself in a way I had previously not understood was available. Bird song, for instance, will not be the same again, because I don't feel separated from it any more. Intelligence, surely, is the use to which we apply our spirit — once we have found its source.

Stone Orchard
September 1970
Radio

What a week this has been! To begin with, I was tired. A friend had died in an accident. I'd written something I'd thought was good while I wrote it — but when I read it, it was awful. The climate had gone mad; in the backyard I saw a ball of fire. On the road, I found a blind and starving cat. [This was Mottle, who became Mottyl in *Not Wanted on the Voyage*.] A poisonous spider appeared in the garden. Another friend caught pneumonia and when I went to visit him in the hospital, he didn't look like himself at all. There he was, in the middle of a great storm, lying on a bed, looking small and ill. Breathing so hard. With clenched fists. And when his eyes opened, he didn't know who I was — or what to say to me or why I was there.

And the night my friend had died, I'd been getting drunk at a birthday party. Nothing to do with him — we'd been out of each other's lives a year or more — but he lay dying for lack of blood and there I was getting drunk.

And then I had to go into Toronto to meet with various people, in the midst of all this — while my head was still under the hammer — and all the way in I was thinking: *oh, why go on? What are we, that we* make *ourselves go on?*

In the city I met with people and, at lunchtime, I went down out of one of those crazy white offices with pictures of birds on the walls and paper flowers on the desks — those places we infuse with photographs and plastic life because nothing real could survive the air-conditioning or the lack of it — rooms with soot-black windows and secretaries with emphysema clutching *The Valley of the Dolls* — and I went down the iron steps and out through the spotted foyer into the dubious sunlight of Front Street and there was music. Faraway, down the street, around the corner — there was music. And I turned in that direction and saw a great crowd of people — and I heard a giant calliope.

When I got there, all kinds of people were crowded up by the side of the road, squinting at the calliope, silenced by its noise. And then there was a busload of clowns to squint at and, after that, a flat truck carrying several bears in cages. The bears' fur had been dyed yellow and pink and blue. And trotting beside them, there were cowboys in black hats with tin .44s and string lariats and rubber noses. Then there was a band, red-coated, white-hatted, gold-braided — a huge and everlasting band that went on for blocks, playing "Let the Sunshine In" and "What the World Needs Now Is Love." While — all the while — the crowd stared and squinted — expressionless.

The band was followed by another busload of clowns — but these clowns were children — children, got up like clowns. They were drinking Coke out of tins and their make-up was running all over their faces and hands and some of them were eating hamburgers and hotdogs and there was lipstick all over the food and these children stared back at us out of their clown faces, eating, drinking, wiping their lips with coloured paper napkins; and they didn't smile or laugh the way real clowns should do. They stared at us — ate their food — and were gone.

After that, there was a hiatus — and an eerie, almost disturbing silence — because it seemed that everything was over, except that no one went away. We all just stood there, faintly hearing the distant calliope and the far-away, far-off band and into this silence there came a shuffling sound — a soft, padding sound — the kind of sound that prisoners make when they stumble out of darkness into light. And it was elephants.

Elephants.

Ten of them. And no one moved.

We all just stood and stared.

Ten elephants came shuffling — led by a giant male with tusks and followed at the end by a baby elephant a quarter of his size. There they were. In the middle of Yonge Street, Toronto. Watched by maybe a thousand, open-mouthed people with voided minds — whose expressions slowly turned to concern, as if the elephants *worried* them.

Each elephant held the other, trunk to tail. And they swayed. From side to side — in a slow step — almost a dance step — crowded up against each other, flank to face. Men with goads and picks were walking by their side. And the elephants' eyes stared about, shy eyes, incredibly shy, with an awkward gaze — uncertain, fear-ful, flicking looks out over the crowd, unaware that they were the giants among the midgets — the beasts among the men. But the men knew it. . . .

They watched with a certain satisfaction the parade of the elephants. *There go the elephants,* they said to one another, pointing out tusks and tails and trunks. Remarking on the largeness of the ears and the smallness of the eyes. Soon, pointing out the features of the ele-phants, the grown-up men had the children laughing. *Oh — such funny looking creatures,* they said, *with their oversized ears and their undersized eyes and their big, huge feet and their tiny tails. Stupid creatures — the way they fall into line that way, holding on like babies to their mothers. Stupid, shuffling down Yonge Street.*

And the elephants looked out and saw the buildings and the hordes of people and they crowded up closer to each other, trunk to tail, and they turned and lumbered around the corner and were gone. And one man said to another: *My god — if one of those creatures ever broke loose! . . .*

I stood there after the elephants had gone, after the crowd had broken up and vanished back to business — and I thought: *my god, indeed. What if one of us broke loose.*

Toronto
October 1984
Interview

. . .I don't remember when this happened — but it was certainly over a year ago. I had been writing another version of this book altogether — not about the Flood — not about Noah — not about the Ark. What that book and this one did have in common was an old, blind female cat and a gin-loving farm wife who thumped out hymns on her piano. Also, a storm — except that the storm in that book was a blizzard. . . .

. . .The gin-loving farm wife was married to a man whose violent abuse was focused on everything that lived. It extended from her to the least of his animals — and, in the blizzard, he deserts them all and disappears. . . .

. . .I was just a short way along in making this tale when my friend Phyllis Webb arrived from Saltspring Island in B.C. to attend a feminist seminar at York University. WFW and I went along to hear her read.

Phyllis had brought some new work with her — poems that I had neither read nor heard before — and it was one of these that revolutionized my concept of this book. It was a poem called "Leaning."

In this poem, Webb creates the image of the whole of modern civilization crowding into the Leaning Tower of Pisa. The Leaning Tower of Pisa begins to fall in slow

219

motion. Either it will crash upon the earth — or launch us all into space. . . . The poem ends:

And you, are you still here

tilting in this stranded ark
blind and seeing in the dark.

Hearing these words — I made a sort of strangled sound — like *oomph!* It was just as if I had been struck in the solar plexus.

In that moment, the whole of *Not Wanted on the Voyage* fell into place. *All* of it.

Why?

Because, in her poem, Phyllis Webb had used the words *ark* and *blind* and *dark* — and all at once, I knew who all my people were and what their predicament was. The gin-loving farm wife was Mrs Noyes — the abusive farmer was her husband, Noah — the blizzard was the Great Flood and Mrs Noyes would not get on the Ark without her cat — the blind cat, Mottyl. . . .

Stone Orchard
January 1984
Notebook

WFW re: characters in *Not Wanted on the Voyage:* Stop walking around them and start walking inside them!

Stone Orchard
February 1984
Journal

Many late-night, early-morning voices on the telephone. Drinking worst it has been in longer than I can remember.

Sometimes I sit in the darkened kitchen, talking with whoever I can find — afraid to turn on the lights for fear that someone will see the midnight oil and spill the beans: *I see that Tiff is up very late these nights. . . .* Mostly, I sit in the wicker chair in the study — wine glass in hand and bottle on table — one light only — just enough to be sure I hit the ashtray with my ashes. This kind of drinking pushes me in and out of oblivion, from total recall to total blank — episodes of infuriating sobriety when no amount will put me to sleep. I fear the only person who isn't awakened by my insomnia is Phyllis [Webb] who is far enough away to be on the up side of midnight when it is 3:00 A.M. in Cannington [P.W. lives on Saltspring Island, B.C.] Her voice is always so calm, no matter how much panic I project, and she will not tolerate a rambling conversation — forcing direction on what we talk about — often something amusing — always attempting to lead me away from "me" towards "the multitude. . . ."

"Tell me what you're writing."

"Oh — not anything. Nothing."

(Laughter.) "Nonsense! You're writing about the Ark and Noah. Tell me where you are in the story."

"Lost at sea." (My attempt at melodrama.) "Everybody's lost at sea and me included. I hate it."

"Hate what?"

"Book writing. Noah. *Everything!*" (My essay on self-pity.)

Phyllis laughs again. The laughter is neither patronizing nor dismissive. What the laughter is about is mostly recognition. The "hatred" I have described is the common hatred every writer feels from time to time. *Here I am in this corner — driven here by this book (this poem — this essay) — and I can't get out.*

What you want to do is write your way out of it — but the writing isn't working, and you panic and, after the panic, you resort to anger. GET ME OUT OF HERE!

I also tend to think, in these moments, I will never be able to write again. The worst experience of this occurred when I was writing *Famous Last Words.* Nights, I used to go and stand in the hallway, leaning against the door jamb outside WFW's bedroom and I would say to him: *I cannot do this. I cannot write this book.* It felt as if my brain had died — and I would then say: *I'm going to go into the garden and pick another pod of peas to replace the one I've got!*

Pea-brain Findley.

Phyllis understands this. Panic. Fear of silence.

But it doesn't last. And I have to trust it also isn't going to last on this occasion. Truly, it seems perverse. Its timing is astonishing. Like impotence, it only falls upon you when you are least prepared to cope with it.

Thornton said that when a piece of work won't gel the thing to do is set it aside, and move on to something else. "There are bound to be passages in every book that you know like the back of your hand," he said. "Move on to one of these — leap in where you have most confidence. That will keep you writing — and by the time you've finished the passage where your confidence is greatest, you'll be able to cope with the passage that was thwarting you."

Above all — do not stop writing.

Stone Orchard
January 1984
Pep talk (me to me)

You are telling the story of Noah's Ark. This is a story that everyone knows. Certainly, everyone knows the basic facts: the flood — God's displeasure — Noah and his wife and sons and the sons' wives — the animals "two-by-two" — the dove — the olive branch and the rainbow.

There is absolutely no justification to retell this story unless you can tell us something new about its people and about the event. *This you can certainly do.* Mrs Noyes and Mottyl the Cat — Lucifer-Lucy — Yaweh's Circus and Travelling Road Show — Noah's magic that always fails — the animals — the concentration camp atmosphere — Noah's emergence as a dictator — the horror of Hannah's compliance with evil, etc., etc. are all valid additions and interpretations of the story.

Proceed.

Proceed simply.

Don't try to "write" — just *tell.*

You couldn't ask for a better illustration of how "simple" your presentation can be (and should be) than *Animal Farm.* Or *Alice Through the Looking Glass.*

Stop explaining. Explain *nothing* — merely reveal.

The key word is TELL.

Stone Orchard
October 1972
Notebook

[*Early on, after Mottle — the blind cat — arrived at Stone Orchard, I began to think of her as Tiresias, who was also blind — a medium and neuter. Mottle, a female, had been spayed.*] I had another flash of insight about Tiresias which came because Mottle lay at my leg last night while I was reading in bed — and I could sense her instinctive knowledge of me as a creature — as being another creature — that aspect of "animal" and "man" that is always missed. To them, we are not always overlords and "gods" whose whims and gifts they depend on. I listened to her speaking to me in that semi-magical way that cats communicate (purring), and I thought: *she accepts me as more than her feeder — her eyes — her opener of doors. I am more than her warmth and security — I am her companion in a far deeper sense — on an entirely other plane than the one I so glibly imagine or accept. I am her fellow animal.* We have a relationship that is as complex from her point of view as any I could ever have with another human being — and this thought made me see that our relationship is also, therefore, complex to me.

I look down, now, from this writing, and see her at the centre of the rug and she is brooding — and, because I have turned in my chair to see her — she hears this; one ear lifts back in my direction. This is subtle — but absolute. What I do next will govern what she does next. If I leave the room, her hearing will follow me. No matter where I go in the house, she will "follow" me that way. I am an extension of her nerve ends.

I know about the brain pan and the "thought cycle" and the whole business of degrees of confinement when it comes to animal intellect. But that is the false connection between us. It is *our* "ignorance" — not theirs — I want to explore with Tiresias.

She has a wisdom of her own that has nothing to do with thought as we know it. Nor with "instinct" as we describe it for ourselves. Whatever it is, it lies on that same plane where we are creatures together in this one place where we share our existence. As human beings, we have forgotten how to play our role in that dimension. Why?

How can it be that Mottle is so utterly *herself* — when with all my human intellect — I so often fail *to be myself at all?*

Tofino
November 1981
Journal

Most embarrassing moment of my life! Just came into the cabin from being on the beach at low tide. As usual, I was crawling around in my shorts on my hands and knees — with my bum in the air and my nose in the sand. All this to garner what I can of a cat's-eye view of the world — so I will get some part of it right when I put the cats on paper. Besides which, I have come to enjoy this new perspective because it reveals so much that I've never seen before. Not even as a child.

So, there I am, cat postured — playing this time at being Mottle — eyes shut tight and one hand groping for safety. I am talking to myself. Why not? The beach is completely deserted. . . .

Suddenly, I hear a woman's voice.

"George?. . ." (The call is hoarse and whispered.)

Then a man's voice.

"Yeah?. . ."

"Come and look at this."

I freeze.

Come and look at what?

"I think perhaps the children shouldn't be exposed to this," the woman is saying, now. "Go and stop them, George, before they get here."

Carefully, I turn my head towards the voice and, slitting my eyes, stare out between my lashes. . . . There is a person standing ten or fifteen feet away, in boots. This is the woman. George — bare, hairy feet — is just preparing to go and "stop" the children.

"Do you think he's sick?" says the woman.

"No," says George. "Don't get involved. I told you, Anita — this is a drug-runners' beach. You hear about it even in Fredericton. He's obviously high on something. Come away. . . ."

The hairy feet move off.

The boots, for a moment, hesitate.

"He looks so uncomfortable, George. His face is all covered with sand."

She must be thinking I am deaf, as well as "blind."

"It surely is a lesson, George, of what addiction does to a person. . . ."

"Yeah. That's right, Anita. Come on!" The boots turn away and follow the feet, but I can still hear the voice. Anita is really quite concerned.

"You think we should call the authorities, George?"

"Why would we do that?"

"Well — he could be *dangerous!* He could do something terrible, George, like go berserk on an overdose and kill us all!"

Their voices — and their feet — were disappearing now beyond my vantage point.

"If he took an overdose, Anita, he would be *dead,*" said George.

"So we shouldn't worry, then?" said Anita.

"No, Anita. Not to worry. Just keep walking. . . ."

As soon as they were gone, I got to my feet and ran up into the trees. What if these people really do call the authorities? What will I say?

I was just pretending to be a blind cat?

Sure.

Stone Orchard
March 1985
Article

On October 15th, 1984, thousands of copies of a novel called *Not Wanted on the Voyage* arrived at a warehouse in Markham, Ontario and almost at once they were being dispatched to bookstores from St John's to Victoria. The book had been completed the previous June and now — just four months later — here it was between covers and its journey to the reader was almost over. But the author's journey to the reader — that all-important *Author's Tour* — was yet to come. Uprooting and disorienting, tiring and fraught with alarming confrontations, touring is dreadful in the prospect. But mandatory. If you write books, it goes with the territory. Damn.

My tour, in behalf of *Not Wanted on the Voyage,* began on the 23rd of October, 1984, in the Motor City of Oshawa, Ontario. By the time it was over — six weeks later — I had travelled over seven thousand miles; stopped in twenty-three towns and cities; read in more than a dozen colleges, universities and high schools — as well as innumerable bookstores, restaurants and libraries; given over seventy interviews and visited fifty or sixty booksellers. I had also lost all sense of direction — and gained fifteen pounds.

I did not fly, back then, so the journeying was done on trains and in cars. Touring, in spite of all the people you meet, can be a lonely ordeal. But I was lucky and had a companion: William Whitehead.

One of our first stops included a visit to an Ontario high school, and one of the first words we heard after my reading from the book was: *scandalous!* And I must admit that, as a reaction, it threw me completely. Given the subject of the novel, if someone had called it blasphemous I might have paled, but I wouldn't have been surprised. *Not Wanted on the Voyage* re-tells the story of Noah's Flood. The book is often upsetting, angry-making and frightening. Noah is a sadistic tyrant — Yaweh opts for his own death and Lucifer appears as a seven-foot gent in drag. I fully realize these may not be the easiest concepts to accept — but *scandalous?* Maybe I'm just old fashioned. Scandalous, to me, still means Scarlet O'Hara dancing in her widow's weeds with Rhett Butler. Granted, Noah's wife drinks a fair amount of gin, likes to thump out Methodist hymns on her piano and teaches her sheep to sing. She is the heroine. A blind cat also plays an important role. The book can be called a myth — a fantasy — a fable. Reading from it — watching people's faces, whenever I could — was a lesson in sharing I will not soon forget. Sometimes, when laughter might have been expected, there wasn't any at all. People in the audience would scowl, turning to their neighbours and muttering: *did he say the devil wears a dress? Did he say God chooses to die?* Once or twice, I heard the scraping of chairs and the hard, hard heels of determined shoes on the floor. Doors would open — and shut: a statement was being made. On such occasions — after the reading was over — there would be such restrained applause, I would look to make sure the audience hadn't come equipped with padded cotton gloves. And revolvers.

Wonderfully funny things happened.

In Calgary, I was to read in the Public Library. The event was to start at eight o'clock in the evening. The library in question is one of the few remaining architectural gems financed by Andrew Carnegie. It sits in the middle of a beautiful park, which on this occasion was covered with a bright, sparkling fall of fresh snow. Going up the path, our shoes squeaked and the air was filled with particles of ice. This was quintessential Canada. Glorious.

Our host had cautioned us there might not be many people in the audience. The last time I had read in this very same building, there had only been ten in attendance — one man remarkably drunk. This time, I was prepared for the worst: maybe two — maybe three — but, pray God, all of them sober. In we went, through the empty building to a room set aside for lectures. There was not a soul — not one. I looked around in dismay. *Oh — this isn't where you read,* said the host. *You read upstairs. This is only where you leave your coats and smoke your last cigarettes.* So WFW and I took off our duffles and smoked our last cigarettes and then the host said: *ready?* The mood, by now, was depressed and tense. If there *was* anybody up in the reading room, perhaps it would be a firing squad.

We approached the door that would open onto the stairs. I gritted my teeth, grasped the handle of the door and pulled it towards me.

Instantly — every burglar alarm and fire alarm in the

entire city of Calgary started to scream: HE'S COME HERE TO STEAL OUR BOOKS! HE'S COME HERE TO SET OUR CITY ON FIRE! Naturally, I had to be prodded up the stairs. And — wouldn't you know it? The one and only time when a performer might have been happy to play to an empty house — the place was packed — standing room only. A hundred and fifty people. Staring.

Interviewers, in my opinion, have for too long taken a bum rap from writers on tour. Some writers say they find them officious and overbearing — graceless and ignorant. *None of the s.o.b.'s have read my book!* That is the usual complaint. This does, of course, happen. But it doesn't happen all that often — and when it does, there are ways of dealing with it. W.O. Mitchell is a past master at this sort of situation. When an interviewer hasn't read the book, Mitchell simply takes over and interviews himself. Of course, being Mitchell, he turns it into a comic triumph — and we all can't do that, but we can try.

There are devious interviewers, too — no point pretending there aren't. But these, too, come few and far between. With experience, you begin to recognize them. To begin with, they tend to be too friendly. Their questions never quite come to grips with why you are really there — or with what you are really about. Smiling, they ask you to talk about your cats and your favourite restaurants. They are much too curious about the way you dress and what you think of the local scenery. None of these questions is asked with any real interest. Ultimately, you have to bring them round to the subject at hand — namely, why you are there: the book. Their eyes shift at this. They go cold. The interview is over. Later — when you read what they have written — you discover they dislike the book — and they go to some pains to say so: publicly. But they do not — ever — tell you face to face they do not like the book. I have never been able to understand this. Wouldn't their interviews have been more interesting if their questions had challenged what they didn't like?

On the whole, touring for *Not Wanted on the Voyage* was pretty good, when it came to interviews. The book had been read and the book was what got talked about — not the weather. To be frank, I'm put off by writers whose publishers have gone to a hell of a lot of trouble and no small expense to send them across the country and to whom the people in the various media have at least given their attention — and then the writers return from their tours and bitch about the whole experience. A lot of books get published in a season — hundreds. And, of the hundreds, maybe twenty or thirty get anything like the attention they deserve. And if your book has been lucky enough to garner any part of that attention — believe me — you are very, very lucky.

The last alarm took place in a town called Sechelt, on the Sunshine Coast of British Columbia. It was here that we had the most difficult and touchy schedule to keep. In order to reach our destination of the evening — the town of Castlegar, where I was to give my last reading — we would have to arise at four A.M., catch a commuters' ferry, pick up a rented car and drive four hundred miles through the mountains. I do not drive and this was where WFW would totally take over. It was in early December — the coldest December, by the way, in local memory. All through the tour, we had been concerned at the prospect of this engagement because of the weather — and we were not alone in this concern. The drive would take eight hours and the route had its climax in a mountain pass which is often closed in the winter because of blizzards or ice storms.

Our motel in Sechelt was located on a small stretch of

road leading down to the ferry terminal and even as we got up at four A.M., the parade of commuters was already passing beyond our windows. WFW went into the bathroom — washed and shaved and had just returned to the bedroom as I was beginning my shower. The water was scalding hot and, in the cold, a great deal of steam was created. Consequently, as WFW went out through the door, a great wave of roiling steam pursued him and, almost at once, set off the smoke detector. For those of you who have never heard a smoke detector at four o'clock in the morning, I can only tell you how lucky you are. If someone should ever want — for whatever ghoulish reason — to produce a fail-safe method of bringing on a dozen heart attacks, I recommend the high-pitched ululations of a smoke detector. We thought — in the classic phrase of our time — *the Bomb has fallen.* Of the two of us, I was the last to recognize the source of the screaming sound but WFW was onto it at once. He even knew what to do to stop it. He dragged a table across the floor — stood on it and placed the tip of his extended index finger on the tiny button provided for just such moments. The only trouble is, the steam was still pouring out of the bathroom and every time WFW removed his finger from the button, the wailing started again. This, even after I had turned off the shower and closed the door. You recall the early-bird commuters, rolling past in their cars? Well, as my first constructive act in this situation, I ran from the bathroom — wet and dripping and freezing — to the window where I yanked aside the curtain and flung the windows wide. I then ran over to the door and flung that open, too, in order to create a draught that would rid the room of its steam. Well — the steam began to abate all right, but the commuters beyond the windows did not — and what they saw, as they went their merry way, was the vision of a living, shivering statue: William Whitehead,

"The Nature of Things" chief writer, standing on his table, posed stark naked in the chilling draught — with one arm extended in the direction of the ceiling as his finger, apparently, pointed at some remarkable feature embedded in the plaster.

As we climbed aboard the train at Revelstoke to commence the long journey home to Toronto, I was suddenly overcome with a sense of loss. I was tired, but as often happens when a good experience comes to an end — there was a sense of exhilaration — an extra shot of adrenalin that wouldn't let me quite relax. I sat by the window, staring out at the mountains for a very long time, unable to sleep: not wanting to sleep. So many people had been met and friends re-greeted — so many funny and touching things had happened — I found myself saying out loud: *"and now the dreaded Author's Tour is over. Damn!"*

Saltspring
October 1988
Journal

We set out after lunch today to see the Unicorn. Phyllis came with us. She had said that, to the best of her knowledge, he was still up there where I'd seen him first in the field across the road from the house we rented in 1985. She had been out driving the other week and was certain it was him.

There is a notebook somewhere with a shopping list from 1985 and down at the bottom, after listing all the other items we required, I had written: *apples for the Unicorn.*

When I first encountered him, I was standing on the upper deck of the house and looking across the valley towards the tops of the hills. In the valley there were sheep — many, many sheep and a handful of cattle.

Being evening, the cattle and sheep had started wending their way towards the ponds where they would drink before going further on to the barnyards where they would spend the night. This had become a scene I loved to watch.

All at once, a pony-sized figure appeared on the hillside. Pure white and nervous, it emerged from the darkness of the woods and stood, taking in the view.

I ran and got the glasses. Through the binoculars, clearly what I was watching was a small white horse — but its features and the shadows made it look exactly like a unicorn. Two or three days later — having spent a good deal of time persuading it to trust me — I had it eating out of my hand. It has blue eyes and milk-white hooves. It is altogether the most extraordinary likeness of a unicorn I can imagine. It even has a pale red blaze in the shape of a horn that reaches down between its eyes from under its forelock. I fed it apples every day that year until the day we left.

The following year, we went to the Atlantic House Hotel for our final visit — but last year we came back here and rented the house belonging to Angela Wood. We went several times to see the Unicorn, but Phyllis did not come with us.

Today, however, we all went up in the car and there he was. He came across the field and met us at the fence. He seemed, as he had last year, to remember me because, at once, he started agitating for the apples he knew I brought with me.

I always twist the apples until they break in half. This way, we had enough today to feed him several pieces each and he was glutted. I don't know when we will be coming back to Saltspring — but I hope that when we do, the Unicorn will be here. I cannot think of him any other way. Magical and not quite earthbound.

Looking back to see him one last time as we drove away, I watched him turn from the fence and walk towards the field. Instantly, he disappeared.

I know he just went down into the valley. But it had the magic timing of a dream.

We drove home in silence. Going to feed the unicorn is not an event you discuss.

·10·

THE
TELLING OF LIES

Stone Orchard
September 1986
Speech

It is four storeys high with white peeling clapboard walls — green roofs — shaded on one side by chestnut trees — giving way on the other side to wide green lawns — and beyond the lawns, about a mile and a half of white sand beach. . . .

My father first went to the Atlantic House Hotel in 1904 or 1905 when he was two years old — or three. When he was older, he did what the rest of the teenagers did — stealing the laundry's ironing boards and taking them down to the beach to use for surfing. Late one summer — Dad was riding the waves when his father called to him from the board walk: *Alan, come in! We have to go home! Our country is at war* . . . August, 1914.

My father loved that beach. *The wind,* he told me, *comes all the way from South America.* Nothing stood between that place and the bulging coast of Brazil. It was 1982 when I waded into the surf where Dad had played

237

as a boy, and I threw his ashes into the air, to fall back into the ocean he had loved. Years before, in the 1930s, I had ridden on my father's shoulders as he'd plunged out into the rollers — teaching me both to respect and not to fear the water.

On and off, I spent a part of my summers there for fifty years. In any given week — in any given year since 1850, Canadian guests at the Atlantic House Hotel were more than likely to outnumber the guests who were American. This was partly because of the excellent rail connections that once existed between the town of Scarborough, Maine and Montreal, Quebec. Partly, too, because one of the hotel's former owners married — back in the 1860s — someone from Ontario. Whatever the reason, Canadians tended to dominate the guest list. In doing so, we brought our peculiar wars along with us. The story goes that a guest from Montreal once said: *I'm leaving now — and I'm never coming back! There are too damned many people here from Toronto!* True. And I was one of them.

When I was a teenager, I used to nervously avoid what had been dubbed *Stonehenge* — the monumental, stone-faced gathering of matriarchs who, long ago, had claimed one corner of the lobby. I remember vividly their piercing, all-seeing eyes, their thin-lipped mouths and the furs around their necks. I was absolutely convinced they had killed the animals they wore with their very own hands — or possibly by spitting venom. The young, of course, can be over-sensitive. But I do remember once, as I passed unavoidably through their territory, hearing one of them say: "who's boy is *that*?" It was not meant kindly.
I used to listen to the night-watchman pacing the halls at regular intervals through the darkness. He always paused

outside my door in order to replace the light bulb the guest next door habitually unscrewed because it shone in through her transom. In *The Telling of Lies,* the young night-watchman is re-reading all of Henry James. After I'd written that into the book I discovered — quite by chance — that Henry and William James and their sister Alice had spent their summers, too, at the Atlantic House Hotel.

My friend Joellen Knight, whose parents owned the Atlantic House, and I used to walk down the beach into the territory of Prout's Neck — an enclave of the wealthy that boasted its own private police force, and also boasted another battery of matriarchs who would scream at us like harpies from the grand houses they called cottages. "Young man! Young woman! You cannot walk along there unless you get permission!" "May we have permission?" "No!!!" The shoreline right-of-way that ran in front of their mansions also ran along beneath the studio Winslow Homer used to occupy at the turn of the century. It was here that he painted his extraordinary seascapes, including the shipwreck scenes. Joellen knew perfectly well that no one owns the sea. So we walked through the water, laughing.

We all used to search the beach for black pebbles with a white ring that ran all the way around. Finding one of these was supposed to bring good luck. Mary Clarke, who was one of the oldest matriarchs, once presented me with such a stone, along with a gull's white feather, and a note in spidery writing that quoted from William Blake: *no bird soars too high if it flies on its own wings.* Years before, when Mary Clarke had been in her seventies, she came downstairs in her wedding dress and asked all the men to dance with her. They did.

In the dining-room, on the bulge of the porch, in the lobby, down on the beach — or anywhere I could sit unobserved — I used to stare at the sometimes baffling, always magical clientele of the Atlantic House. It made, as all such places do, a wonderful microcosm — and, thus, a wonderful place to make up stories. On the beach, for instance, watching the people arriving every morning to initiate the sprouting of a garden of beach umbrellas, I used to think it would make a splendid setting for a murder — a killing that would take place, undetected in the midst of all that happy, noisy activity. A body found at the end of a day in a place where — all day long — a throng of people had played. . . .

As a tribute to the generations who made the Atlantic House such a wondrous place — as an "exercise" in story-telling — as a look at some of the tensions between my country and America — I ultimately wrote *The Telling of Lies* and set it at the barely fictional Aurora Sands Hotel. The milieu was a gift. I only had to close my eyes and I was there.

The Atlantic House Hotel is now a thing of the past. They have torn it down and put up condominiums for millionaires. Consequently, I will never see that bit of the Atlantic shore again. But as long as I live, so will my memories of sand and sea and a white clapboard haven.

One of the keenest images — never to be forgotten — comes from the last summer spent there by our former Governor-General Jules Leger. On an August afternoon, the beach was hit by a sudden and typically violent thunderstorm. Inside the hotel, all the lights went out. The sky was green. The wind — and the waves it caused — were quite alarming. Everyone remembered the hurricanes of '54 and '38. When I glanced out the window, I

240

saw a tall, gaunt figure standing on the lawn, his sand-coloured raincoat whipping around his legs and one arm dangling free — the arm that had been paralysed by a stroke. It was Jules Leger.

For once, he was not surrounded by the small children who seemed to instantly collect wherever he went. He stood alone, facing the sea and drinking in the wind — defying all the worst the elements had to offer. He went down onto the sand and, choosing his place with some deliberation, he stood there amidst the waves until the storm was over. So far as I am concerned — he is standing there still; just as is the Atlantic House Hotel — for those of us who loved it.

Scarborough, Maine
August 1983
Notebook

Scene: overheard on the Bulge (the hotel's open porch that "bulged" out onto the lawns in the direction of the sea):

He is more than half blind, pouty lower lip, white hair, balding — all the hair there is brushed back — caved-in chest — uses magnifying glass to read.

She is emaciated, hatchet-faced — horn rims — wearing a patchwork-design pink, green and yellow sweater — carries a dog. Man, woman and dog are strangers to me.

Both the players have identical baritone voices.

He: (reading sports page) Did you know there are 280 officially approved golf balls?

She: (reading international news section) Mmm. (Pause) If they listed all the African nations — I wouldn't know half of them.

He: I like the coloured ones best.

She: (Pause) What? They're all coloured. Or might as well be.

He: Especially the orange and green ones.

241

She: What?

He: Well — then you don't have to bend down to see who's who.

She: What *are* you talking about?

He: Balls.

The End.

The Hallwards. Bernard — over six feet, erect posture, grey suit (inevitable) — white, white hair and moustache. Tiny little teeth when he smiles. Hands always posed together, touching at fingertips.

Alice — very small — deaf. Blind, too; wears extraordinarily thick glasses. Has a cane. Lifelong limp. (Accident? Birth?) Head sinks back into shoulders — she stares up like a child. Back of head remarkably childlike. Dear, dear, endearing — maddening — old people.

Edna — their companion — animated, graceful, patient. Suspect she wears old-fashioned corset.

The scene: the Hallwards, in their nineties, and shouting deafly at each other and at Edna. Mrs H., when Bernard has disappeared: "Where *is* he? Where? I ask you?" "He's gone for a walk, Alice." "A *walk!* A WALK! A walk? But he mustn't go for a walk. He mustn't. We must find him." "Now, now, my dear — why must we find him? He's perfectly all right, I assure you." "No. No. He mustn't go walking, Edna. He *mustn't*." "Why?" "Because he has a *heart.* Just like everybody else!"

The Hallward table in the dining-room had to be relatively easy to reach. This was so Bernard and Edna could aim Alice at the door when she was finished eating, give her a

242

push and more or less trust she wouldn't walk into the rest of us on her way. Once given her push — Alice would move like a bullet. Blind as a bat. And waving her stick. You couldn't make Alice up, if you tried!

Scarborough, Maine
August 1983
Notebook

Gary Merrill, the actor, occasionally walks along the beach from his house to visit at the hotel. He often wears a tweed skirt — his response to some of the more trivial aspects of feminism — and he brings, besides his lady friend, a miraculous picnic basket from which an apparently endless supply of martinis and canapes is produced for all.

When Merrill wore his skirt, by the way, he did so without a trace of female exaggeration. He was decidedly *not* in drag. It was a brown tweed skirt that covered his knees. He wore it with shoes and socks — a shirt, and very often, a tie.

Once, in the days before the skirt had made its first appearance for our benefit — he asked the rather grand — but charming — Mrs R—— to accompany him to dinner at Portland's swankiest restaurant. When he arrived to collect her — he was wearing the skirt. He stood in the lobby waiting while Mrs R—— was making her way from her room. Everyone present waited with bated breath. At last Mrs R—— came down and stood aghast.

"Is it a kilt?" she asked.

"No," said Merrill. "Not a kilt. A skirt."

"But we can't *both* wear a skirt!" said Mrs R——.

"Why not?" said Merrill. "Yours is black and mine is brown."

They went as they were.

This made history.

Scarborough, Maine
July 1977
Journal
Dining-room: three old women, all eighty or older. Two
are seated, one like a ramrod,
the other wide-eyed and child-
like, at supper. The third, who is large and birdlike in a
shapeless dress, stops beside them. All speak with exag-
gerated animation. They hold hands and touch one
another excessively as if for reassurance.

"I have always been your most devoted friend," says
the one who has just arrived.

"Yes. Yes. I understand. I feel the same way," says
Ramrod.

"What has she said, dear?" Wide-eyed asks.

"She says that she feels the same way," says Ramrod,
shouting.

"What way?"

"That we are devoted, dear."

"Oh, yes, I am devoted, too."

Patting of hands and forearms. The standing lady bowing so she can hear and be heard.

"I saw that you had been expected," Ramrod says to
her.

"But what route did you come by?" All in precise and
beautiful English . . . very few adjectives used. Just the
enquiries and the answers — the direct sentiments of
age. Finally:

"Goodbye. . . ."

"Goodbye. . . ."

". . .Goodbye."

Pause. The standing lady leaves.

"That was nice of her," says Wide-eyed.

"Yes."

"To stop that way and say hello. . . ."

"Yes. It was good of her, dear," says Ramrod.

". . .And goodbye. . . ."

"Goodbye. Yes. . . ."
They eat.

Scarborough, Maine
August 1983
Journal

Two Dianas. *Diana Marler's dream* (Diana and John Marler — two of the most delightful people at the the Atlantic House — he, a distinguished Montreal lawyer who, during World War II, had fallen in love with, and subsequently married, a beautiful English girl).

The dream: John had become a world-famous artist — and when Diana went to his studio to see for herself how this unlikely status had been achieved, he unveiled his greatest work. It was *The Last Supper* — à la Leonardo da Vinci — except that it was painted from the other side of the table, with everyone's back view . . . and their hands all covered with hair.

Diana: But John . . . why?
John: Well . . . I can't do faces.

Scarborough, Maine
August 1983
Journal

Diana Walls (younger daughter of another Montreal family, who, as she began her teenage years, was obviously on the way to becoming a great beauty. I watched the Walls getting ready to leave for home.)

The last thing Diana Walls did at the sea was to write in the sand with a feather.

Scarborough, Maine
August 1983
Journal

On the beach at Atlantic House, Maine — 10:30 A.M. Foggy and clouded over — but warm, with a calm sea.

Loons — about six or eight pair — out in front of us diving in unison, pair by pair. Cormorants flying low over the water and a few sandpipers "chipping" and running along the sand at the edge (the "movable edge"). Large herring gulls and terns flying lazily overhead, making for the rocks just being exposed by a receding tide. Earlier, at breakfast-time, there were lobster boats — though none are in evidence now. The foghorn at Cape Elizabeth is sounding and one very determined man is riding out to sea on a sail-board, bright orange and white — the man in yellow trunks and what appear to be tall, black socks — though these are probably some kind of foot-gear that allows him to keep a purchase on the surface of the board. He has gone out with alarming speed in the direction of Ram Island, even though there does not seem to be much wind. The water is typically ice-green in close to shore and a kind of slate colour further out.

WFW is sitting beside me, on my left, wrapped in a poncho, happily reading a murder mystery by Anthony Boucher and as I glance over, I can see the words *Murder coming!* written on the back in huge red letters.

A child is drifting out to sea in a large, round rubber raft — entirely careless of the shore. Toby's catamaran is drawn up, high on the sand, with its jib still raised. Four blue chairs and a yellow-and-white umbrella wait for their people to arrive on our left. A small, beige dog has just inspected us and moved on down the beach. A whining, sour-faced woman and a tall, paunchy man with white hair and trousers have gone past one way — complaining to each other of the fog. Now, they turn back, wearing incongruous and rather sinister dark glasses. The woman, who wears a pink sweater and a blue skirt that just manages nicely to clash with the blue of her husband's shirt, gazes towards me with her turtle-mouth poised upon a word and is silenced by Sebastian, who sits on the sand at my side. The turtle mouth snaps shut. The couple passes on — and she begins to speak again — *that*

man . . . *had a* Teddy bear . . . *what are we* . . . coming
to? . . .

Well — I don't know what we're coming to, madam —
but I do know this: your predecessors at this hotel were a
lot more fun than you! Janet (Baldwin) dancing on the
sand — Fred Hudon and his wife building driftwood bat-
tlements against the sea — the hordes of charming Hydes
who could fill half the dining-room — Portia Hallmeyer
and her steamer trunk of booze — Tatty Leveritch, beautiful as an actress, saying: *you always build your castles in
the sand just where I built mine.* . . .

Maine gear includes washed blue colours and lots of
tan and white and sand colours — a few greens (the
shade of grass cut an hour ago) and blue canvas shoes.
White hats — shorts — polo shirts mostly — and the children in excessively bright orange or red or pink bathing
suits, probably chosen so parents can see them at any distance.

A green Winslow Homer fishing dory has just come in
close to shore and moved back out to sea, making for Seal
Rock. Two people, one in a yellow slicker and the other in
an orange life jacket. One wears a sou'wester hat. Timeless and eerie.

In the receding tide, Old Proprieter (the rock at the
mouth of the bay) is just beginning to show and consequently, white froth out by the bell-buoy.

A small aircraft, invisible, passes overhead. Three children — one of them enormously fat — run past, trailed
by two others who feign indifference at having been left
behind and another who is panic-stricken — and calls out
the tide's coming in! The tide's coming in! — much as one
would cry *the British are coming!* Not a very bright child,
since the tide is now racing seaward. . . .

Barbara Walls is coming along the sand in a royal blue
bathing suit. She also wears a bright green robe. She

stops to speak with Mary Jane Schmidt — who says something funny. Barbara throws her head back and laughs. A photograph of joy. She reaches her place and waves to us and sinks in the warm sand. There is a moment of universal contentment. Then . . . two men — two women — entering the scene as if on cue.

I am truly sick of couples who look like this: the men in tailored blue jeans — pale, carefully tapered shirts — haircuts that cover the tops of their ears but are razor-edged at the neck — eyes that look haunted by some missed opportunity to take advantage of fate, while their fingers clutch belt-loops that contain either a Pierre Cardin tie or a thick leather belt with a five-hundred-dollar silver buckle. These men are always taller than they seem, because they have developed what appears to be an increasingly modish "stoop" that speaks of ease and carelessness they have never known. Their mouths could take out a patent on the shape of what can only be described as "stoic petulance." They are silent, mostly; watching.

Their wives — or what they prefer to call their "ladies" (*this is my lady* or *this is Dwight's lady* or *she used to be Arnold's lady*) are thus: the eyes displayed in fish-bowl glasses — usually tinted. These glasses have been designed by Cardin or Balmain or by Mister Halston. The glasses have nothing to do with seeing — but only with showing. They denote such qualities as "brightness" (*she's a very bright lady. . . .*) — "shrewdness" (*quite the business-lady. . . .*) and infantile "I-wouldn't-hurt-a-fly" naïveté. The eyes themselves are *always* blue and have never known laughter. (They are too "bright" to *really* think anything is funny — consequently all the laughter is in the mouth and nose.) The mouths are made up to look un-made-up. They glisten faintly — and have "charming" little dimples at their corners — probably etched in with eye-liner. These women sit and walk and stand in parody of men (who also sit and walk and stand in parody of "men") and their hair is inevitably "looped" in some shiny way to emphasize the length and youth of their necks. Chins are carried "forward." Clothes are loose and "unthreatening" — worn with silver chains.

The men have lowered, quiet voices and the women speak entirely from the throat. They never truly look at one another — though they stare very boldly at others — casting remarks *sotto voce* for one another's benefit, without so much as inclining in one another's direction. They are pathologically polite, given an introduction — and pathologically aloof five minutes later. None of them has a last name — and the "name-game" is now to drop first names and leave people guessing. . . . *(Henry* is a favourite, these days — and *Nancy,* of course, stops people dead in their tracks.) Otherwise, the names all have to do with private inner circles, where fear can be spread like sauce over a new suit when someone says *Tony told me all about it at dinner last Thursday* . . . or *Sonya says it's all a carefully manufactured lie* . . . Tony and Sonya, of course, can be anyone — but not if one of the Tonys — not if one of the Sonyas — has power. The name game is insane — and I'll be glad when people go back to saying things like: *I don't think so* . . . and *not in my opinion.*

Anyway, I'm sick of them. They proliferate through hand-shakes, I suspect — and nodding acquaintance with a few magazines.

We left home last Saturday (30th) at about 8:30 A.M. Tired and over-anxious to put the year behind us. I'm still looking for a new publisher — WFW has been working on deadly projects and we can't quite make out the future, though parts of it can be guessed at and have positive aspects. The main thing is the tiredness — the "endlessness" of things that are now, in fact, mostly over.

We drove via Fort Erie to the New York Thruway and south to Naples, where we stayed with Stan and Nancy [Colbert] overnight. The new house is *splendid* — with a wonderful view of a lake and the highlands beyond. Secluded without being cut off — and charmingly set amongst trees and meadows. They gave us a great supper of Cornish hen and vegetables, plus a pie made by a local woman who must know magic! We had good talks and a superb rest.

Onward the next morning — to New Hartford, an adjunct of Utica, N.Y., where we had lunch with Joellen at St Margaret's House — a Jacobean mansion set in a series of formal gardens and quite lovely. [Joellen Knight, daughter of the former owner of the Atlantic House, had joined an Episcopalian order.] Jelly had been given permission to eat with us alone and had set up a table in the library — where the window-sills were set with African violets all in bloom, and where the light was exquisite — indirect and warm and reflecting sunshine. We ate beautiful vegetables and sliced ham (we were wayward!) with raisin sauce and then ice-cream with local raspberries afterward, tea and coffee and chocolate-chip cookies. It was truly lovely and we laughed a lot and enjoyed ourselves thoroughly. Afterwards, we walked in the various gardens — while a "civilian" lady paced back and forth in one prospect, reading the Bible aloud — and, in another prospect, the chaplain walked amongst flowers. We sat, at one point, in a rose garden — Jelly and WFW on the grass, me on a bench — and Jelly told us about how her mother had died (it was "peaceful" and she was happy.) Jelly said Frances had been partially immobilized and forced to lie quiet — and that she had still been memorizing poetry until the last week. She would remember something — a verse or a line — and ask to have the rest read to her until she had it committed to memory. Joellen was given leave to go and be with her, but had left, thinking Frances was improving — when she got word of the death and went back.

Jelly then talked to us — in a rush that was marvellously co-ordinated and connected in that crazy way that good narrative has of maintaining the theme while seemingly going off in all directions. The "theme" was *reconciliation* — and it ran through all kinds of stories about her family . . . and finally, into a dream she'd had:

She saw "all these strings and ropes" in the air and people tugging at them, trying to climb up. Above, with the ropes and strings attached to it, was "the seat of the mighty" — a great, floating empty chair. And all these mad, crazed people trying to clamber up to sit there. Then, separately "a kind of love-seat" and lying in it — "waiting" — the Lamb of God — peaceful and utterly contented — with this "wonderful expression on its face — of love." And the empty place beside it — vacant for anyone who chose to be there. She was calmed by this dream and made very happy by it.

Scarborough, Maine
August 1982
Journal

They have hung Dorothy Warren's photographs of the Atlantic House in the dining-room. At last, we can see them all — or, at least, a good many of them — together. The images are stark, for the most part — declarative — simple: *here is the sea — the sand — the old hotel. Here are its people.*

Some of the pictures are misted — fading off to distance — timeless. There is one of Mary Clarke, aged seventy, perhaps, with her back — as always — to the camera. She faces the sea, her arms like the arms of a schoolgirl, flat against her sides. She wears a cotton dress, a ribboned hat and square, black shoes. Straight as an arrow, she stands beside the water, gazing out across its surface. No emotion. No regret. No longing for another time. Simply: *me and the sea, apparelled as you find us — less than formal, more than casual; lifelong, nodding acquaintances, pausing this afternoon to acknowledge one another's presence....*

In all the photographs, Dorothy maintains a discreet distance between herself and the subject. Her presence is non-obtrusive. None of the photographs is posed. Yet all the images have character.

There is one of "The Colonel and His Wife." Typically, they are seated on the lip of the dunes above the beach. There is evening light. They sit beneath their umbrella, looking off towards Prout's Neck. Halfway House can be seen beyond them, dark and mysterious against the sky. The Colonel and his wife are sitting ramrod straight. Were they, as some suspected, held in place by drink? Like Winston Churchill before them, was it sherry and brandy that kept them balanced upright through the day and knocked them flat at night?

Another picture shows the *Stonehenge* circle of dowagers — not in their evening mode of furs and stoles — but in their morning mode of cotton and white shoes. Mrs Clarke — Mrs Wells — Mrs Warren — Mrs Little — Alice Riley — Polly Clark, etc., etc. Each one the doyenne of her separate world — a chair's worth of power — but each one wielding it with all the assurance of an empress. Remarkable women of another age....

Dorothy shows all this without a trace of comment. *Here,* she says. *See this — and make of it what you will.*

...with Dorothy down the beach. She carries, as always, a camera. She wears blue shorts, a polo shirt and canvas tennis shoes. Sometimes, a hat — more often, not. Now in her seventies, she has the figure of a woman in her forties and the energy of someone in her thirties. Not that Dorothy is about to run the beach! But she stands erect and strides along with unflagging pace and, when she pauses to investigate a shell or stone, she bends straight over from the waist as if she was in gym class. Truly extraordinary. And all this with a heart condition.

"I won't go in myself," she says, when I stop to swim. "But I'll watch you from here."

Dorothy sits on a piece of driftwood.

She then instructs me that, before I dunk myself, I should scoop up water and splash it over my diaphragm.

"That way, the shock of the cold won't be so great when you put yourself under. . . ."

No one has ever told me this before. I try it, and it works.

When I have swum, we sit for a while in the sun, Dorothy up on her log and me on the sand beside her. She tells me of her continued enthusiasm for Ruth Draper and how, having now published Draper's letters, she is exploring the possibility of another book — this one about Ruth's love affair with Lauro de Bosis, the Italian poet and patriot.

The subject is fascinating — bearing, as it does, all the ingredients of high drama — the actress and the poet — the political naïf and the activist — the older woman and the young, charming womanizer. And then Lauro's flight over Rome — October 1931 — the rain of his falling pamphlets — *Bread for the starving of Rome!* — Lauro's defiance of Mussolini's air force and of how he disappears into the sea. Icarus. Wonderful story. Wonderful storytelling.

Another actress — this one living — played a part two or three years ago in my acquaintance with Dorothy Warren.

Mildred Dunnock has been a guest at the Atlantic

253

House on and off for many years. Unfortunately for me, she has always been here at times when I was not. Consequently, I had never met her. I had spoken of her to Dorothy, who was aware of how much I wanted to meet Miss Dunnock. One day — Mildred Dunnock and her husband turned up at the Atlantic House to have lunch with friends. WFW and I always have lunch on the beach — so we missed her arrival. I, however, came up around two o'clock to collect something from the room and while I was there, the telephone rang.

Timothy? It was Dorothy Warren.

Yes, Dorothy?

Get down here at once! I'm phoning from the lobby. Janet Baldwin has Mildred Dunnock trapped in the driveway and won't let her pass until you arrive!

I wish I had a tape recording of that. And a film of what went through my mind as I raced down the stairs — three flights.

Janet Baldwin has Mildred Dunnock trapped in the driveway. . . .

I pictured Mildred Dunnock backed up against a pillar, with Janet holding a shotgun.

Of course, when I arrived, totally out of breath and utterly disarrayed — I discovered Mildred Dunnock sitting in her motorcar, calmly chatting with Janet Baldwin, who stood — charming and weaponless — to one side. They were laughing.

In the long run, Miss Dunnock — who was waiting for her husband — sat with me on the steps of the front porch and we talked for half an hour. It was, for me, worth every second. Now, I wonder. With Dorothy Warren and Janet Baldwin working as a team . . . today, Mildred Dunnock — tomorrow, the world!

. . .this morning, Dorothy came by our table in the dining-room. She had been going through some of her papers up in her room and had found something she thought I might "enjoy as a souvenir of another time."

After America had been swept into the war in 1941, Dorothy had joined the army. She had been put in charge, at one point, of transporting three hundred WACs from New York City to London. The journey across the Atlantic was made on board the *Queen Mary*, through waters infested with German U-boats. *Weren't you afraid?* I asked. *Of course not*, said Dorothy. *I had more trouble keeping the men on that ship away from my WACs than I had with any U-boat.*

And so, this morning, after I had opened the package she had left beside my plate, I was not surprised — though I was delighted — to discover its contents. My "souvenir" was a small blue booklet entitled HOW TO ABANDON SHIP.

In it, the ground rules are laid out for officers concerning their duties in the event of disaster at sea.

I looked across the dining-room at Dorothy. She was serenely munching toast and gazing at a book. The thought of sinking ships was impossible to countenance. I can well imagine her thinking, as she came upon the booklet amongst her papers: *well — I certainly won't need that any more.*

As, indeed, she won't.

If anyone is here to stay, it is Dorothy Warren.

Stone Orchard
September 1982
Journal

. . .it has occurred to me with sudden clarity that Dorothy Warren is the very model of the woman who solves the mystery [in *The Telling of Lies*]. But do I dare tell her this? What if she says *no?* Then I wouldn't have my leading character. . . .

She said yes — with certain conditions. Vanessa van Horne is not, of course, a portrait of Dorothy Warren — for that would not be fiction. But I could not have written her if I had not known Dorothy Warren first.

So now I have put the rest of father's ashes in the sea and we have brought home a photograph which shows me doing this with the ashes making a kind of "rainbow" above where I am standing in the surf. It was a beautiful day, with an off-shore breeze and the sun very bright and the tide receding. Consequently, it was possible for me to walk a long way into the water and to have the confidence Father would be carried out to sea, not back to shore.

In a way I can't quite decipher yet, I'm glad that Mom wasn't there. Not because anything went wrong and not because I think she could not have coped, but only because — I guess — I had wanted something I could do for Dad by myself. And this was it. WFW stayed on the shore taking photos, but I was not aware of this. Today, he showed them to me and I'm pleased he took them. The image of the ashes in the air is beautiful and not the least bit sad. Triumphant. Father loved such things: the sense of flight, the sky, the water, the sand. I said to him: *go with all our love* — meaning Mother's and Michael's and Margie's and mine — and that was all. Nothing more. The sea-birds said the rest.

Poor Margie would be so distraught if she knew what I had done. She thinks that all of him has gone into the family vault! But there's been a part of him at Stone Orchard since the spring and, now — at last — a part of him in the sea. Dad wanted that. Margie didn't. *It's improper to scatter people far and wide,* she says. He was the last of her brothers and she is now the last of her immediate family. The long arm is broken.

More than twenty years before I was born — as long

ago as 1904 — they all stood there on that beach and, barefoot on that sand, they faced the sea: Goggy and Grandfather, Margie and Tif and Stuart — one of them holding Father, who was just a baby then of two or three. And they looked out over the ocean, pointing at the horizon — watching the ships out there and thinking of South America and Europe — thinking, I am certain, of the century before them — none of them knowing it would destroy their way of life and everything they hoped for. Stuart would die on a kitchen table, the doctors operating there to remove a tumour in his brain; Tif, Margie's twin, would be destroyed in a war they had not even dreamed of, then, and sent home, broken, to die; Grandfather Findley would be felled by cancer in 1921, leaving Goggy a widow for more than thirty years and Margie to struggle against the loss of all their money and her independence. She has borne all this grief in a frozen silence, though she would not be silent now if she knew what I had done with her brother's ashes. And, I guess, I cannot blame her for that. While I'm certain Margie would not articulate her grief this way, there must be a desperate need to gather whatever remains — however slight it might seem — into a package or a box: an entity with edges she can hold: a gathering of what she was born with to carry to the grave. Still — it is done, and I have been obedient to Father's own wishes.

No one came by when I was doing it — thank heavens. I can all too well imagine someone looking at Father's ashes and the gulls in the air above me: *what's Tiff up to now?* they might have said to WFW. *Is he trying to feed those birds? . . .*

One of the last times I saw Dad at Sunnybrook, he told me he'd been "walking on the beach" just before I arrived. Only in his mind, of course. They kept him so

257

heavily sedated at the end, I think he was living most of the time in a kind of dream-state — pleasant, I suspect. He would often say: *I've just been talking to so-and-so* and this could mean anyone — his father or some friend. Nevertheless, he always knew who was there in the flesh and he never faltered over names. He seemed not to be afraid. His dying had taken so long, I guess, that he wanted whatever happens at the end to be done with and over. He had always been so admiring of Uncle Tif and of their father and the way both men had died. *They did it well,* he would say — and I'm sure he wanted to *do it well* for their sake as much as for his own. My father accomplished that, and I am proud of him for it. . . .

All this puts me in mind of the image of my parents as they were when I saw them last together, in the garden at Stone Orchard. It was just two years ago, in the spring of 1980.

At some point, I went out and found Mom and Dad in the garden. They were seated on a wooden bench surrounded by peonies, delphiniums and cats and there was a split-rail fence behind them. The picture is very clear to me and I even know that Mom was wearing something blue — though, with Mother, that would not be hard to guess.

"We've been trying to remember something," one of them said. "A poem," said the other.

"Oh?" I said. "What?"

"It's Euripedes," said Mother. "A fragment," said Father. *"Earth the most great and heaven on high."*

"When we first were married, we used to say it together in the dark," said Mother — and then to Father: "do you want to try it now, dear?"

They began in perfect unison:

Earth the most great and heaven on high,

Father is he to man and god;
And she, who taketh to her sod
The cloud flung rivers of the sky,
And beareth offspring, men and grass
And beasts in all their kinds, indeed
Mother of all. . .

At this point they faltered.

"I'm sorry," said Mother, "I've forgotten."

"And every seed," said Father.

"And every seed?"

"And every seed."

Before they began to speak again, Father turned away and looked into the field behind the garden. He and Mother linked arms, as if to be sure they got the rhythm of the words right. Mother looked at her feet and closed her eyes. "*And every seed,*" they said, in unison again,

Earth-gendered back to earth shall pass,
And back to heaven the seeds of sky;
Seeing all things into all may range
And, sundering, show new shapes of change,
But never that which is shall die.

Father had written this fragment down for me many years before that afternoon and I had used the last line as the epigraph for *The Wars* — but I had never heard them speak it this way before, together. Now that Father is dead and his ashes are scattered, it gains in poignancy, especially the thought that *all things into all may range.*

· I I ·

INSIDE MEMORY

Toronto
January 1982
Article

Summer: There is no grim reaper here — only the gardeners sweating over their mowers and, time to time, the sound of shears amongst the hedges. Far away, beyond the palings leaning hard against the shaded walk that runs up Yonge Street, you can hear the singing subway cars heading, like Orpheus, underground. Someone is seated, taking advantage of the cool beneath the trees, on a low retaining wall down in the sunken garden, wondering where they are — lost, but not afraid of being lost. Merely bemused. Surely this is a park — for so it seems. Except that over on the hillside a funeral is taking place, which looks incongruous. So many birds are singing. Two or three people whisper by on bikes, skirts flying, trousers flapping. All the dark riders from the limousines — even the limousines themselves — turn their backs and look away. *In the midst of life we are in death.* . . . Indeed. Except that here, the words seem wrong: reversed. Surely what is meant is: *in the midst of death we are in life.* There is even laughter here — or what can pass for laughter on a summer afternoon: squirrels scolding the intruders who have come to stand beneath their trees, singing hymns — disturbing the peace.

My brother learned to drive in this place. This was in 1949 or '50. He owned, as nearly everyone seemed to own back then, a small grey Austin with inexplicable gears. *British.* And very demanding. Not that the hand-book didn't explain the gears; not that a person couldn't comprehend the explanation. It was the precision, the *exactness* that was inexplicable. Nothing the book explained was right unless you performed the ritual with unerring niceness. Then the car gave a kind of *well, at last you've got it* sigh and whirred away up the hill towards the Massey Mausoleum, not — being British — aware of the consequences of smashing something built by a Massey. And, of course, when it came to the brakes there was that same, damned niceness neither my brother's feet — nor mine — could manage. Once, however, the machine had been tamed we spent our summer evenings taking advantage of this city of the dead — Mount Pleasant Cemetery — with its microstreets and avenues, its minibridges and its squirrel pedestrians, while my brother perfected to a hair's breadth the car's neurotic desire to be driven by the perfect driver. Then — oh fatal moment (in a cemetery, no less) — when my brother turned to me and said: *it's your turn now.*

You will note the vines that have overgrown the Massey Mausoleum. They hide a mass of scars. All mine. I was learning how to reverse. To a niceness.

I have never driven since.

Autumn: When the leaves come down you think of death. It's unavoidable. There was a time of crisis in my life (not important what it was) when I used to go and walk the cemetery end to end from west to east and north to south. I would enter from the Yonge Street gate and visit all the graves I knew. Sometimes I'd stand and stare at them — windblown, caught in the tails of smoke from leaf fires still legal then — and try to conjure up the people underneath. Not just the people, but the sense of lying there, of being there: *someone.* Someone remembered: not forgotten. Someone vibrant, trembling in the earth — crying out *me!* through a stone mouth. *Cubitt Sparkhall.* Who can he have been, with such a marvellous name? And all those Victorian ladies: the Emmelines, the Adelaides, all the Isabellas and Elizas lying beside their husbands — folded hands and braided hair. And the babies. And the children. The plague deaths of 1918. Hundreds — *hundreds* lying down together. Life is over. Life is gone — that hadn't even been begun. And nothing but the earth to see through; hear through; feel through; reach through up towards the falling leaves. And the weight of my feet. And they not knowing who I am.

I walk away towards the tunnel, down past Dominion Coal and the old board fence erected there just to force the curiosity of children, and I pass beneath — or under (which is right?) — the mumbling avenue, emerging on the other side of Mount Pleasant Road amongst the graves where my old friend Zuleika, the aloof white cat, used to try to catch whatever mice there are in grave-yards, and I come upon the grave of some old enemy there and I stop. And something shrivels near my shoulders. Pride? And I think of all my hatred, buried with him there. In such a little space. Beneath a stone so small it barely tells his name. And I think: there's a lesson there — and you'd better learn it. Fast.

The whole place is made of echoes. Not a single sound that does not make you turn and wonder where it's coming from. And all the family stories here. The man with three wives . . . each wife loved more modestly, less earnestly: *dearly beloved wife . . . loved wife . . . wife of. . . .* And him down last of all: falling like a clanging lid on all their lives.

And the gardeners come and go, like soldiers in their trucks, with their rakes like weapons, leaving behind their fires. So I turn away from them and go back the way I came, passing the Lukes' Memorial — the tablet of which makes so much effort to reassure the living that death is nothing to fear: *Emmeline — in the full enjoyment of her senses . . . Marie-Louise — without pain of body. . . .* And the image is made so strong of two very proper women — sitting up to die. And, finally, the crisis breaks in me (whatever it was) and I start to laugh. Not rudely — but with pleasure. Which of her senses, I wondered, was Emmeline enjoying to the full at the moment of her death?

And which would I? If I could.

Winter: This year's oak leaves never seem to fall till next year's spring. They hold with such assurance nothing can knock them down. I love all trees in winter — seen against the snow. But the oak trees are best. And something called a small-leaved lime. *Tilia cordata mill.* There's an avenue of these that makes a fine display in winter: stark as stones. And there's a stone marked *Tree.* I guess of all the places in the cemetery, this is my favourite place: standing at one end, looking along towards the other. I don't know why this is. I mean, I don't know why I love it so. Maybe it has to do with the sense of being amongst the succession of things. But I could stand there for hours. I always hate to turn away from them. Walking under them is being a procession of one. That's why I never look back. Maybe they'll follow me.

My father died this year. A winter death. Which meant we went and did it all in overcoats and scarves — with our breath in the air around him. His people — mine — are buried in the Mausoleum. There's an iron fence and FINDLEY is written, stark as I've ever seen it; very plain — the best reminder: *this is you: that's all.* And in behind the iron fence — an arm's length, just — are my father's parents and his brother and his son. Locked behind marble facings, each with a name and dates. This is not where he will be. There's only room for another, and his sister will be buried there. I reach in past the iron rails and touch my father's father's name. *Thomas.* And go.

WHITE. There's a stone in the snow marked WHITE. And I know that when summer comes, I will find a stone marked GREEN.

Spring: Has Mister Peplow's cross merely fallen over? Or did he topple it, climbing out in response to some trumpet call — some *tuba mirum* — missed by the rest of us? Have we missed the Reckoning? That — it strikes me — would be most interesting.

No. There is no grim reaper here. Only the gardeners sweating over their mowers and, time to time, the sound of shears amongst the hedges. In the Mount Pleasant handbook of Rules and Regulations for visitors, it states that: *controversies with workmen or others on the grounds are to be avoided.* Well, I have tried very hard to imagine what sort of controversy might arise between myself and the man who pushes the mower or the woman who wields the shears, and I have failed. Unless it might be that I should find her trying to trim away the cosmetic vines that hide my sins against the Masseys. But, no. She wouldn't dare.

The only voice I have ever heard in that place that is given to rising is the voice of the peacock, shrieking in its cage behind the Jackman plot. But the shrieks are rare and the sound of them is the only sound remotely reminiscent of a soul in torment. Not a bad record for a city of stones that contains 150,000 dead: a city that is meant by its very definition to be — for some, at least — the gates to an everlasting hell of fire and brimstone. (This, after all, is Toronto.) On the other hand, remember the toppled cross of Mister Peplow. It could be the peacock who roused him from his rest.

If this is cold comfort, I offer the following to those who fear Peplow has beaten us all to the final roll-call. It concerns my aunt: a woman of no mean vitality. She has sworn to us all she will breathe her last while playing a game of bridge. And how can we doubt that a woman of such determination will fail to hear the Last Trump?

Stone Orchard
December 1975
Article

Thornton Wilder had a twin brother — stillborn. This silent figure hovers over his work like a blind, mute ghost. His other half was always with him. You sensed this when he himself fell silent. Someone else was there. There were two faces, too. One was amused and gentle — often mischievous — and the other was harder — stronger — blazing with pain, intelligence and discipline. This could seem, at times, an angry face — and I think, perhaps, in some ways it was. But his anger was rarely directed outwards. I think it mostly affected him, silently, inside: at the desk, perhaps — in his bed, at night — or sitting alone at the kitchen table.

Stone Orchard
December 1989

Caroline and Frank were my mother's aunt and uncle. Far and wide they were seen as *the two most beautiful people in the world.* This was everyone's opinion and it continued right to the end of their lives.

There was something almost mystical about the aura of romance that surrounded them. It extended from their persons to their clothing to the way they entered a room. When Frank and Carrie came to visit, they brought their whole journey with them through the door: the old hotels, the restaurants, the roaring trains and all. Even the idea of proximity was tantalizing: *Frank and Carrie are coming up the walk! They're standing on the porch! They're ringing the bell! They're here!*

The family name was Bull. There had been five brothers: Frank and Clarence, Claude and Harry. The fifth was my grandfather, Fred. They were all involved, one way or another, in the world of music and pianos. Fred started his business life as a salesman for Nordheimer's, travelling by train through Southern Ontario. In the long run, he bought the Williams Piano factory in Oshawa and settled down in that town to raise a family with his wife, Maude Fagan, who became — in her senior years — a guiding light for me. My mother was the third and last of their children.

Uncle Frank went to work with my grandfather at the factory. At first, he went out on the train route and sold pianos the way my grandfather had. But Frank was also an inventor *manqué* and, in the long run, that is what he did. He invented things — never an easy profession to articulate.

The most prized of his achievements was a gizmo that made it possible to alter the tempo of a player-piano without having to alter the tempo of your pedal-pumping. The gizmo saved a lot of music-lovers from cramps in the thighs and calves. But this came later in his life, after he had met and fallen in love with Caroline Smith of Paris, Ontario. Uncle Frank's other talent was singing, though he only sang at dinner parties in other people's houses. Sometimes, he also acted as a vocal coach — and, as things turned out, it was an avocation that stood him in good stead.

Caroline Smith — whose family had come from a plantation past in the southern state for which she was named — was the *Emma Bovary* of Paris, Ontario. She fed on books and theatre and music and, just as Emma had, she doted on stories and plays and songs that presented the lives of their heroines in an overblown romantic light. The novels of Mrs Henry Wood and Elinor Glyn were popular then, and songs such as "A Bird in a Gilded Cage" and "She Was Poor But She Was Honest."

It was also the time of touring theatrical companies led by the great actor-managers such as Martin Harvey, whose choice of plays and leading ladies was ineffably romantic. The heroines in such material always suffered romantic loss — and often lost their lives as well as their one true love. If you have ever seen Lillian Gish in *Way Down East,* cast adrift in a blizzard on the treacherous ice-floes of a raging river, then you have seen the film adaptation of one of Aunt Carrie's favourite plays. *Way Down East* was a staple of theatrical menus in the 1890s and the early1900s. For Caroline Smith, who was still very much a tragic Southern belle in her dreams, it was the stuff of life.

It is easy to imagine, then, what it must have been like when her father — the very model of a Victorian martinet — told her Frank Bull was not an acceptable candidate as her suitor. A piano salesman! A mere musician! *Go!* the enraged Mister Smith is said to have shouted at my Uncle Frank, *and never darken this door again!* But Frank and Carrie were passionately in love — and there was nothing for it but to elope.

Naturally, since romantic love is not intended to be

easy, they had to elope in the dead of winter — in a blizzard. (This is Canada, after all.) Having fallen under her spell in her later life, when her magic was still very much intact, I could believe that Aunt Carrie commissioned that blizzard. Snapped her fingers and there it was. She could also, I'm sure, have summoned forth a raging river, ice-floes and a pack of ravening hounds. She would change her name to Eliza! As it was, the blizzard was enough.

They fled through the streets of Paris, Ontario in a horse-drawn sleigh that Uncle Frank had hired from a livery stable. They were pursued in another sleigh by Caroline's father. Mister Smith was in such a towering rage, he'd brought along a brace of pistols and fired them into the swirling blizzard that blew about the lovers as they raced for the station.

Arriving seconds before a westbound train was about to depart, Uncle Frank threw down the reins to a baffled young man who was standing in the station yard. Then he ran with Aunt Carrie and they literally flung themselves onto the already moving train just as the irate Mister Smith came roaring out of the storm. Emma Bovary could not have asked for more.

Uncle Frank drew all his money out of his wallet and asked the conductor *how far will this much carry us?* The conductor counted the cash and, after a little calculating, told them they could go as far as Minneapolis, Minnesota.

So, Minneapolis, Minnesota it was. But when they got there and after Frank had telegraphed my grandfather asking for enough money to tide them over, it dawned on them that — all romantic notions aside — there had to be a means of support that would save them from the streets. "The streets," in Victorian parlance, was a euphemism for destitution. Here it was, mid-winter and there they were, mid-continent and in foreign territory. What

271

could Frank do in such a place and such a season, aside from shovel snow?

This is where his avocation proved to be their solution. (Aways have an avocation up your sleeve.) Uncle Frank decided it was time to exercise his talent as a vocal coach.

But who in high society — the only venue for a vocal coach in those days — would hire a man whose name was *Frank Bull?*

"Who did you say?"

"FRANK BULL!"

Well — as Eliza Doolittle might have put it: *not bloody likely.*

But Uncle Frank was Uncle Frank, after all — an inventor. He came home, one day, to the second-class hotel where he and Carrie had been living and he presented her with his card.

"What's this?" she said. "I don't need your card. I'm perfectly aware of who you are."

"No, you're not," he said. "You think I'm Frank Bull."

"But you *are* Frank Bull. I married Frank Bull!"

"No you didn't," he said. "Take another look. . . ."

Aunt Carrie glanced at the printing on the card before her, gasped and sat down.

"You mean to say," she said, "I'm married to a foreigner? . . . I can't even say it!" she said. "I can't pronounce it, Frank! What is it?"

Uncle Frank gave an extravagant bow.

"Madame," he said, with a curious mid-European accent Carrie could not begin to identify. "You see before you *François von Buell! Vocal Coach to the Royal Houses of Europe!*"

"François von Buell?????"

"Yes," said Uncle Frank — and explained: "That's me in Dutch and French."

Carrie was in shock. And remained in shock for several days.

But Frank was in luck. Offers poured in as he advertised the arrival of François von Buell, fresh from his triumphs in the courts of Europe — ready, for a certain fee, to act as vocal coach in the courts of Minneapolis, Minnesota.

Stone Orchard
December 1968
Journal

Last night, John Steinbeck died.

He was sixty-six. 1902.

Of Mice and Men is a kind of masterpiece — far greater as a creation, in my mind, than his "big book," *The Grapes of Wrath.*

He stood for things I rather liked — he was shy; he went the other way when the lionizers appeared. He obeyed his own mind, and by all appearances, his own instincts.

He seems to have been a graceful man — in the best sense of that phrase. You could not draw a line through him — either as a man or as a writer. True to himself, he adhered to waywardness — and he drew his own lines.

Stone Orchard
February 1989
Article

Glenn Gould once said the key of F minor was the key to his own personality. He explained this choice by saying that F minor was *halfway between complex and stable, upright and lascivious, grey and highly tinted.* Indeed, when you recall Beethoven's *Appassionata* Sonata for piano — written in the key of F minor — a kind of aural portrait of Gould can be made to appear: the passions are profound, but austere — the displays of intellect are dazzling, but carefully controlled; the mystery is absolute; the music folds back into itself and is gone.

Summing up his key analogy, Gould said that F minor also embodied "a certain *obliqueness.*" Again, the statement proves how well he knew himself, because the lines he drew through his life and his music were all obliquely drawn. This was a sign, perhaps, of his native genius: the genius of which the music-loving world is the endless beneficiary — but equally, the genius to which Glenn Gould was forced to submit from the moment he was conscious. His was not the happiest of lives, but it had its moments of laughter and, certainly, it had its moments of wonder.

Now, we have the story of Gould's extraordinary life in a new biography written by the American journalist and social historian Otto Friedrich, whose previous writings have dealt with subjects as diverse as Berlin in the 1920s, Marian Hooper Adams, Alice B. Toklas and Hollywood in the 1940s. But the very eclecticism of Otto Friedrich's previous writerly concerns makes him the perfect candidate to tell Gould's knotted story. Most importantly, he gives us all of Gould there is to tell without, thank goodness, once resorting to Edellian *psycho-jecture* when facts are not available. In *Glenn Gould: A Life And Variations* Friedrich sets both the man and his view of music before us with all their complexities intriguingly, if maddeningly, intact. And where he draws blanks, the blanks are allowed to speak for themselves. Which they do.

Someone once described the phenomenon of genius as "a rarified spirit's search for embodiment." Over time, given the fact my life has largely been lived in the worlds of theatre and books, I have had occasional glimpses of that rarified spirit's embodiment during encounters with Tyrone Guthrie, Edith Evans, Thornton Wilder, Margaret

Laurence and a very few others. Always, whatever form the genius takes, there are signals given: qualities that let you know at once with whom you're dealing. Some of these can be off-putting at first. For instance, a sense of inviolate aloofness (think of Baryshnikov); a private, often eccentric vocabulary (think of Marshall McLuhan); coolness (think of Meryl Streep).

One of the most alarming of these signal qualities is a certain testiness that emerges, probably unbidden, from these men and women — creatures not of habit, but of concentrated energies. On the way to making their unique discoveries, interruption is the worst of their enemies. It is anathema. *DON'T INTERRUPT!* they will yell at you. *LEAVE ME ALONE!* (I have heard these cries on stages and on platforms, in writers' living-rooms and actors' dressing-rooms. Garbo — you should pardon the expression — is not alone in this.) The language of these shouts and ballyhoos can range from the scatological to formal death-threats. I once had a shouting match with the director Peter Brook (rehearsing Osric in *Hamlet,* I was apparently thwarting his image of the perfect homosexual), in which he threatened first to emasculate, then to sodomize and finally to feed my carcass to the Leather Queens of Brighton, England. Half an hour later, his vocal passion spent, he asked me brightly out to tea. Brook's notorious exactitudes were — as they remain to this day — worthy of whatever anguish they caused. If, as one of his actors, you believe that — you stay with him and you grow. If you don't believe it, you leave. Yes: I debated leaving. Hurt and confused, I hated him. But, in the end, I stayed — and never once regretted it. To whatever degree I was capable of growing then, I grew and Peter Brook got his Osric. What he didn't get was to feed my carcass to the Leather Queens of Brighton. I survived — and so did he. And so did they.

That incident has provided me with more than anecdotes; it has led me towards the infinite reward of letting down my guard in the presence of such men and women — one of whom was undoubtedly Glenn Gould. Not that I had to endure the brunt of whatever violence Gould harboured, though in our brief aquaintance I saw it turned more than once on others. He had a way with words, when he chose the destructive mode, that was almost appallingly cruel. Cruel, but not sadistic. Cruel because he could write people off — dismiss them, life and limb and heart and soul, with a judgement call that wrote them out of history entirely. *So-and-so,* he would say — naming some name, the voice coming brittle, disparaging, amused down the wire the way it did: *it's too bad. It's too sad. He can't make anything happen — and he's taking up all that room!* His behaviour, afterward, to whatever person had been named would reflect this judgement; the person would become invisible — ceasing, somehow, through lack of communication, to exist.

Why? It wasn't, in retrospect, something Gould did to other people — it was something he did to himself. He cut himself off. Over and over — both in my own small experience of Gould and in the larger, wider experience of him afforded all of us in Otto Friedrich's evocation of his life — Gould puts the world of other people aside and locks himself in his room. Even as I wrote that sentence, I was thinking — hoping — I meant it theoretically — rhetorically. But, of course, his apartness was all too real. It became, over time, his whole way of life. His trademark.

Gould had more than one way of creating apartness, of gaining what Otto Friedrich calls "the value of solitude." As told in *A Life And Variations,* Gould made the discovery at an early age that he could push the immediate world away by means of sound. Once, while young Glenn was attempting to master a difficult passage of music and getting nowhere, the maid turned on the vacuum cleaner and, in his urgent need for silence, the boy took advantage of the dreadful whining and made of the noise a kind of wall — or barrier. Inside the "wall," he found he could work in perfect seclusion, safe as houses sitting in a desert.

Later in his life, when he lacked the patience to drag out the vacuum cleaner, or even to *own* a vacuum cleaner, he developed the sure-fire technique of setting two radios — one on either side of the piano — turning them up full blast and settling into his work at the keyboard happily walled in his private cell. The thing he needed most was to be alone with the music — all of the music, even the parts he wasn't playing.

This was also why we always heard the famous humming and singing everytime he gave a concert, every time he cut a record. Nothing could stop the whole of the music from making its appearance, whether it came from his fingers or his mouth. (The great jazz pianist Erroll Garner used to do the very same thing. Doesn't anyone remember?) Crouched in front of the keyboard, looking like an Arthur Rackham illustration of a strangely oversized dwarf, Glenn Gould locked himself beyond the reach of everything else alive and became the living embodiment of music. That was everything; everything that mattered. The rest, by the time he was reaching the end of his life, was a midnight phone call — hours and hours of whatever he had to say to whichever of his friends would stay awake with him and listen. Gould, like many men and women of genius, was an insomniac and — just like many insomniacs, though never admitting it was true — he was afraid of sleep.

When he came to create the music for the film of my book *The Wars,* Gould fell in love with one long sequence in which there was a scene where Martha Henry, playing Mrs Ross, comes out of church and sits on the steps with her companion, in the snow. Mrs Ross is distraught because the Bishop has come to preach the sermon and in the sermon he has extolled the virtues of war. Since Mrs Ross's son has just gone off to fight in World War I, she is not ecstatic about what the Bishop has been saying and she protests by stomping out of the service. Sitting on the steps in the midst of a very cold Canadian winter, she experiences a strange epiphany. A child with an almost alarming quality of innocence comes and stares at her, until Mrs Ross can no longer bear the burden of her own despair and anger. Rising, she invites the child to join her in the church and, as they enter, the whole congregation rises and begins to sing: *"Praise God from whom all blessings flow."* Less than a minute later, Mrs Ross's son is forced to shoot a horse on board his troopship — the first of an ever-increasing number of violent deaths that follow as the war progresses. For days, Glenn watched this sequence over and over and over. The proliferation of contrasts both attracted and appalled him. The sequence had been shot, in part, in St Paul's Church on Bloor Street in Toronto. Glenn himself had played the organ and conducted the singing. When he had been engaged to provide the score for the film, he had refused to sign his contract unless there was a guarantee that, in all the filmic carnage involving animals, none of the animals should really be killed or harmed. The guarantee was given — and we got our music.

I don't recall how long it was afterwards — it seemed about five minutes — when all of us were back at St Paul's on Bloor Street East to mourn for Glenn at his memorial service. WFW and I had been working for weeks on a Harry Belafonte Special for television — locked against our will into the same night hours that had seemed, till then, to be Glenn's exclusive territory. (Television editing is like that — you take the editing machines whenever they are available.) That was when Glenn had his stroke. All week, we waited. And then he died.

Sitting in the crowded church, there seemed to be a lot of silence. There wasn't, of course. People spoke; we shouted hymns; Maureen Forrester stood somewhere to my right and sang "Have Mercy, Lord" from the St Matthew Passion. Then, I think, the silence I so clearly remember did in fact descend and out of that silence everyone sitting — hundreds of us, each one sitting alone — heard the first painfully haunting notes of the *"Aria da capo,"* the melody from which Johann Sebastian Bach had extrapolated the Goldberg Variations — commissioned, it cannot have been incidental to Glenn, by one of Bach's patrons who could not sleep and wanted solace in the night. We knew, of course, who was playing. The barely audible humming gave him away. Glenn Gould had come full circle.

In writing *Glenn Gould: A Life And Variations,* Otto Friedrich has achieved what must have seemed an impossible task when he first set his hand in motion above its pages. The creation of any successful biography involves, of necessity, encounters with any number of nightmares for a writer: facts that cannot be verified; people you need to interview who die two days before you arrive; intransigent keepers of the flame who refuse to divulge the one vital thing you must have access to. . . . But the making of any successful biography also entails the will to follow through until you have found the man or the woman you are looking for, entire. And Otto Friedrich has done that.

279

Early on in this book, we are told that Glenn Gould liked to underline certain passages or lines in what he was reading. One such line occurs in a book with the unlikely title *Anarchy, State and Utopia* written by Robert Nozick. The line is this: *To exist for a while is better than never to exist at all.* Glenn Gould existed in real life. We know that for certain. He continues to exist on his records and in his films and radio broadcasts. Now, he also exists in Otto Friedrich's rich and splendid biography, for which both Gould and Friedrich must be praised.

Stone Orchard
February 1985
Article

MARIAN ENGEL
1933 — 1985
I haven't decided, yet, what my adventure is going to be.
These were among the last words recorded by Marian Engel, in an interview she gave Peter Gzowski in October of 1984, four months before she died. She was speaking of the various adventures she had been watching her friends undertake in the "last half" of their lives: adventures for those over fifty — people whose children had grown up — whose relationships were altering shape — whose obligations and ambitions were taking off in new directions. People who faced, in other words, plain old middle-age. They were also the adventures of those who had gained their maturity — who could now, by virtue of having made mistakes and "learned their lessons," take a second look at life and say: *these are the things I really want to do in the time remaining* — and: *these are the chances I'm willing to take.*

Life after fifty was limited for Marian Engel — and she knew it. She had known it would be limited for a number of years, having made the discovery that cancer had invaded her body shortly after she returned from her stint as Writer-in-Residence at the University of Alberta in

1979. But if life was to be limited, Marian's sense of adventure and her need for it were not. They were limitless. It was after the discovery of the cancer, for instance, that she set out to research *The Islands of Canada,* her "coffee-table book" published in 1981. This research entailed an immense amount of travel, some of it under difficult circumstances — but the adventure of it all, the travel, the discovery of new places and the meeting of new people meant a great deal to her. It was also an adventure which gave her a chance to share new things with her children, one or both of whom accompanied her on some of her island journeys.

Because of her father's work (he was a teacher of auto mechanics, kept on the move because of the Depression), much of Marian's Engel's early life was spent as a nomad. But not an unhappy one. The effect of living in many different places seems to have galvanized her imagination — and, as all incipient artists will, she watched and she listened and she took life in with relish.

Born in Toronto in 1933, she lived out her childhood in a variety of towns and cities in south-western Ontario. Galt, Port Arthur, Sarnia, Goderich all turn up one way or another in her fictions — melded and given other names — but the essence of a *kind* of town emerges, unique to Southern Ontario. Her portraits of these towns are always vital, caring and honest to the last degree. Their streets, their stores, their restaurants and beauty salons; their houses and their lawns; their sidewalks and the people walking there are drawn with the sort of casual exactness that only comes when the subject is part of the writer's personal background. The air of research is altogether absent. This is what might be called *blood-writing* — when the search for detail is effortless and uncontrolled as heartbeats.

Nothing Marian wrote, on the other hand, could be called simplistic: nothing was innocent of complexity — of wholeness. She never fudged the negatives of places or of people, because she knew the power of the negative to influence the line a person's life would follow. The leading figures in Marian Engel's books rarely lived in these Southern Ontario towns of hers — but they were always returning to them, either in fact or in thought. Her characters always kept in touch with the past: with where they had come from, the good and the bad of it — and this was one of the salient factors that gave her characters their edge.

Marian graduated from McMaster University in 1955 with a B.A. and consequently went on to McGill, where she wrote her Master's thesis under the supervision of Hugh MacLennan. The subject of this thesis was *The English Canadian Novel Since 1939* and the conclusion — both amusing and ironic — is unavoidable: all subsequent theses on this subject will, of necessity, give a central place to the novels of Marian Engel. Her relationship with MacLennan was a good one, both as a student and friend; "healthy," because it made room for more than one philosophy. Receptive, amused, argumentative, mutually respectful and enlarging, it lasted until her death.

Following her graduation from McGill, Marian took a teaching post in Missoula, at Montana State University, but this adventure ended after a year because she was not prepared to waste her energies on the internal politics of her department. She was interested in teaching and in writing — devoted to her students and her work, but she had no devotion whatsoever to the politics of who got to sit at the Master's right hand at high table. Other teaching jobs ultimately led her to Europe, where she spent some time in the Balearic Islands (on Ibiza); the South of France (at Aix-en-Provence); and in London, Paris and Cyprus. It was during this period that her marriage to Howard Engel took place and most of her subsequent travels in Europe were geared to Howard's assignments with the CBC. It was also during this period — the late 1950s and early 1960s — that Marian began to write her first novels.

She had written before, of course, having pretty well always known she wanted to be a writer. In fact, by 1954, she had already published a number of stories, (under her maiden name, Passmore), in magazines such as *Seventeen* and McGill's *The Muse*. Her first novels went unpublished and it was not until her return to Canada that her novel-writing established its own voice and began to find a serious audience.

For a while, Marian's travels were over and she and Howard Engel settled down to life in Toronto and the raising of a family. Twins — William and Charlotte — were born in 1965 and it was shortly after this that Marian began to "noodle around," as she said herself, with the ideas and the pages that would become her first successful novel, *No Clouds of Glory*. This was in 1968.

The decade of the 1970s was perhaps the most vital of Marian Engel's life. It began auspiciously, with the publication of her second novel — and one of her best — *The Honeyman Festival,* followed in 1973 with the founding of The Writers' Union Of Canada, in which she played a central role.

It was a perilous time for Canadian writers. To begin with, our numbers were swelling and this meant more and more voices had to be heard. At the same time, our publishing houses were being taken over — or threatened — by outside interests. Contracts were hard to come by — and the terms by which they were governed were not, on the whole, in the writer's best interest. Culturally, our country was on the verge of a new and powerful flowering. On the other hand, it was also on the verge of being swallowed whole. Lack of funding, lack of protective rights, lack of a collective professional focus threatened to cut us down at the very moment when we were learning to stand on our own.

It was in this moment that Marian Engel, Graeme Gibson and a handful of others gave articulation to these problems and The Writers' Union began to take shape. Marian Engel's energy was central amongst those that hammered out the collective means by which these problems could be solved. As a consequence of her leadership in these matters, she was elected as the Union's first Chairperson at the inaugural meeting in Ottawa.

The seventies also saw Marian's separation and divorce from Howard Engel — and this meant a whole new way of life. Her children stayed with her — consequently, Marian faced all the complicated problems of becoming a single parent. The housing, feeding and schooling of her family were to remain her central concerns until she died. But she was also concerned that she achieve these things exclusively by means of her writing. That she succeeded was a triumph. Writers, not only in Canada, but everywhere, have a hard enough time just getting by on their own. But it can be done — and is done every day. The picture is not all black. But "getting by" is — at times — appallingly complex. And, of course, there is the question: is "getting by" enough?

By its very nature, writing is necessarily freelance work. We don't have salaries. There is no such thing as a weekly pay-cheque. But we do have extraordinary resources, because the whole field of writing can be open to us. This doesn't mean that we all have talents in all the fields of writing. Not by a long shot. But fields — besides the ones in which our major talents lie — can be open to us. And Marian Engel seized on these as ways of supplementing her income. Journalism, criticism and writing for radio all played a part in this period of her life — as well as teaching. Having lost a house she particularly loved — on Brunswick Avenue, in Toronto — she subsequently bought another, which she came to love as much, on Marchmount Road.

It was also during this time that she wrote her last novels: *Bear, Joanne, The Glassy Sea* and *Lunatic Villas.* When she died, she was working on yet another project — a single novel that was turning, almost against her will, into three separate books.

Marian Engel gained many honours in her life: a Governor General's Award, The City Of Toronto Book Award and, latterly, the Order of Canada. She was a Trustee of the Toronto Library Board and Writer-in- Residence at both the University of Alberta and the University of Toronto. But greater honours than these, perhaps, were bestowed upon Marian Engel by those who knew and loved her. These had to do with the way in which she faced and endured her illness — the imminence of her death — and death itself.

Marian died with a teeming brain and a whole world of writing left to do. She died, in effect, with her pen in her hand and her notebook on her knee. About a year before this death, she had written these words about her state of mind:

Time has done some work. We shall see if it is good or ill that has been produced, if impatience has been replaced by wisdom, and lack of energy replaced by richness. Anything could happen. I write because I

*have always written. I try again because I don't
know what else to do. It is both a trial and a joy.*

In the end, it is all behind us: the thinking and the
making, the doing and the writing. The drawing of lines
— of final lines — is inevitable. We can be thankful that
Marian Engel left a collection of short stories to be published after her death — *The Tattooed Woman*. Her final
months were spent in selecting its contents — and it
caused a good deal of excitement — a good deal of
intrigue and not a little bewilderment. *Which stories
shall they be?* she would ask us over and over. *Do you
think there should be a unity — or should I just throw in
the stories I like, a sort of grab bag?*

Much of the time the book was being planned, Marian
Engel was bedridden — sometimes in hospitals, sometimes at home. The coming and the going between one
place and the other became a kind of routine. The walls
of my kitchen were plastered with pieces of paper reading: *Marian — Rm 414* and then a telephone number.
Also: *M. home Tuesday, 3:00 P.M.* Back and forth and back
again. And the stories went with her — sometimes piles
of them — sometimes just a shopping bag with one or
two or three. Whichever bed she currently occupied
would have all these pages beside it or spread out over
the covers — though there wasn't much room on the covers: Marian liked very much to occupy as much of the
covers as she could with her own arms and legs. She was
a great one for sprawling — childlike with toys — except
the toys were her stories.

Which, which, which? she would ask. But, even while
she was asking — you could tell she wasn't paying the
slightest attention to your answers. She already had her
answers. She knew perfectly well which stories she want-

ed to include. The asking of the question was just a diversionary tactic. *Maybe if I ask for their opinion, they'll leave me alone to do my choosing.* You could tell this, because when you did give an answer, somehow she would counter it: *No. I've already decided against that one. . . .* Or: *do you really like that one. Really?* The implication here was: *what peculiar taste you have.*

You learned fairly quickly to shut up.

Some of the stories couldn't be found. They were deep in boxes or deeper still in Robert Weaver's filing system at the CBC. Others had to be found and sent from her agent, Virginia Barber, in New York. Some were hiding under her bed. Neatly, I might add. Hiding there neatly.

Ultimately, she made the choice of "unity." The stories have a collective "oddness." But "oddness" is a word of which you must be careful. Marian Engel's sense of oddness is very often one of mere apartness. Her people lived apart, making their peace with life and what passed for life with a kind of wonderful valour. She never gave them short shrift, she never short-changed them; she never demeaned them.

The great wonder is the way they went about their lives, working out their problems as if what they were doing was ordinary and everyday. But, of course, it wasn't. A person does not — as rule — decide to draw attention to herself, when she feels her husband leaving her, by scarring herself with razor blades. But, in Marian Engel's hands, this woman with the scars becomes a marvel of self-control. Her scars become works of art: *she* becomes a work of art. And it is that facet of Engel's imagination that sets her people apart from all the other people in fiction. She could show you their hurt in ways that you would never forget. Cannot forget. And won't — because, like the Tattooed Woman herself — the scars she makes are as much on you as on herself. When you come away from her work, however, you have not been disfigured — but transformed.

Stone Orchard
December 1986
Journal

Christmas card from Isabel Wilder [Thornton's sister], today. Somewhat oversized writing — but legible. All it says is: I'M SO OLD! LOVE, ISABEL.

Yes, and Thornton has now been dead eleven years.

Wilder is my name,
America's my nation,
Hamden is my dwelling place
And heaven's my destination.

Thornton Niven Wilder
April 17, 1897
Madison, Wisconsin.
Hamden, Connecticut,
December 7th, 1975

The last time I saw Isabel was before Thornton's memorial at the Battell Chapel in New Haven. Winter. The pews we sat in creaked. Isabel and Amos Wilder [Thornton's brother] sat up front, Isabel so small she was barely visible. Beforehand, when we spoke, she stared up into my face from somewhere around my belly button! Or so it seemed. *Thornton would be so glad you're here,* she said. *And I am glad,* she added. *But what a long journey you've made!* I said, *no.* I said it had been a wonderful journey — which it was — driving down through small-town America — through images Thornton had loved and made his own. *It was fine,* I said. *We loved it.* Then her face clouded. *Do you have letters?* she asked. I said I did.

Will you be careful of them? she asked. *Yes,* I said, *of course, Miss Isabel. Why do you ask?* She looked away, and then back up at me. *I don't want Thornton spread all over God's creation,* she said. *I want to know where every bit of him is.* . . . Then she stopped. *I'm being foolish,* she said. *No you're not,* I said. *I know exactly how you feel.*

What will she do now, without him to care for? She has been a faithful, valiant friend to him. Thank God she was there when he died. *He went upstairs, lay down to rest and died,* she said. *He'd been in New York and suddenly felt so tired he just came home. Otherwise, he would have died at the Yale Club!*

People can die so quietly — behind our backs. Well. Then we all went off to the service in our boots and galoshes.

Stone Orchard
January 1987
Article

MARGARET LAURENCE
1926 — 1987
In what has become one of the best-known passages in Canadian writing, Margaret Laurence brought *The Diviners* — towards its conclusion:

> "Morag walked out across the grass and looked at the river. The sun, now low, was catching the waves, sending out once more the flotilla of little lights skimming along the greenbronze surface. The waters flowed from north to south, and the current was visible, but now a south wind was blowing, ruffling the water in the opposite direction, so that the river, as so often here, seemed to be flowing both ways.
> *Look ahead into the past, and back into the future, until the silence.*"

Last week that silence came for Margaret Laurence — though only she would have been aware of its presence.

289

For the rest of us, the silence was filled with the sound of her voice.

A strange place it was, she wrote of the place where she was born, *that place where the world began. A place of incredible happenings, splendours and revelations. . . .*

Jean Margaret Wemyss (pronounced *Weems*) was born in Neepawa, Manitoba on July 18th, 1926. Her family always called her Peggy and, even now, if you go to Neepawa and make enquiries — those who knew her as a child still speak more freely of Peggy Wemyss than they do of Margaret Laurence.

When Peggy Wemyss was four years old, her mother died and even though her father knew he hadn't much time to live, he remarried. He, too, was dead before his daughter and her brother had left their childhood behind. In a memoir, *Dance on the Earth,* completed before her death, Margaret Laurence pays particular tribute to the women who shared in her Prairie upbringing — her birth-mother and her father's second wife, whom Margaret always called "Mom."

All three of these parents had a lasting and creative influence on Margaret Laurence's sense of the world into which she was born — its demands on human beings and their right to make demands of it. She maintained that the world you were a child in stayed with you all the days of your life and that its light was the light you always saw by and its dark the dark that coloured all your days.

You never forgot where Margaret came from. She had a western way of looking at things — of seeing things: places, people, ideas. Distance played a role in this: in how she saw and what she saw. Perhaps in what she didn't see. For Margaret Laurence, stuff up close didn't loom as large as stuff along the horizon. . . . Portents were more important than events. During events, a person is occupied — wheeling and dealing; coping — or not. Portents imply that something can still be done to ward off disaster. Much of Margaret Laurence's writing was about just this: people attempting to ward off disaster: maybe not always succeeding. Hagar — Rachel — Stacey — even Vanessa — certainly Morag: all of them are watching the horizon: worried — sometimes tormented by it, but all of them imbued with the guts and the ingenuity to thwart what is looming there. None of them is foolish enough to turn away and say *I'll think about that tomorrow.* Margaret Laurence was the same — except in one aspect. She played a game of chance with her health and lost. To her, this was basically not of much consequence. To the rest of us, it mattered. To Margaret — not a whit.

I live with a westerner myself, and I'm sure there are special strengths that accrue in those who grow up with the prairie in their eye. Those of us born and raised in the east have other strengths — (and weaknesses: it isn't, after all, a contest). But there is something unique in westerners — aside from their strengths — that others cannot acquire. And I really do think that "something" has to do with reading the horizon.

Margaret Laurence read the horizon with a calm, professional appraisal. *There's going to be a storm,* she would say, walking into the house and starting to close all the windows. The rest of us — out on the lawn — would go on sitting in the sunshine, dubious and smiling. Then the storm would come and soak us to the skin. Margaret never said: *I told you so.* She'd laugh it off and hand us each a towel. But I think she got bored with the rain in other people's clothes. If you see what I mean. . . . Saying things twice was not her *métier.*

What alarmed her most — what she coped with least successfully — was that other portent on the horizon: *some things may never be understood.*

I think we make a dreadful mistake in assuming Margaret Laurence always coped. She didn't always cope and would have been deeply offended by the mere suggestion that she did. She lacked a certain kind of patience required in order to cope with certain situations.

She couldn't cope, for instance, with "serious" people. I think it would be fair to say she distrusted them. Distrusted them because their "seriousness" was stated and stressed. So far as writing was concerned — writing and everything to do with writing — if it wasn't a serious concern, a serious endeavour to begin with, why the hell would you bother talking about it in the first place? Therefore, on the subject of writing, serious conversation was anathema. *Are you going to tell me the sky is seriously blue, kiddo?* she'd say. *What's this: you hope I understand the birds are seriously flying today? This is news? You want me to talk about serious birds?* . . . Oh, yes. She hated it. On the other hand: *if you want to seriously gossip . . . trash the government. . . . If you want to tell me one or two seriously outrageous jokes, I'm all ears.* All ears for laughter. The one sure sign of a serious writer.

It is my feeling, she said, *that as we grow older we should become not less radical but more so.* Long before she died last week in Lakefield, Ontario at the age of sixty, Margaret Laurence — both the writer and the woman — through her books and in her everyday life — had achieved a kind of radicalism the rest of us can only respect. Some of her writings — most notably *The Diviners, A Jest Of God* and *The Stone Angel* — had incurred the wrath of all wrong-thinking people and her life — as a dedicated feminist, a Canadian, a Human Rights activist and advocate of Nuclear Disarmament — had become a beacon for others.

Back in the days when The Writers' Union of Canada was about to become a reality, Margaret Laurence was there at its founding. Crazily, I can't remember where that meeting was. It may have been Ottawa. It may have been Toronto. I do remember the lecture amphitheatre in which we held those early sessions. I can still see Margaret Laurence where she sat in juxtaposition to others — and I still recall the appalling nervousness that overcame her, every time she rose to speak. She had what can only be called a debilitating shyness, when it came to public speaking. Who knows why? She was not a shy, inverted person. Still — her nerves tormented her.

Her questions from the floor of public forums were inevitably tense with the drama inherent in any person who can barely stand up because of her fear, but who knows that she must rise to the occasion. Her body often betrayed her, forcing her to hold fast to the back of the chair in front of her. Whenever it was known beforehand that Margaret was going to make an appearance, a chair and table were provided. Any witness could see she was shaking — even from far away as fifty feet. Robin Phillips, the noted director, once choreographed an entire evening of readings given by writers in opposition to censorship, around the fact of "Margaret Laurence's table" — which sat just where it should — left of centre from the audience's point of view.

That every writer, that night, making her entrance or making his exit had to contend with this table — (the one they all have to face every day of their working lives) — was a marvellous symbolic gesture. That it was Margaret Laurence's table made it doubly symbolic of what that evening was about. No other writer in our country's history had suffered more at the hands of those professional nay-sayers, book-banners and censors than she had. And that suffering — make no mistake of it — took its toll, both professionally and personally. So be it. She was prepared for that and, in the long run, she triumphed because she knew, when all was said and done, that her books had been written, as she said herself: *in order to clarify, proclaim and enhance life — not to obscure and demean and destroy it.*

I cannot close this without remarking on one other brief event.

During Margaret Laurence's tenure as Chancellor of Trent University, I happened to receive an honorary degree one year. This meant that I was seated on the stage behind her as she conferred her blessing on each of the hundred-plus students who also received their degrees that day.

As each of the students approached the Chancellor, Margaret Laurence was on her feet to greet them: shaking hands with and speaking to every one. Many leaned forward to kiss her. All were enamoured of her. Not for her fame and not for her position. Only for herself.

How rare that is I need not even ask.

That convocation day at Trent, there were no clouds. No distant storms. Only the sky and the students. If Margaret was reading the horizon, the portents were auspicious: joyous: positive.

She stood for that — in more ways than one.

My lifetime here is a short span, she wrote, *but I am not here as a visitor. Earth is my home.*

Indeed it was — and is. And we are the better for it. All of us.

Stone Orchard
January 1988
Journal

The poet, Gwendolyn Mac-Ewen, had died in December 1987, and the event described here was her Memorial Service on January 20, 1988, for which Phyllis Webb has flown in from B.C. . . .Yesterday to Toronto. Pick up P.W. at Michael's [Ondaatje] and down for supper at restaurant across the road from St Lawrence Centre. Michael and Linda [Spalding] joined us halfway through the meal — Michael involved in arrangements for event, which started at eight in the Town Hall section of the Centre. Meeting with P.W. inevitably sad, depressing . . . mortality hovered over every gesture — every word — and every sip of wine. . . .

. . .Gwen was only forty-seven when she died. It is all so crazy and wrong — but she had stripped her life to the bare essentials — her poverty was absolute and, having given fair warning in her last book, *Afterworlds*, she made her final moves and gestures, went into the dark and died there.

She was a splendid writer — never less than adventurous — always evocative of her own unique vision — always trying for the upward curve that inevitably eluded her. We had some kinship as explorers and I adored her as a person, however difficult she could be from time to time when the drink and depression overcame her and she was swept away. Whenever Gwen tried for sobriety, the world turned cold and grey and its people seemed to her like a race made up entirely of indecipherable aliens. Nothing could cheer her. The last conversation we had — when I phoned to tell her how *Afterworlds* had blown me away — was filled with despair and anger. Age was her implacable enemy — *what is left*, she said, *when you're nearly fifty and condemned to everlasting sobriety?*

Nothing a person could say to her or tell her was of any use. The sun itself (which she loved) had become the central banality. Light, warmth and animals — nothing she loved was of any use to her any more. Her campaign to save Toronto's alley cats had "failed" — it didn't matter how many cats she had, in fact, saved, befriended, comforted. If one remained on the street, the whole campaign had failed. She refused to hear the word "hope."

The same, it was clear, was true of her campaign to save herself. There was always that part of her that had been so deeply wounded, total recovery was impossible. For Gwen, there was an element of solace in bitterness and sorrow — turned to as if they were the only constant and, therefore, the only certainty to be depended on. There is a kind of safety in despair. I know it well, myself. The causes of despair are the only promises kept with unfailing regularity. Or so it seems, in the dark.

Well.

The others who read last night were Bob Weaver, Margaret Atwood, Al Purdy, Mary di Michele, Joe Rosenblatt, Martha Henry, Dennis Lee, Margaret Avison, Barrie Nichol, P.K. Page, Michael O., Barry Callaghan and Phyllis. The house was packed. I gave Gwen a toast in red wine. (The Management tried to take the wine away from me, but I said *it's a prop* and they let me keep it!) Phyllis read last. She read from *Afterworlds*. It was devastating.

Before we had gone down into the hall, we had all sat together in a room upstairs and someone had said: *we have to stop meeting like this. . . .* The deaths have been overwhelming — Marian, Margaret, Gwen. . . . All of them years before their time.

The last time Gwen and Phyllis and I had been together was when we all went up to visit Marian Engel, who was then — for the umpteenth time — in the Eaton wing of the Toronto General Hospital. WFW and I had brought a cake — a spectacular chocolate *Doyenne* cake which WFW had found at Dufflet's on Queen Street.

Marian was on, I think, the fourteenth floor. At any rate, she was very high up and the view from the windows was almost lovely — early spring afternoon light spread out across the city and the lake — and M. in her bed, legs sprawled, a multitude of pillows and the sheets in typical Marian disarray — much laughter — reminiscence — general avoidance of the fact that M. was coming down to the wire and could not survive a great while longer. We had all known one another intermittently for years. So the cake was a kind of celebration: *here we are, together.*

M. had a passion for chocolate and the *Doyenne* was incredible. Smooth, hard chocolate icing had been spread over two thick layers of dark chocolate cake and in between the layers, raspberry filling. But more than that, a raspberry glaze had been applied beneath the icing and when the cake was cut, the raspberry glaze spilled down the sides of the cake and oozed out over the plate. One sugared violet sat at the nether end of a swirl that had been the cakemaker's final gesture. Beautiful.

We had all assumed that plates could be found in the hospital and forks and napkins, too — but, no. They could provide us with nothing.

Consequently, Marian Engel's room on the fourteenth floor of the Eaton Wing was the scene of perhaps the most bizarre banquet in the history of the TGH. Two of the country's most important poets, two of its most celebrated novelists and one of its most prominent documentary writers all bent forward over their servings of chocolate *Doyenne* cake and, using wooden tongue-depressors, ate them from toilet-paper plates!

"And a good time was had by all."

Sic transit gloria mundi.

Stone Orchard
February 1988
Article

KEN ADACHI
1928 — 1989

The complexities in Ken Adachi were entirely Japanese — though, even as I put these words on the page, I can hear the whispered laughter that was part of his personal signature. He laughs — (it is still present laughter) — because the only thing that was overtly "Japanese" about Ken Adachi was his face. But the balances on which he weighed his gestures were decidedly Japanese: the disciplined demeanour fronting for the passionate enthusiast; the sense of discretion which acted as the governor of rage and laughter alike. He was one of the most remarkably self-controlled people I have ever known.

In remembering the public man, the greatest disservice we could do him would be to forget the private man — the man, in his own words, who was "the victim since childhood of a particularly virulent strain of racism." Ken Adachi spent the middle years of his boyhood in what was called, with uniquely Canadian arrogance, a "detention camp." As if detention were not incarceration. And yet, when he wrote about the history of Japanese-Canadians, including the years of imprisonment during the Second World War — Ken Adachi's attention was characteristically focused on others. In *The Enemy That Never Was*, published in 1976, he told the story of his people with admirable — even remarkable — objectivity, never once falling back on his own experience, or his own hurt to score points or reinforce his arguments. Also, in what remained of his life, he worked unstintingly in behalf of the Japanese-Canadian community's struggle to wrest not only an adequate apology, but financial recompense from the Canadian Government for what had been done to them. Thank all the gods — Ken Adachi was here when, at last the apology was given and reparation promised.

Ken Adachi was a man of active passions — literature being at the top of his list. He was a teacher, a writer, a journalist and a critic. He also loved jazz and cats and American musical comedies. He was an avid fan of baseball, soccer, hockey and even of cricket — a sport he could only follow on television or through the papers. On squash and tennis courts, he put away opponents half his age with awesome ease. On the track, he could leave his wife, Mary, (no mean athlete herself), gasping for breath while he ran on without her, all in spite of yet another passion — cigarettes. Ken without a tennis racket or a cigarette in hand was just an impostor, caught without his insignia.

The room where he worked at home was entirely private — tall, with books on multiple shelves and the table surfaces covered with piles of correspondence, record jackets, sports magazines and ashtrays. The comforts it offered were entirely those of a private creature whose life beyond its walls was governed by a code of gentle silence: *don't disturb me and I won't disturb you.* Most of what he talked about outside this room was discussed without the overt enthusiasm you got when you were in there with him. He talked more freely there — urging whatever he was reading outside of his work upon you. In there, he offered the music he loved — or he dragged you into the sphere of some young writer you'd never heard of, whose cause and career he had taken up. He had innate respect for writing and for writers and, if he became your champion, he would press your name and your work into every hand that passed. He was especially effective in bringing young writers forward, writers who were elsewhere receiving blank stares and diffidence, until they fell into Ken Adachi's purview. David Adams Richards, Jane Urquhart, Neil Bisoondath, Maria Jacobs — and I must add Timothy Findley (some years ago) — have all received, along with dozens of others, the benefit of Ken's attention as they waited in the wings, unread.

Whatever the burden of his turmoil may have been, he never laid it out on the table tops to be examined. He never drew you into any conspiracies of gossip concerning the foibles and problems of others. He never pried for the sake of gratuitous curiosity. He would, however, pry with determination if the prying was apt to produce some positive result. He cared about his friends and only regretted their private lapses and public failures if they caused his friends unhappiness.

His only fault — his most grievous fault — lay in his propensity for silence. When I learned that Ken Adachi had taken his own life, I raged against this silence almost as if I hated him — and I only say that here because it tells, for those who did not know him, how greatly loved he was. Speaking to others after the event, I found that my rage against his silence was echoed again and again. But the silence, after all was Ken's, and we have to accept it now as having been deliberate and — somehow — a generous example of his integrity. He wouldn't have troubled us for all the world.

I cannot close this without a word for Mary Adachi; about Mary, for her.

Mary Adachi was some years Ken's junior. Who knows how, but there seemed to be no difference in age between them. He was as young as she was — and she may well have been the reason. They moved entirely as themselves — one with one; superbly successful individuals who were absolute necessities in one another's lives. This was the prize of their marriage — one of the gifts they have given unwittingly to those who knew them and even to those who merely witnessed their presence. Now, we have Mary; then, we had Ken. That is what is. And we accept it. It is my belief that is what Ken Adachi wanted us to do. And I believe that Mary Adachi wants that, too.

Stone Orchard
January 1987
Speech

The Philosophical Society of Trent University has invited, over a time, a variety of speakers to address its membership in a series of lectures given under the general heading My Final Hour. *The idea is that, provided the chance to do so, how would each speaker sum up his or her experience of life and what would each one say about the future? I dedicated this address to the memory of Margaret Laurence, who had died earlier that month.*

1: Well — here it is: my final hour.
   And what do I have to say for myself?

2: *But I Daniel was grieved*
   and the vision of my head troubled me,
   and I do not want to keep
   the matter in my heart
   for the heart of the matter
   is something different.
   Neither do I want happiness
   without vision.
   I am apocryphal and received.
   I live now and in time past
   Among all kinds of musick. . . .

3: From time to time, during this address, I shall be quoting more from that extraordinary poem. It was written by Phyllis Webb and she called it *I Daniel.* It tells what it feels like and what it means to be that most ill-defined and imprecise embodiment of humankind, the writer. Perhaps *to be one — is to know one* . . . as they say.

   I think I would know one anywhere. Another writer, that is.

But I cannot tell you *how* I'd know.

And that's the truth. I really cannot tell you what it is that gives a writer away. But something does.

A mark — like Cain's?

I trust not.

A *password?*

Don't be ridiculous.

And certainly not a secret handshake.

No. It cannot be defined by any other means than nameless recognition.

Still — let me see if I can do this: let me try to define some part of it, at least.

4: There is a way of seeing space — of leaving space — of making space around everything a writer sees; of leaving room — of *making* room for everything to be itself: alone. Shakespeare said that; or something very like it. Gloucester says it in Henry VI, Part Three. . . . He says: *I am myself alone.* In other words, he says: I am so much myself, there isn't any room inside of me for any part of me to be like anyone else. Besides, I have no time for that. A writer credits whatever he sees as being unique; he looks for each and every one of us — for each and every one of every kind of being and for each of every thing that is. The writer cannot see the mass, as such, because the writer never *looks* to see the mass; the writer looks to see the parts — and the writer looks at every part and every person; each of them *alone.*

And so, there is a way of looking — not of seeing, but of *looking* — that gives the writer away. The *seeing* — the way of seeing — is unique to every writer and cannot be told in any other way but with the pen. Or whatever passes, writer to writer, for a pen: a stick, a nail, a piece of lead, a piece of chalk — an IBM Selectric or an Epson Word Processor.

5: For fifteen years of the fifty-six that have brought me to this final hour, I was an actor. Perhaps you are not aware that an actor must always be prepared to audition. The phone rings and your agent says: *you're to go down and read for Olivier at ten tomorrow morning.* Something has to be up your sleeve or else you're up the creek. So you've always got to have your audition pieces ready — and one of mine was that speech of Gloucester's from Henry VI, Part Three.

In case your history is shaky, let me remind you that Gloucester would end up on the English throne — as Richard III. Not what you'd call the nicest man you've ever met. . . . Which is precisely why, so long ago, I was drawn to him; the way that birds are drawn towards the jaws of cats.

Whatever else you can say about Richard III, you have to admit he knew who he was.

I came across him first when I was fifteen or sixteen years old. This was at a time when I was being informed by other people — and, sometimes, very harshly — that I was not like them; that I was not, or so it seemed, like anyone.

This part of me that others would not accept and could not cope with was called — by them — an *aberration.* I had known about it all my life, but they had not. They had not, because this *aberrant* part of me had not been revealed in its physical manifestation until my mid-teens. This had to do — as you might have guessed — with the focus of my sexual attentions: a focus not apparent to others until I was sexually active.

For most of my life till then, I'd maintained a careful, watchful distance from others — from *most* others, with notable exceptions. During my childhood, the notable exceptions were: the maid in the kitchen, the tramps at the door, the rabbits in the garden under the porch, the dog at the foot of my bed — and my maternal grand-mother — a woman, it so happened, who was descended from the kings of Ireland. Now, at the age of fifteen, I withdrew completely.

The subject at hand is not my sexual orientation. That is something to which I have been peacefully reconciled since I could think; perhaps since I was three. The subject here is other people's lack of reconciliation to the person I was. The whole person.

Nor is the subject here, in the strictest sense, myself — myself and only myself. The subject here is all of us; all of us and reconciliation; all of us and reconcilation with who we are — the whole of who we are and what becomes of us when others break us into parts.

People who once had loved me, all at once despised me.

I felt the sorrow of the leper and the rage of the out-cast. There would never, I swore, be reconciliation between myself and others. The effect, you see, of apart-ness can truly be devastating — and yet, whole govern-ments pass laws in behalf of apartness; this kind or that kind — it is almost immaterial. Everything *else* that I was — which felt to be about 99.9 per cent of who I was and what I was about — went into exile with the 0.1 per cent of aberration. But I could not tell the others in my life — I could not explain to those who had set me apart — and I could not even tell or explain to myself what it was that I felt, because I had no words; I had no means of articula-tion.

And it was then that I came across Richard, Duke of Gloucester: perhaps the most *aberrant* human being in all of English literature.

I devoured him whole. It seemed that I was already intimate with all his dreams and aspirations as a man. I understood — acutely — what it was that drove him to divorce himself from decency. And I remember to this day my reaction to that first encounter. I blushed. I blushed because I thought I had been seen. And then I felt a rush of immense excitement. The more of Gloucester I read, the more I understood that I was reading the definitive articulation of everything I had not been able to articulate about myself and how it felt to be *my* self alone.

6: "*Oh, why is he telling us this? It seems so petty and so small. In his final hour, he should rise above the history of his rage.*"

I think not. And besides, in my final hour, the subject here will not be rage — but *reconciliation.* I think I have come to live almost entirely for that word.

I am telling you this because — by the time of my final hour — I will have to have come to grips with what this means; with what it has meant to live with — and to try to overcome the manifestation in me of the person who speaks these words of Richard, Duke of Gloucester: monster. And here they are. At the very end of Henry VI, Part Three, Gloucester murders the king. He stands above the body and says:

> *Down, down to hell and say I sent thee thither. . . .*
> *I, that have neither pity, love, nor fear.*
> *Indeed, 'tis true that Henry told me of;*
> *For I have often heard my mother say*
> *I came into the world with my legs forward:*
> *The midwife wondered and the women cried*
> *'O, Jesus bless us, he is born with teeth!'*
> *And so I was; which plainly signified*
> *That I should snarl and bite and play the dog.*
> *Then, since the heavens have shaped my body so,*
> *Let hell make crook'd my mind to answer it.*

I have no brother, I am like no brother;
And this word 'love,' greybeards call divine,
Be resident in men like one another,
And not in me: I am myself alone. . . ."

7:   *But I Daniel was grieved*
     and the vision of my head troubled me,
     and I do not want to keep
     the matter in my heart
     for the heart of the matter
     is something different. . . ."
I am a hiding place for monsters.

8: When I was in my twenties, I went to Hollywood. Like anyone else, I got there by a circuitous route: "by stages" you might say. By stages in Kingston, Stratford and Toronto; London, Oxford and Edinburgh; Dublin, Berlin and Moscow; New York, Chicago and San Francisco. *Join the Theatre and see the World!* And I really thought I had.

But I was very good at keeping my distance by then. Yes — I was *very* good at that. I was so alarmed by the thought of love that I only slept with strangers. And if I fell in love — and I did that twice before I was twenty-eight. . . .

"*What? Only twice!*"

Yes: only twice. . . .

Before I was twenty-eight. . . .

. . .if I fell in love, I would find some way to unleash the monster and let the monster do its work of driving love away.

Someone once said that *hell is other people.*

That was Sartre.

And he was right.

But love is other people, too.

306

That was Findley.

And he was right.

But the monster did not agree with Findley. He agreed with Sartre.

And here I was in Hollywood. The long transition had begun from actor to writer — still in the exploratory stages: tentative — unfocused, but under way.

I was living with an actress, then. And one night, we went to visit a friend of hers. He was a writer: a writer and a producer — a man named Ivan Moffat and he lived on the heights above Santa Monica in one of those classic Hollywood houses made of glass and wood: all jutting decks and every room, so it seemed, on a separate floor.

Ivan Moffat was a man I'd heard a lot about and someone I admired. He'd co-produced and written screenplays with a director who headed my list of greats in that particular field: a man, now dead, whose name was George Stevens — a director responsible, above all else, for a film called *A Place in the Sun*. Also — and not incidentally — for *Shane* and *Giant*. So, when I went to meet Ivan Moffat with my friend Patricia Cutts, I was going to meet a kind of personal god. And we went to meet him in this house that personified the whole of every glittering dream I'd ever had about Hollywood.

There was a bonus. Another god — less personal, more public. And this was Christopher Isherwood.

We were late — unavoidably, due to Patricia's shooting schedule at MGM — and Mister Isherwood, standing in Ivan Moffat's living-room, was not amused. He made a scene about the value of his time — (as opposed to the value of ours) — and we were made to feel that great men have no time to dally with people they had never heard of. This was an insight I could have done without — coming from a man whose writings I admired and whose alienation and apartness echoed so utterly my own.

307

In disliking him for his behaviour, I was forgetting that he, too, had been all his life a hiding place for monsters; his monsters not at all unlike my own. And so he drifted away into his apartness and I made no effort ever again to get in touch with him. It was only after Christopher Isherwood had died that I was mature enough to forgive his rudeness and his bad temper. But, of course, I had already lost all chance of his friendship.

Still — that is incidental to the bulk of what I tell.

When Isherwood had retired into his own domain — (behind a wall, I think I must add) — Ivan, Patricia and I went on to eat our dinner in the twilight. We talked of everything under the setting sun. We had such a marvellous time together — laughing, drinking wine and swapping tales.

I couldn't take my eyes from Ivan Moffat's face. He was a handsome man — but worn down, troubled beneath his mask of smiles and glittering eyes. His hands shook. From time to time, for all that he was engaged in the conversation, his eyes would shift away from us and gaze out over the city down below — where all the lights were coming on and from which there rose the scent of flowers and gasoline, of perfumed ladies and eighty-thousand people smoking cigarettes. The golden lights, the scent and the sound of everyone's private music playing down below us created an atmosphere of almost tangible sadness — of memories and dreams — of great ambitions failed and greater ambitions yet to be fulfilled. For me, this atmosphere was redolent with stories: books unwritten — parts not played. For Patricia, I think it was an atmosphere that seemed about to deliver the highest prizes of her profession; she was truly on her way to stardom. But for Ivan, the atmosphere appeared to be creating a sequence of thoughts — of memories he could not bear to deal with. He became increasingly distracted;

increasingly determined to erase these memories with some — it hardly mattered which — activity.

In the past — I don't know when it was — there had been some dallying between Patricia Cutts and Ivan Moffat. And it was this "activity" he now threw into gear. The dallying — picked up wherever they had left it in the past — would last and satisfy them for about a week. But it seemed to be exactly what the moment required.

And so, with tact and with amusement, they retired into the lower reaches of the house. But, before they departed, Ivan produced a bottle of brandy — indicated his records, his stereo, his books and his vast collection of movie scripts — including *A Place in the Sun* — and he said: "feel free."

When they had gone, I revelled in what — to me, in that particular place, in that particular time — seemed absolute paradise. I was where I had always wanted to be: high above the lights of *Hollywood, California*, safely ensconced in the very heart of my ambitions. Whether these were the ambitions of the actor or the writer hardly seemed to matter. I was *there*. I had *arrived*.

So, I put on the records: I opened and began to drink the brandy. In a word, it was wonderful and I had played like this for maybe an hour — listening to the laughter rising from the floor below — when I chanced upon a set of books that altered, as things turned out, my life forever.

They were books of photographs.

I say that, now, so easily. . . .

Official-looking photographs — each one carefully mounted on a separate page and the pages bound in plain cloth covers.

There wasn't any written indication — anywhere — of when the photographs had been taken; not of when, or where or why. But my instinct — quite correct as instincts go — told me that Ivan Mofffat had taken these pictures himself. And he had.

9: I was staring, through photographs, into the heart of Dachau. After its liberation, Ivan Moffat had been the first official army photographer through the gates.

How can this be explained to those who were not alive before that time: before there was a war, before there was a Dachau, before there was a Bomb? How, for instance, can a person explain *there was a time when Nagasaki was just a city in a pretty song?* It cannot be done. It is impossible. Even in a world where Nagasaki and Hiroshima, Dachau and Auschwitz are names that tell of horrors distant as the Inquisition, it cannot be told what it meant to see those photographs that night.

Such images, in all their appalling intimacy, had not yet entered the public domain. The pictures we had seen — the ones the public saw — the ones they showed at Nuremburg — were bad enough. But these in Ivan Moffat's books were beyond all comprehension. Someone — a part of me tried to believe — must have been creating a fictional obscenity. Surely, no one could actually do such things as were seen in these photographs.

Of course, I could give the pictures a context. I'd already heard what everyone else had heard and seen what everyone else had seen; *had been allowed to hear, allowed to see.* But nothing — not my nightmares, not the worst of my imagination, not the worst of my experience — had opened the door on the remotest possibility of what I saw that night.

I was looking into hell — and hell was real.

And I saw all this in *Hollywood, California* — high above the magic of its lights and the perfume of its heady scent and I saw it through the sound of someone singing: *I get no kick from champagne . . . mere alcohol doesn't*

*thrill me at all . . . so tell me, why should it be true . . .
that I get a kick out of you?*

I never recovered from what I saw that night.

Perhaps I should say: thank God. I cannot tell.

But, at last, I had been joined — through a unique revelation of horror — to the rest of the human race. I was never to see myself again as a being apart. How, after all, can you be *apart* when everyone else is standing *apart* beside you?

This was a kind of epiphany. I did not know how to say it then, but the vision of Dachau in Ivan Moffat's photographs told me that I was just like everyone else. We are all a collective hiding place for monsters.

This is the worst and the hardest of reconciliations: the one that forces you into the company of murderers.

Still:

*Neither do I want happiness
without vision.
I am apocryphal and received.
I live now and in time past
among all kinds of musick. . . .*

10: My earliest memory of death is this:

I am five years old. My mother's father has died. There has been a schism in her family for many years. My grandfather's death is loaded with other sorrows besides the sorrow of loss: the sorrow of reconciliations never to be completed — the sorrow of many questions never, now, to be answered.

What I remember of that time is this:

I am standing looking down a long, dark hallway — dark, but not sinister. This happens in a house I love.

Way off down this hallway I can see a place in sunlight. Standing in the sunlight I see three women, dressed in white. They are standing in a circle, arms extended to embrace one another. All three heads are bowed and all three women weep.

Held in their hands are large bouquets of flowers — the flowers all white — the whole scene vivid in sunlight. My mother is being comforted by her sisters-in-law.

How am I to know, at such an age, that what I am seeing has been lifted from mythology — a view of grief as old as time? The sight of those three women standing there has delivered, indelibly, the notion of what can be done when there is death.

We can grieve, in spite of sunlight — we can mourn in spite of life — we can embrace, in spite of death; we can bring white flowers and weep.

But how can monsters bring white flowers to Dachau? Because, in spite of our complicity, we must. Or there will be no reconciliation.

11: Another verse of Phyllis Webb's poem begins:

> *The coin is dropped into my palm*
> *I become the messenger, see —*
> *here, now in my own hand*
> *the printout of the King's text*
> *which he has forgotten*
> *and I remember.*

Which he has forgotten and I remember.
This tells, fairly, what a writer does.

In my final hour — unless I succumb to senility — my problem will not be what I have forgotten, but what I recall I have not told.

When Margaret Laurence learned she was going to die, she rejoiced in two things only. The first was her certainty that she had raised her children to stand on their own feet; they knew — and she knew — who they were.

The second was an equal certainty that she had done her work; that her work was finished. She had written and published what she had to say and she had completed — to be published after her death — a memoir of her time on earth and a journal of the weeks that led to *her* final hour.

If you loved Margaret Laurence — and I did — you could rejoice with her in these two convictions.

But I shall have no such convictions. To begin with, I have no children. Nor do I have any more to say than Margaret Laurence had, or more to say than *anyone* has who writes. But, because the matters of which I write have an endless resource in what appears to be a bottomless pit of memory, I cannot shut them off. Sometimes, I wish I could. But the damn stuff keeps on being delivered!

And, when my memory fails — there is always yours to plunder — or someone's. The communal memory also prods me with its news.

It is a truth: a writer is a witness. A witness of the present, a witness of the future; a witness of the past. Memory provides that witness with veracity. Yes; even our memory of the future.

The other invaluable thing about memory is that it keeps you connected to the innocent side of events: the side preceding events that allows you, constantly, to rediscover the freshness of your initial wonder; the keenness of your initial alarm.

I have always believed my duty, as a writer, is to remain — to some degree — naïve. I mean that it is irresponsible, debilitating — and, above all, dangerous — to become inured to the way of the world.

Thornton Wilder wrote: *the one thing an author is*

not allowed is to look at the tragic background of life and the constitution of human nature for evil with surprise — *for surprise denotes that he is newly come from a conviction it was otherwise.*

Does this refute what I have just said?

I think not.

Goodness can still surprise us. Especially when we know it should be otherwise. Memory informs us it should be otherwise. But a writer's memory, if whole, can still remind us of what — collectively — we have forgotten. We have forgotten that once — if only once — we saw the world before us: whole and green and alive with promise.

Greenness is not a quality of hope alone. It is the property of memory. Even if deprived of sight, we all remember green. The very first breath we take is suffused with it. Earth and air and fire and water are green. And that is good.

12: How do I know I know what I know?

I cannot say. I do not know.

I know this much, however, and in my final hour it will hold tremendous importance for me; it is what I would say most urgently, if I could speak to someone then:

I know that human imagination can save us; save the human race and save all the rest of what is alive and save this place — the earth — that is itself alive.

Imagination is our greatest gift.

Again, I fall back on Thornton Wilder, who said that: *cruelty is nothing more than a failure of the imagination.*

Yes.

I believe that. If you can imagine harmony, you can achieve it. Harmony, after all, can be well defined as an absence of cruelty. If I am a hiding place for monsters —

and I am — then I can also be a hiding place for harmony.

Or, at least, I can imagine such a thing.

In recent times, the subject of banning books and censorship has been the cause of grave and increasing concern. The gulf between those who favour and those who oppose these things is growing wider and deeper. For myself, I am on the side of opposition. Nothing can make me believe another human being should have the power to prevent me from reading what I want or what I need to read. (I need it in order to grow.)

The focus of most campaigns in favour of banning books and of censorship is children. Those who want to govern what our children read are rightly concerned with the future. They have chosen, however, a strange way to show their concern. One of their number once approached me and fervently urged the destruction of my books. Not, it must be clear, the destruction only of what I had written — but of all the books I owned. A single book, the Bible, should — and *could,* in this person's belief — replace them all. Such incidents are rare, I trust. But however rare, they are tragic. Tragic, because to urge the destruction of books — in whatever context — is to urge that we despair.

At its worst, this campaign has now produced — aside from its proscription of books whose naming would take all night — a new and desperate tactic: namely a war being waged against all literature and teaching that enhances or encourages imagination in the young. To quote the makers of this war: *imagination — in the young — is dangerous.*

Really?

Surely, if we can imagine Dachau, we can also imagine harmony.

Why, then, should it be that — of these two — the

315

one we lack is harmony?

13: Some years ago, I wrote a book called *Famous Last Words* and I'm going to read from it, now. This quote concerns a time before this time and it tells what others had to say in their final hour.

Famous Last Words is a novel about what appeared to be — and, indeed, may well have been — the final hours of Western Civilization. The story, for the most part, takes place in Europe during and following the Second World War. But this particular passage tells of another ending, long before that.

Hugh Selwyn Mauberley — a fascist sympathizer, a novelist and a character lifted holus bolus from the mind of Ezra Pound — is in Spain during the Spanish Civil War. This incident takes place in 1938. Mauberley is travelling with a friend — a woman whose name is Isabella Loverso. Isabella Loverso is not a fascist sympathizer. For Mauberley, the insights gained from the scene that follows were the first that actively turned him away from fascism.

During a bombardment, Mauberley and Isabella have taken shelter in the caves at Altamira; the caves famous for their paintings and inscriptions from the ice age. Here is what he tells:

"Some of the local peasants had taken up residence there. Others made it their daily shelter during the raids. As a consequence, some had brought candles while others had commandeered lamps from the local public buildings, setting them out in rows along the floor. It was a muted, gentle atmosphere and all the talk was in whispers, falling away at the height of the bombardment into silence. The air was cool and far, far away you could hear the sound of water. Somehow, the presence of that sound was a comfort. Everyone's patience flourished and we sat in rows, while some even slept.

"And there above us, clustered in juxtapositions the meaning of which are lost beyond the barricades of time, were the drawings of all those animals whose shapes have long since been altered and disappeared from the view of men. 'Bison' I knew they were called, though little enough like any bison I had ever seen; and 'deer' that were recognizable as such, though longer of leg and more delicate of hoof than the deer I remembered passing over *Nauly*'s lawns; and 'men' as simply drawn as any stick men made by the children of the human race since the dawn of time and pencils. And waving blades of grass — or were they trees? — and constellations here and there of fingerprinted stars: black dots.

"And out of the corner of my eye I caught a glimpse of something irresistible above my head, seen in the ebb and flow of the swinging light: the imprint of a human hand.

"God only knew how long ago it had been put there. Maybe ten — and maybe twenty thousand years before. *This is my mark;* it said. *My mark that I was here. All I can tell you of my self and of my time and of the world in which I lived is in this signature: this handprint; mine.*

"*I saw these animals. I saw this grass. I saw these stars. We made these wars. And then the ice came.*

"*Now the stars have disappeared. The grass is gone: the animals are calling to us out beyond this place — the frozen entrance to this cave. . . .*

"*In days or hours we will have died. We cannot breathe. The lanthorn flickers. All the air is gone. I leave you this: my hand as signature beside these images of what I knew. Look how my fingers spread to tell my name.*

"Some there are who never disappear. And I knew I was sitting at the heart of the human race — which is its will to say I *am*."

14: As Doctor Johnson reached his final hour, he wrote of prayer in his journal.

He wrote that prayer must be a vow.

I believe that vows are prayers.

I also believe that human beings can make the difference — consciously — between the success and the failure of this experiment: life.

What difference?

Which?

Make choices. Choices — and a vow.

The last words written in Doctor Johnson's journal are these:

"Against despair."

Nothing is harder, now in this present time, than staring down despair. But stare it down we must. Unless we do, there can be no reconciliation.

15: Be grateful, in your final hour, for life. Not for your life alone, but for the fact of life: for everything that is.

After all is said and done, I know I will have no answers. None. I don't expect to have them. What I will have, and all I have now, is questions. What I have done — what I have tried to do — is frame those questions — not with question marks — but in the paragraphs of books.

. . .then I Daniel looked and saw —
but what do you care for the grief
of what I Daniel understood by
books the number of the years of desolation?
Confusion of faces, yours among them,
the poetry tangled, no vision of my own to speak of.

The hand moved along the wall.
I was able to read, that's all.

I am still — and will always be — myself alone. But, as myself, I know, now, I am not alone.

Goodbye.

And thank you.

·NOTES·

page 3: CBC's "Matinee," the week of November 11, 1970.

page 39: An abridged version of this piece was broadcast on CBC's "Speaking Volumes" in March 1990.

page 58: CBC's "Matinee," the week of January 6, 1971.

page 65: The Last of the Crazy People was my first published novel. I had written it in 1962 and '63 at Richmond Hill, Ontario. Publication, however, did not take place until 1967, when Grace Bechtold sold the hardcover rights to Meredith Press, New York. The Bantam paperback was published in 1968.

page 79: CBC's "State of the Arts" in their series "A Sense of Place" on September 21, 1986, and SCRIPSI, Special Penguin Issue, August 1989.

page 99: CBC's "Matinee," the week of February 8, 1971.

page 156: An edited excerpt from a script for CBC's "Matinee," the week of August 7, 1970.

page 159: The Leacock Symposium at the University of Ottawa in May 1985.

page 163: Launch for *The CanLit Foodbook* edited by Margaret Atwood, proceeds from which support The Writers' Development Trust and the Canadian Centre of P.E.N. International.

page 167: A new version of a piece that appeared in *Canadian Literature*, No. 91 (Winter, 1981).

page 187: The Globe and Mail, June 1990.

page 190: Based on an article published in *Toronto Life,* May, 1984.

page 193: Part of the programme notes for A *Tribute to June Callwood,* June 5, 1987 — one of the fund-raising events that preceded the opening of Toronto's AIDS hospice, Casey House, which was initiated and developed by June. It was named for Casey Frayne, who had been the victim of a tragic motorcycle accident, and the son of June and her husband, Trent Frayne.

page 216: Based on a script for CBC's "Matinee," the week of September 9, 1970.

page 226: "Alarms and Excursions — Some Adventures in the Book Trade," *The Globe and Mail,* April 13, 1985.

page 237: Notes for a talk given to a Penguin Books sales conference just before the release of *The Telling of Lies.*

page 263: From *Toronto Life* magazine, April 1982.

page 268: From Thornton Wilder's obituary, *The Globe and Mail,* December 10, 1975. He had died December 7th.

page 273: Saturday Night, May 1989.

page 280: Based on a piece in *Books in Canada,* April 1985, and the preface to Marian Engel's *The Tattooed Woman.*

page 286: From "Why and How and Why," Canadian Writers in 1984 — The Twenty-Fifth Anniversary Issue of Canadian Literature.

page 289: Based on two pieces written shortly after the death of Margaret Laurence, one published in *Maclean's* magazine, January 1987, and the other in *Canadian Woman Studies,* Fall 1987.

page 297: Quill & Quire, April 1989.

page 301: This speech was delivered in Peterborough, January 26, 1987, and published in *The Journal of Canadian Studies,* Spring, 1987, Vol. 22, #1.

waiting with everyone else for the
Commissar to appear, Little Wilf
was busy with his notebooks.

Wherever he went, wherever he
sat — in streets, in bars, in public
toilets — Wilf made notes. He listened
with a stethoscope and he watched
through a magnifying glass. He
collected graffiti. His ~~also was~~
theory was that you could sum up
the age you lived in by reading its
walls. The truth, which loves to hide,
had found the perfect hiding place.
It was just another ~~bit~~ bit of
gossip in ~~comment~~ the litter of
women and dirty jokes on the
partitions of a comfort station.

Little Wilf never missed a trick.
His eyes were like two window docs
on an abacus: clickety-click — they
moved so fast a pair of Chinese
fingers ~~too~~ might have been tied
to his brows. He watched and ~~the~~
listened and ~~by~~ waited. He was
very poor. The thing was, there